D1546658

THE ART OF ENCHANTMENT

Diaghilev's Ballets Russes, 1909-1929

Nancy Van Norman Baer

with contributions by

Joan Acocella

John E. Bowlt

Elena Bridgman

Lynn Garafola

Dale Harris

Simon Karlinsky

Nicoletta Misler

Richard Robson

Richard Taruskin

The Fine Arts Museums of San Francisco

Universe Books

THE ART OF ENCHANTMENT
Diaghilev's Ballets Russes, 1909-1929
has been published in conjunction
with the exhibition organized by
The Fine Arts Museums of San Francisco
M. H. de Young Memorial Museum
3 December 1988 through
26 February 1989

Front cover (detail) and
introductory illustration:
Mikhail Larionov,
Project for the curtain
for *Le Soleil de Nuit*, 1915,
cat. no. 66.

Frontispiece:
Léon Bakst,
Costume design for
Puss-in-Boots in
The Sleeping Princess, 1921,
cat. no. 24.

The costumes in this exhibition
are generously lent from
The Costume Galleries,
Castle Howard, England.
Their restoration was made
possible by the L. J. Skaggs and
Mary C. Skaggs Foundation.

The exhibition has been made
possible by gifts from the National
Endowment for the Arts, a Federal
agency; Mr. Robert L. B. Tobin;
Mr. and Mrs. George F. Jewett, Jr.;
and The Golden Grain Company.

Transportation of this exhibition
has been provided by British Airways.

Publication of this catalogue has
been made possible by a generous
grant from Louisa Stude Sarofim.

Trade edition published by
Universe Books
381 Park Avenue South
New York, N.Y. 10016
Distributed to the trade
by St. Martin's Press.
ISBN: 0-87663-761-6
Library of Congress
Catalogue Card
No. 88-30376

Produced by the Publications
Department of The Fine Arts
Museums of San Francisco:
Ann Heath Karlstrom, Publications
Manager, and Karen Kevorkian,
Editor. Design by Desne Border,
San Francisco, California. Display
type in Gill Sans and text type in
Electra, photocomposed by
Wilsted & Taylor Publishing
Services, Oakland, California.
Printed on Centura Dull 80# by
Village Craftsmen/Princeton
Polychrome Press, New Jersey.

*Library of Congress
Cataloguing-in-Publication Data*
The Art of Enchantment:
Diaghilev's Ballets Russes, 1909-
1929/[compiled by] Nancy Van
Norman Baer: with contributions
by Joan Acocella . . . [et al.].
Catalogue of an exhibition held at
The Fine Arts Museums of San
Francisco.
Includes bibliographies.
ISBN 0-87663-761-6
1. Ballets russes—Exhibitions.
2. Ballet—Costume—Exhibitions.
3. Ballet—Stage-setting and scenery
—Exhibitions.
4. Diaghilev, Serge, 1872-1929—
Exhibitions.   5. Fine Arts
Museums of San Francisco—
Catalogues.   I. Baer, Nancy Van
Norman.   II. Acocella, Joan
Ross.   III. Fine Arts Museums
of San Francisco.
GV1786.B3A77   1988
792.8'074'019461—dc19
88-30376 CIP

792.809
Dia
Art

●

CONTENTS

▼

Jean Cocteau,
Serge Diaghilev, 1930, cat. no. 38.

Preface

▼

UNDER THE DIRECTION of impresario Serge Diaghilev, the legendary Ballets Russes defined the golden age of ballet in the early twentieth century. *The Art of Enchantment: Diaghilev's Ballets Russes, 1909-1929* allows us to explore the comprehensive nature of an art form characterized by extraordinary innovation based on a vision of the modern performance stage as a medium for interdisciplinary collaboration. The works of art in the exhibition, as well as the catalogue essays, illuminate the importance of the Ballets Russes in bringing together some of this century's best-known designers, choreographers, dancers, and musical composers in the creation of a modern aesthetic.

The Fine Arts Museums of San Francisco are proud to recapture the excitement and magic of Diaghilev's early productions that introduced the best of modern Russian culture —art, music, dance—to Western Europe at the beginning of this century. Noted perhaps as much for his personal flamboyance as for his theatrical *succès de scandale*, Diaghilev created a legend that continues to fascinate. He has received little recognition, however, for his contribution as an art historian and avant-garde literary editor, nor have the historical and aesthetic roots of his enterprise been fully acknowledged. The works of art, costumes, photographs, and archival material in this exhibition, and the catalogue's interdisciplinary nature, stimulate a renewed assessment of the scope and breadth of Diaghilev's vision.

Nancy Van Norman Baer, curator of the Museums' theater and dance collection, organized both the exhibition and the catalogue. She has been instrumental in establishing The Fine Arts Museums as an international forerunner in the field of dance-historical exhibitions with the success and critical acclaim of *Pavlova!* in 1981, *Dance in Art* in 1983, and *Bronislava Nijinska: A Dancer's Legacy* in 1986.

Certainly the exhibition owes much gratitude to those individuals and institutions who have generously lent us fragile and rare works of art. We are especially privileged to have the loan of historic dance costumes from Castle Howard Estate Ltd. in England, made possible by the cooperation and generosity of the Hon. Simon Howard. Other lenders to the exhibition are Robert L. B. Tobin, George Riabov, Parmenia Migel Ekstrom, Masha K. Engmann, Sylvia Westerman, Mr. and Mrs. Nikita D. Lobanov-Rostovsky, the Nicholas Roerich Museum, the Severin Wunderman Museum, the Nijinska Archives, The Museum of Modern Art in New York, the Institute of Modern Russian Culture, Paul M. Hertzmann, Inc., the Mills College Library, and The Bancroft Library.

Support for the presentation of this exhibition has been provided by the National Endowment for the Arts, a Federal agency; Louisa Stude Sarofim; Robert L. B. Tobin; Mr. and Mrs. George F. Jewett, Jr.; and The Golden Grain Company. Costume restoration at Castle Howard was made possible by the L. J. Skaggs and Mary C. Skaggs Foundation. The confidence of our lenders and supporters serves as inspiration to those dedicated to the preservation and scholarship of dance history within the realm of art history.

HARRY S. PARKER III
Director of Museums
The Fine Arts Museums of San Francisco

● Acknowledgments ▼

AN EXHIBITION OF THIS SCOPE involves the cooperation of many institutions and individuals. I especially want to thank Castle Howard Estate Ltd. for having made available their remarkable collection of Diaghilev-era costumes for research and exhibition. Through the generosity and cooperation of the Hon. Simon Howard we have been able to bring to life an extraordinary era—one that revolutionized theatrical design and strongly influenced modern art movements of the early twentieth century. I am most grateful to my colleagues at Castle Howard, in particular Richard A. Robson, Curator of The Costume Galleries; Lyndall Bond, Keeper of Textile Conservation; and Michael Hunter, Assistant Curator of The Costume Galleries. Mr. Robson deserves special accolades for having shouldered administrative and design responsibilities in mounting this show.

The organization of this exhibition has brought great pleasure, largely because of new and strengthened personal relations. Several private collectors have generously granted access to their collections and have shared their infectious enthusiasm for the art and artists of Diaghilev's Ballets Russes. In particular I wish to thank Robert L. B. Tobin, whose collection has inspired my work over the past eight years and whose support has made possible the realization of my endeavors. Among those who have also shared their treasures are Parmenia Migel Ekstrom, Masha K. Engmann, Mr. and Mrs. Nikita D. Lobanov-Rostovsky, George V. Riabov, and Sylvia Westerman.

A number of others were also helpful in advancing the cause of this exhibition. I wish to thank Tony Clark, Severin Wunderman Museum; Elaine Dee, Cooper Hewitt Museum; Daniel Entin, Nicholas Roerich Museum; Linda Hardberger, McNay Art Museum; Ann Jones and Pic Swartz, Tobin Collection; Francis Mason, Dance Research Foundation/ *Ballet Review*; Irina Nijinska, Nijinska Archives; Martin Antonetti, Mills College Library; Anthony Bliss, The Bancroft Library; Judy Kinberg, WNET/13; Helgi Tomasson and Richard Carter, San Francisco Ballet; and Selma Jeanne Cohen, Douglas J. Engmann, Stephen Steinberg, and Rouben Ter-Arutunian. I also wish to acknowledge the Archives for the Performing Arts, San Francisco; Paul M. Hertzmann, Inc.; The Institute of Modern Russian Culture; The Museum of Modern Art, New York; and the Stravinsky-Diaghilev Foundation.

Enormous appreciation is due my colleagues who contributed essays to the exhibition catalogue, as well as Louisa Stude Sarofim who underwrote its publication and Desne Border who created the handsome design. I particularly wish to thank two authors: Lynn Garafola, for her ongoing support and advice, and John E. Bowlt, for his ready and detailed answers to all inquiries. In addition, I extend my appreciation and admiration to Joan Ross Acocella, Elena Bridgman, Dale Harris, Simon Karlinsky, Nicoletta Misler, and Richard Taruskin.

I am extremely grateful to members of the staff of The Fine Arts Museums of San Francisco for their effort and professionalism in realizing this project. Deep appreciation is extended to Debra Pughe, Exhibitions Support Department Manager; Bill White, Chief Technician and Exhibition Designer; Ann Heath Karlstrom, Publications Manager; and Karen Kevorkian, Editor. I also would like to thank Director Emeritus Ian McKibbin White, who proposed the exhibition concept, and Director Harry S. Parker III, who has given his wholehearted support to this show. I am grateful for the encouragement offered by the Board of Trustees, especially Mrs. W. Robert Phillips, President of the Board, and Mrs. William B. MacColl, Chairman of the Trustee Exhibition Committee, and to Stephen E. Dykes, Deputy Director for Administration; James Forbes, Deputy Director for Development; Thomas K. Seligman, Deputy Director for Public Programs and Planning;

Steven A. Nash, Associate Director and Chief Curator; and Debbie Small, Manager of Government and Foundation Relations. Other staff members who have contributed to the success of the exhibition are Kathy Baldwin, Karen Breuer, Nic Caldararo, Laura Camins, Therese Chen, Elizabeth Cornu, Renée Dreyfus, Judith Eurich, Debbie Evans, Pamela Forbes, Robert Futernick, Bill Huggins, Linda Jablon, Robert F. Johnson, Connie King, Charles Long, Paula March, Lucy Martell, Joseph McDonald, Jane Nelson, Maxine Rosston, Michael Sandgren, Kate Schlafly, Gus Teller, and the technicians, the security force, the Docent Council, and the Volunteer Council. In particular I wish to thank curatorial assistant Elena Bridgman, whose authorial contribution, research, manuscript review, and personal insights have been invaluable.

To the sponsors of the exhibition I also owe my sincerest gratitude. The early support of Louisa Stude Sarofim and Robert L. B. Tobin gave me courage and confidence that was reinforced by the support of Mr. and Mrs. George F. Jewett, Jr.; Verinder Syal, The Golden Grain Company; and the National Endowment for the Arts, a Federal agency. In addition, the L. J. Skaggs and Mary C. Skaggs Foundation underwrote the conservation of the costumes at Castle Howard, thereby initiating the development of the exhibition concept, and British Airways provided exhibition transport.

My deepest personal thanks go to my husband, Alan, for his continuous support, and to my parents, Grace and Allen Van Norman, who instilled in me a love of art and dance.

N. V. N. B.

SINCE 1959, as a result of major gifts, The Fine Arts Museums have assembled a rich and varied collection of art associated with the dance. The foundation for this collection was laid by Alma de Bretteville Spreckels who, with her husband, Adolph B. Spreckels, built the California Palace of the Legion of Honor. Inspired by her friendship with the innovative American dancer Loïe Fuller, whom she met in Paris in 1914, Alma Spreckels began collecting dance sculpture and drawings as well as costume and set designs for opera and ballet productions. Because of her aesthetic sensibility and close connections with artistic circles in Paris, Mrs. Spreckels was able to purchase—over the next four decades—a number of excellent works, in particular those of the Russian artist-designers of Diaghilev's Ballets Russes.

Mrs. Spreckels's collection grew to such proportions that in 1957 she established a private Museum of Dance and Theater on the lower floor of her Washington Street home in San Francisco. Inspiration for this museum came from a 1937 visit to the Paris Archives Internationales de la Danse, which were subsequently destroyed during the German occupation in World War II. Although Mrs. Spreckels's new museum was initially not open to the public, she intended it to become a city museum with herself as the primary benefactor. After the formation of a Board of Directors with architect George S. Livermore as president, the Museum of Dance and Theater was officially incorporated and discussion of an appropriate location was begun. Among the sites considered were the Chalet at Ocean Beach and the Sharon Building in Golden Gate Park, as well as the area opposite the main entrance of the Legion of Honor, where a new pavilion was to be constructed.

After two years of planning, personal reasons including failing health and the death of her only son caused Alma Spreckels to put aside the idea of building a separate museum of dance and theater in San Francisco. Instead, she permanently transferred her collection to the Legion of Honor in two large gifts—one in 1959 and the other in 1962. When the Legion of Honor merged with the M. H. de Young Memorial Museum in 1972, these works became the Theater and Dance Collection of The Fine Arts Museums of San Francisco.

Several generous gifts have served to augment and extend the Spreckels collection. In 1977 Mr. and Mrs. Nikita D. Lobanov-Rostovsky presented to the Museums forty costume and set designs by the second generation of Russian stage designers. These works admirably complement the Spreckels collection, introducing fine drawings by younger Russian artists working in the theater. That same year, an important collection of historic dance costumes worn by Loïe Fuller and Anna Pavlova was placed on permanent loan to the Museums by The Bancroft Library at the University of California, Berkeley. In 1981, in support of the *Pavlova!* centennial exhibition organized by the Museums, eighteen large-scale drawings of Anna Pavlova by the American artist Malvina Hoffman were given to the collection by the Hoffman estate. And, in 1985, twenty theatrical designs by the Russian artist Boris Anisfeld came to the Museums as a gift from his daughter.

The series of dance-related exhibitions organized by The Fine Arts Museums has brought ongoing visibility to the Theater and Dance Collection. *In Celebration of Loïe Fuller* in 1978, *Russian Theater and Costume Designs* in 1980, *Pavlova!* in 1981, *Dance in Art* in 1983, and *Bronislava Nijinska: A Dancer's Legacy* in 1986 have resulted in widespread recognition and have served to establish the Museums as the foremost originator of exhibitions relating dance and the visual arts.

NANCY VAN NORMAN BAER
Curator, Theater and Dance Collection

THE BALLET COSTUMES ON DISPLAY in this exhibition are part of the largest private collection of historic costume in Britain, The Castle Howard Costume Galleries. Without the efforts of George Howard, who inherited the estate after World War II, and his wife, the Lady Cecilia Howard, this remarkable house would have died, stripped of its treasures, its dignity, and its spirit. Not only did they ensure the continuing glory of the estate, reopening it to the public in 1953, but they also founded the Costume Galleries in 1965.

Castle Howard stands on the site of the old village of Henderskelfe, land that has been retained by the same family for hundreds of years. Charles Howard, the 3rd Earl of Carlisle, was a man of immense power and ambition, and to match his position he decided to build a country seat as one of the most flamboyant of status symbols. Designed and begun in 1699, it grew from the imagination of three men–the 3rd Earl of Carlisle, Sir John Vanbrugh, and Nicholas Hawksmoor. Vanbrugh, originally a soldier, was also a playwright. As a result of his success, he was invited to join the exclusive Kit Kat Club, where it is possible that he met the young Lord Carlisle. Castle Howard was the first house Vanbrugh built, and he received much inspiration from the Earl, as well as solid advice from the experienced architect Nicholas Hawksmoor. Successive members of the Howard family completed the house, employing the services of architects including Sir Thomas Robinson, the 3rd Earl's son-in-law, who built the West Wing.

The Earls of Carlisle continued to live at Castle Howard until the beginning of the present century when, following the death of the 9th Earl and his widow, the estates were divided–the Earl of Carlisle living at Naworth Castle near Carlisle and the Hon. Geoffrey Howard taking Castle Howard. During World War II a girls' school occupied the building, and the house was disastrously damaged by a fire. When George Howard inherited it, he and the Lady Cecilia had the courage to refurbish and refurnish it, and the even greater courage to establish a permanent residence and bring up their four sons there. Now, after Lady Cecilia's death in 1974 and George Howard's in 1984, the Hon. Simon Howard lives in the house and administers the running of the estate.

The costume collection at Castle Howard includes examples of domestic, ecclesiastical, occupational, theatrical, and military dress. The main part of the collection dates from the early eighteenth century to the present day, but a research collection of textiles also reflects a broader period. In order that the vast collection of costumes may be seen, the displays are changed each year. For the most part they depict scenes that give the atmosphere of the period, with the introduction of furniture and paintings.

It was in 1968 that George and Cecilia Howard became interested in the sales of Russian ballet costumes in London and founded within the Costume Galleries a remarkable collection, which has subsequently been augmented by purchases and gifts. Many of the costumes on display in San Francisco have not been seen by the public since they last were worn in performance.

Castle Howard takes great pleasure in being able to make it possible for these costumes to be exhibited by The Fine Arts Museums of San Francisco. They are a part of our international heritage, and we are proud to be entrusted with their care. We know that all visitors who see this exhibition will enjoy it and come to feel perhaps a small part of the thrill and excitement generated when these costumes first appeared on the balletic stage.

RICHARD A. ROBSON, B.D.
Curator of The Castle Howard Costume Galleries

THE ART OF

ENCHANTMENT

Diaghilev's

Ballets Russes

1909-1929

A CULTURAL EDUCATOR OF GENIUS[1]

Simon Karlinsky

▼

NOTE:
In this essay, names of Russian ballets and artists are given in English rather than French, in accordance with the author's wishes.

1 This text cites portions of my essay "Sergei Diaghilev, Public and Private," which appeared in CHRISTOPHER STREET 4, *no. 7 (March 1980) and was reprinted in* THE CHRISTOPHER STREET READER, *ed. Michael Denneny, Charles Ortleb, and Thomas Steele (New York, 1983). Quoted by permission of* CHRISTOPHER STREET *magazine.*

Other parts of the text are drawn from my article on Diaghilev forthcoming in the INTERNATIONAL ENCYCLOPEDIA OF DANCE, *ed. Selma Jeanne Cohen et al. Quoted by permission of the publisher, University of California Press.*

2 Jacqueline Lee Bouvier, "People I Wish I Had Known," THE WORLD IN VOGUE, *ed. Bryan Holme et al. (London, 1963), 301.*

3 This was done in the two books in English, published in 1979 to commemorate the fiftieth anniversary of Diaghilev's death: Richard Buckle, DIAGHILEV *(New York); and John Percival,* THE WORLD OF DIAGHILEV *(New York).*

Diaghilev, Lausanne, 1915.
Courtesy, Parmenia Migel Ekstrom.

THE NAME OF SERGEI DIAGHILEV is linked with ballet in most people's minds, but it is not always clear in what capacity. After Diaghilev died in Venice on 12 August 1929, where he was interred at the Orthodox cemetery, people in London and New York were reportedly heard to remark, "What a pity, I never saw him dance." Those better informed had long known that the bulky, heavyset Diaghilev was neither a dancer nor a choreographer. In 1951 a young art student named Jacqueline Lee Bouvier won an essay contest sponsored by *Vogue* magazine. In her essay, she described Diaghilev as an "alchemist unique in art history," whose specialty was achieving "an interaction of the arts, [and] an interaction of the cultures of East and West." The same essay cited Diaghilev's ability to get the best out of his composers, designers, and dancers, and to incorporate it into "a unified yet transient ballet masterpiece."[2]

This view is not wrong. But it is incomplete, only taking into account Diaghilev's activities from the period after 1909, when he was thirty-seven years old, when he was involved exclusively with ballet. In the West Sergei Diaghilev is remembered and honored as an impresario who exported Russian ballet to Europe and America, brought to the public view a galaxy of fine painters by commissioning them to do his sets, caused some of the greatest musical masterpieces of our century to be composed, and discovered or developed the talents of the best choreographers and dancers of his time. In Russian cultural history, however, Diaghilev was a central figure in the momentous cultural revival that began at the end of the 1890s, which affected the visual arts, philosophy, art history, literary criticism, and even the art of typography. To restrict the significance of Diaghilev to ballet alone[3] is to misunderstand the nature of his achievement and to diminish its scope.

Sergei Diaghilev was born on 19 March 1872 at Selishchev Barracks, a military settlement in the province of Novgorod where his father, Pavel, a military officer (figure 1), was stationed. Sergei was an exceptionally large-headed baby and his birth cost his mother, Evgenia (née Evreinova), her life. Two years later Pavel Diaghilev married Elena Panaeva (figure 2), a cultivated woman and a gifted amateur singer. The stepmother raised Sergei as though he were her own child. She supervised his early musical education, instilled a love of the arts, and was Diaghilev's closest confidante until her death in 1919.[4]

After graduating at the age of eighteen from *gimnaziia* (the equivalent of high school) in the provincial town of Perm, Diaghilev (figure 3) enrolled at the law school of St. Petersburg University. Law studies were a pretext, for his ambition at the time was to become a singer or a composer. He settled at the home of his father's older sister, Anna Filosofova, a veteran of the feminist movement of the 1860s who had helped to found the first women's college in Russia and secured better living conditions for women factory workers. The youngest of her five children, the tall and strikingly handsome Dima (Dmitry) was the same age as Diaghilev and was also about to enter law school. To reward the two young men for finishing high school their families sent them on a grand tour of Western Europe.

In Italy, during summer 1890, an intimate relationship developed between the two cousins. Lasting fourteen years, Diaghilev's love affair with his cousin Dima was the most durable and surely the most formative such relationship in his life. Through Dima, Diaghilev joined the intellectual coterie formed by Dima's classmates, who were later to form the nucleus of both the World of Art (Mir iskusstva) movement and the journal of that name that Diaghilev and his cousin were to edit. In this group were the future art historian and stage designer Alexander Benois; the dilettante musician Walter Nouvel, who was to remain Diaghilev's closest personal friend and who assisted him in his ballet

4 *Diaghilev's voluminous correspondence with his stepmother and a "Chronicle of the Diaghilev Family" which she wrote in 1909 are now in the manuscript collection of the Institute of Russian Literature, USSR Academy of Sciences. Cited selectively by recent Soviet scholars, these documents should serve as a basic source for any future Diaghilev biography.*

5 *This attitude is well illustrated in the unpublished diaries of Dima Filosofov, cited in Natalia Lapshina,* MIR ISKUSSTVA *(World of Art) (Moscow, 1977), 300-301.*

enterprises; and Konstantin Somov, later a famous painter. About the same time Diaghilev joined the group, so did a Jewish art student, Lev Rosenberg, later known as the painter and stage designer Léon Bakst. Benois and Bakst were heterosexual; the rest were not. The artistic temperaments of all created a highly charged emotional atmosphere.

What had bonded these young men of diverse background was their love of the arts and their shared dissatisfaction with the way the arts were perceived and written about at that time. At the end of the 1880s and in the early 1890s cultural life in Russia was politically polarized and artistically provincialized. On one hand it was academically stagnant because of a taste for patriotic, storytelling painting, conventional, well-made plays with bourgeois morals, and Victorian novels. On the other hand, criticism was dominated by a school of critics who are now called revolutionary democrats in the Soviet Union, but who more meaningfully may be called radical utilitarians. Forerunners of twentieth-century Socialist Realism, the influential Russian critics of the end of the nineteenth century demanded that all art be socially relevant, address current problems, and be patriotic and strictly realistic in form. Their criteria entirely overlooked values such as originality or profundity. They preferred that the didactic message, which they saw as the aim of all art, be couched in familiar and accessible terms. Their insistence on topical relevance precluded any serious interest in the arts of earlier periods or of other cultures.

The young men around Diaghilev and Dima Filosofov in the World of Art group saw both of those approaches to art—official academic and countercultural revolutionary—as equally limiting, provincial, and philistine.[5] The aim of their association was mutual education and expansion of their cultural horizons. They quickly discovered large areas of important art ignored by the critics of their time: the Russian icons, church frescoes, and church architecture of the earlier centuries, held to be backward and superstitious, not beautiful; the eighteenth-century and early nineteenth-century romantic painters, who supposedly lacked realism and social significance; and some Western phenomena, which also had been held to share these defects, such as the Pre-Raphaelites in England, the music of Wagner and his followers, and, after some hesitation, the French impressionist painters, such as Degas and Monet. In literature, the World of Art group was among the first to realize that the great Russian writers of the nineteenth century—Gogol, Turgenev, Tolstoy, and Dostoevsky—were important not only as topical social commentators or indicters of the inequities of tsarist Russia, but also as magnificent and original literary artists, each of whom had his own vision of life that could not be fully explained by the catchall term *realism*. The rediscovery of the past and an interest in the new trends in the West, attitudes typical of the entire World of Art group, provided the background for the evolution and broadening of Sergei Diaghilev's tastes during the first half of the 1890s.

6 *Diaghilev's encounters and correspondence with Tolstoy are in Ilya Zilbershtein and Vladimir Samkov, eds.,* SERGEI DIAGHILEV I RUSSKOE ISKUSSTVO *(Sergei Diaghilev and Russian Art) (Moscow, 1982), 2:7-16.*

7 *A number of these reports are cited by Iuri Novikov in* SERGEI DIAGHILEV: THE EARLY YEARS, *ed. Joan Ross Acocella, trans. Roberta Reeder, forthcoming. I am grateful to Dr. Reeder for showing me an early draft of this still incomplete manuscript.*

8 *Cited by Novikov in* SERGEI DIAGHILEV: THE EARLY YEARS.

figure 3
Diaghilev as a young man, ca. 1890.
Courtesy, Parmenia Migel Ekstrom.

9 *Vasily Yastrebtsev,* NIKOLAI ANDREEVICH RIMSKII-KORSAKOV. VOSPOMINANIIA, 1886-1908 *(Memoirs) (Leningrad, 1959), 1: 207-208. A slightly garbled translation of this passage into English can be found in V. V. Yastrebtsev,* REMINISCENCES OF RIMSKY-KORSAKOV, *ed. and trans. Florence Jonas (New York, 1985), 90.*

10 *Zilbershtein and Samkov, 2:413-414. Yastrebtsev's memoirs and the sources cited here invalidate the frequent assertion that Diaghilev studied composition with Rimsky-Korsakov.*

Diaghilev's musical ambitions led him to study singing with the famed Italian baritone Antonio Cotogni and composition with Nikolai Sokolov. In 1892 Diaghilev and Filosofov visited Leo Tolstoy and discussed social and moral issues with him. Tolstoy was so impressed that he entered into a brief correspondence with Diaghilev.[6] After this, the young Diaghilev made a constant practice of seeking out Russian and foreign celebrities, such as Tchaikovsky, Aubrey Beardsley, and Oscar Wilde. He did this not out of vanity (as some memoirists have suggested), but in order to see what he could learn about art from these men. One does not always find the infallible taste of the later Diaghilev in the reports on these encounters in his letters to his stepmother.[7]

Thus, meeting Brahms and Verdi on his trips to Western Europe in 1893 and 1894, respectively, he thought both of them too aged and uninteresting. On the other hand, Emmanuel Chabrier, whose opera *Gwendoline* Diaghilev thought would be a new departure for French music, aroused his wild enthusiasm. Diaghilev's account of how he ingratiated himself with Chabrier and his wife in order to sit in their box at the premiere of *Gwendoline* already shows the mature Diaghilev's fabled ability to charm people and to get them to do whatever he wanted.[8] His almost annual visits to Bayreuth opened for him the possibilities of the Wagnerian "unified work of art" (*Gesamtkunstwerk*), a synthesis of the musical, the visual and the dramatic, which, though imperfectly realized at Bayreuth festivals, was basic to Diaghilev's later concept of ballet.

By 1894 some of Diaghilev's music had been played at private recitals and he had appeared as a singer at a public concert. But his musical ambitions suffered an irreparable blow in autumn of that year, when he showed his compositions to Nikolai Rimsky-Korsakov and asked to be taken on as a private pupil. As recorded in the journal of Rimsky's disciple Vasily Yastrebtsev, the composer told Diaghilev that he had no talent and that the pieces he had brought were absurd.[9] Despite Diaghilev's defiant response to this judgment,[10] he soon abandoned his music studies. The center of his interest during the next few years shifted from music to painting.

Diaghilev's involvement with painting was threefold. By dabbling in the stock market and investing in the new and unfamiliar commodity of electrical technology, he managed to increase the modest inheritance his mother had left him to such an extent that he could start building a private art collection. Between 1896 and 1898 he published a number of critical articles on art in the periodical press, an activity that he later continued in his pathbreaking journal, *World of Art*. In 1897 and 1898 he organized a series of memorable art exhibits in St. Petersburg. The first of these featured English and German watercolor artists, the second showed Scandinavian art, and the third and most popular was devoted to contemporary Finnish and Russian painters.

In his art criticism, collecting, and exhibitions, Diaghilev's approach was consistent. He showed a keen interest in all forms of art manifesting the artist's individuality, and disdained art that was conventional or motivated either by ideological pieties or chauvinistic nationalism. By the second half of the 1890s, members of the World of Art group made a few disjointed attempts to bring this universalist aesthetic to public attention. Filosofov published some literary criticism, Benois and Somov exhibited paintings and watercolors of eighteenth-century scenes treated in a modernist manner, and Diaghilev edited the yearbook of the Russian Imperial Theaters. The resulting book was a triumph of typographical art: one of Diaghilev's often overlooked contributions to the appearance of books and journals, a contribution much recognized in the history of typography in Russia.

In 1898 Diaghilev put to use his fund-raising abilities, which were to serve him well during his later years as ballet impresario, and persuaded the generous patroness of the arts Princess Maria Tenisheva and the millionaire merchant Savva Mamontov to finance his journal, which he edited jointly with Filosofov, other members of the World of Art group serving as art critics, music critics, designers, or illustrators. *World of Art* was published for only five years, but historians of Russian literature, art, and culture—at least those in the West—see its appearance as triggering a major turning point in Russian cultural attitudes. D. S. Mirsky, the most authoritative historian of Russian literature, points out that between the 1860s and 1890s literature and the arts were valued in Russia only if they expressed ideas that were considered currently relevant. This explains, for example, why such a major literary figure as Anton Chekhov had difficulty getting recognition. The reigning radical ideologues thought Chekhov lacked topical relevance and therefore judged him politically harmful. However, by the end of the first decade of the twentieth century, Mirsky argues, Russian society was aesthetically one of the most sophisticated in Europe. He gives the main credit for this to Sergei Diaghilev.[11]

11 D. S. Mirsky, A HISTORY OF RUSSIAN LITERATURE, *ed. Francis J. Whitfield (New York, 1966), 409-412.*

The two-pronged offensive against academicism and conformity on the one side, and the supposedly revolutionary insistence on the propagandistic and didactic aspects of art to the exclusion of everything else on the other, caused an enormous stir when *World of Art* began publication. Attacks came from diverse quarters, right and left alike. The patriarch of radical-utilitarian music and art criticism Vladimir Stasov, who had since 1847 championed realistic, nationalistic, and ideologically committed art, had earlier blasted Diaghilev's 1898 Russo-Finnish exhibit as "an orgy of depravity and insanity, with a few good, talented paintings that stand out like vivid and brilliant pieces of lovely fabric pinned to a tattered and dirty blanket." The paintings of the great visionary Mikhail Vrubel (whose work was later prominently featured in *World of Art*) were for Stasov "outrageous, ugly, and repulsive." The early issues of *World of Art* were greeted by vitriolic denunciations by Stasov, for whom the journal was "dominated by nonsense, ugliness, and filth," its editors "inept, inexperienced, and lacking in all taste," and the art works reproduced in its illustrations (by Degas, Monet, Aubrey Beardsley, Bakst, Somov, and Benois, among others) looked like "the work of a three-year-old child holding a pencil for the first time." "If such art prevails," Stasov concluded in one of his articles, "humanity as a whole will have to be locked up in insane asylums."[12]

12 V. V. Stasov, IZBRANNYE SOCHINENIIA V TREKH TOMAKH *(Selected Writings in Three Volumes), vol. 3 (Moscow, 1952). The cited passages are drawn from articles "Vystavki" (Art Exhibits, 1898), 215-228; "Nishchie dukhom" (The Poor in Spirit, 1899), 232-238; and "Podvor'e prokazhennykh" (The Leper Colony, 1899), 257-263. These articles were originally published in the newspaper* STOCK EXCHANGE NEWS.

Anton Chekhov, in a letter to his friend Alexei Suvorin (the publisher of the conservative newspaper NEW TIMES)*, wrote that he was "physically repelled" by the abusive tone of the literary and art critics of his time, citing*

Simultaneously, Stasov's sworn enemy, the ultra-conservative columnist Victor Burenin, writing in the reactionary newspaper *New Times*, launched a series of equally bitter attacks on *World of Art*, characterized by the following passage:

Of course the pretensions of WORLD OF ART *or, more precisely, the pretensions of a Mr. Diaghilev who edits this journal, are not only astounding but also extraordinarily stupid. . . . I do not know whether Mr. Diaghilev belongs to the category of semi-literate adolescents or of fraudulent dilettantes. But there's no doubt that this upstart dilettante is the most comical and at the same time the most unbridled of modern self-appointed judges of art. It is none other than Mr. Diaghilev who preaches decadence and foments the mercenary self-promotion of artists.*[13]

Both the far left and the far right sides of the political spectrum perceived Diaghilev's rejection of didacticism, realism, and nationalistic pride as a threat and strove to discredit the journal and the movement it represented by dubbing it "decadent," a label that stuck for many years.

World of Art and the annual art exhibitions it sponsored managed not only to change

both Stasov and Burenin (see next note) as prime examples of what he meant. "That's not criticism or a world view; it's hate, insatiable animal spite," Chekhov wrote. "Why must they write in a tone fit for judging criminals rather than artists and writers? I just can't stand it. I simply can't." (Michael Henry Heim and Simon Karlinsky, eds., ANTON CHEKHOV'S LIFE AND THOUGHT [Berkeley and Los Angeles, 1975], 250).

13 Quoted from Zilbershtein and Samkov, 1:312. Burenin kept reviling WORLD OF ART in his columns for several years. Then, in 1900, his column mentioned the "ultra-swinish" personal relationship between Diaghilev and Dima Filosofov. According to the memoirs of Sergei Makovsky and Piotr Pertsov (cited in Zilbershtein and Samkov, 2:310, 506), the two cousins, after reading the column, put on their frock coats and top hats and went to Burenin's residence. Burenin himself opened the door, whereupon Diaghilev, without saying a word, put his large-sized hat on Burenin, pulled it over him down to his shoulders and departed. After this, Burenin never again mentioned Diaghilev in any of his writings.

14 On the emotional triangle between Diaghilev, Filosofov, and Zinaida Gippius, see Vladimir Zlobin, A DIFFICULT SOUL: ZINAIDA GIPPIUS, and my introductory essay to that book, "Who Was Zinaida Gippius?" (Berkeley and Los Angeles, 1980).

15 On important art journals, such as THE GOLDEN FLEECE, APOLLON, and others, which were all successors of WORLD OF ART, see Valentine Marcadé, LE RENOUVEAU DE L'ART PICTORIAL RUSSE (Lausanne, 1971).

the course of Russian culture but also to lay the groundwork for all of its spectacular achievements during the first three decades of our century. As noted, artists and historians rediscovered the Russian icon, the architecture of churches and palaces of earlier centuries, and the beauty of the baroque and rococo periods. The French Impressionists and Post-Impressionists were the journal's main blind spot—it began writing about them only in its last year of publication—but otherwise the journal informed its readers of the arts of the past and the present in a comprehensive way never before attempted by a Russian publication. The literary section of World of Art, edited by Filosofov, became the rallying point for the nascent symbolist movement in Russian literature. The journal opened its pages to major symbolist poets, helping to assert their reputations, and it also published the work of an important group of religious philosophers, thus bringing back into Russian culture the dimensions of mysticism, metaphysics, and fantasy, which had been banished by utilitarian critics.

It is often claimed in the West that World of Art (both the movement and its journal) represented an art-for-art's-sake aesthetic and that Diaghilev was opposed to socially committed art. Nothing could be more erroneous. Diaghilev's art criticism shows that he was fully aware of the social aspects of art. What he fought against was the enslavement of art and of the artist by simplistic political dogma. For much of the nineteenth century, the fate of art in Russia was decided by people who neither liked nor understood it, and for whom beauty and complexity were morally suspect. Everything about World of Art, from its philosophy to its outward appearance, was a refutation of that hegemony (which was, however, enthroned again after the Revolution). An auxiliary of World of Art was the concert series "Evenings of Contemporary Music" organized by group members Walter Nouvel and Alfred Nurok. It existed from 1900 to 1912 and it introduced to the Russian public such composers as Debussy, Ravel, Schoenberg, and, in 1907, Stravinsky.

In 1903 there came an editorial crisis in World of Art that paralleled the crisis in the relationship between Diaghilev and Filosofov. Filosofov had joined some of the leading contributors to World of Art to start a religious journal called The New Way. Two of these contributors, the poet Zinaida Gippius and her husband, the novelist and critic Dmitry Merezhkovsky, set out to break up the relationship between Diaghilev and Filosofov, using as their lever Filosofov's ever-growing involvement in religious and revolutionary politics, a subject that held little interest for Diaghilev. The tug of war between Gippius and Diaghilev for Filosofov's affections lasted for three years, culminating in a victory for Gippius that left Diaghilev with deep emotional scars.[14]

In 1904 World of Art ceased publication. Its viewpoint and its mission were taken over and enhanced by several other important art journals that appeared between 1904 and 1917.[15] After the demise of his journal, Diaghilev summed up its cultural policy by organizing the most grandiose and influential of his art exhibitions, the display of Russian portraits of the eighteenth and early nineteenth centuries that opened at the Tauris Palace in St. Petersburg in March 1905. Diaghilev traveled throughout Russia to locate 4,000 portraits, of which some 2,000 were exhibited. The result was the rediscovery of scores of fine Russian painters whose work had not been collected or studied in the nineteenth century, because of its supposed deficiencies in psychological depth and social significance. It is because of Diaghilev that these paintings are today proudly displayed in Soviet museums and reproduced in scholarly monographs and on postcards. Art historians date from this exhibition a whole new attitude in Russian galleries and museums about methods of hanging and displaying paintings and sculptures.

With the end of both *World of Art* and his relationship with Filosofov, Diaghilev turned to Western Europe for his next projects. In 1906 he took an exhibition of Russian art ranging from ancient icons to modernist paintings to Paris, Berlin, and Venice. In 1907 in Paris he arranged five historical concerts of Russian music from Glinka to Scriabin, with the appearances as conductors and soloists of Rimsky-Korsakov, Glazunov, Rachmaninov and Scriabin. In 1908 he brought to the Paris Opera an opulent production of Musorgsky's *Boris Godunov* with Feodor Chaliapin. These performances consolidated the popularity of Russian nineteenth-century composers in the West. Diaghilev's next project was to take abroad a season of opera and ballet. The very idea of exporting Russian ballet to the West struck many of his contemporaries as outlandish.

In the early decades of the nineteenth century, ballet was a respected art in Russia. Choreographers, such as Charles Didelot and Adam Glushkovsky, were highly regarded by the intellectual community. Major writers, Pushkin and Gogol among them, wrote of the ballet with interest and enthusiasm. But at the end of the century this situation no longer existed. Even the choreographic genius of Marius Petipa could not rescue the ballet of the time from the absurdities that had become a part of its convention: the convoluted plots about supernatural beings who expressed themselves in stilted pantomime, the low quality of most ballet music (the scores of Tchaikovsky, Glazunov, and Riccardo Drigo were rare exceptions), sets and costumes inappropriate to the historical period depicted, and a corrupt star system that constantly sacrificed artistry and logic so that a prima ballerina who portrayed a beggar or a peasant girl was often allowed to appear in a pearl necklace and diamond tiara. Socially aware Russians of the turn of the century regarded ballet as a plaything of elderly lechers who liked watching legs in tights.

Alexander Benois and Walter Nouvel were rare instances of intellectuals who loved ballet and believed that it had the makings of a true art form. They at first had a hard time converting Diaghilev to this view. In October 1896 he complained in a letter to Benois that Nouvel's enthusiasm for ballet was "unendurable."[16] But in 1901, when he served briefly as an aide to the director of the Imperial Theaters, Prince Sergei Volkonsky, Diaghilev asked to be put in charge of a new production of *Sylvia* by Delibes. However, his plan to have the production designed by Bakst, Benois, and several other World of Art figures was vetoed and Diaghilev was dismissed from his position at the Imperial Theaters. Diaghilev made other attempts in the next few years to get access to the Imperial Theaters. His aim was to introduce into opera and possibly ballet productions an artistic synthesis of their component elements, the kind of synthesis that Wagner had dreamed of and that had been achieved in drama by Stanislavsky and Vladimir Nemirovich-Danchenko, whose Moscow Art Theater opened the same year that *World of Art* began publication.

By 1907, however, an innovative choreographer was working in Russia, trained at the Imperial Ballet School but interested in achieving a fusion between ballet and the nascent art of modern dance, as exemplified by Isadora Duncan. As Vera Krasovskaya has observed, Mikhail Fokine disliked the traditional ballet of the late nineteenth century as strongly as the World of Art group disliked the academicians and realist painters of the same period.[17] Much of Fokine's reform of ballet reflected the impact of the World of Art on the whole of Russian culture and it was only natural that he should make common cause with the artists of that group. It is, in fact, hard to think of a closer theatrical embodiment of the World of Art aesthetics of ca. 1895 than the ballet *Le Pavillon d'Armide* (1907), with a libretto, scenery, and costumes by Benois and choreography by Fokine–an opulent glorification of the seventeenth and eighteenth centuries, with a story line taken from the romantic poet Théophile Gautier.

16 *Zilbershtein and Samkov, 2:18.*

17 *Vera Krasovskaya,* RUSSKII BALETNYI TEATR NACHALA XX VEKA *(Russian Ballet at the Beginning of the Twentieth Century) (Leningrad, 1971), 2:158ff.*

Fokine had at his disposal an array of brilliant young dancers who believed in his ideas and were eager to appear in his ballets, among them Anna Pavlova, Tamara Karsavina, Sophia Feodorova, Bronislava Nijinska, Vaslav Nijinsky, Adolph Bolm, and Georgy Rozai. So when Diaghilev's plan to bring to Paris several Russian operas in the spring of 1909 was cancelled because of insufficient financing, he and his associates decided to fill most of the season with Fokine ballets, most created earlier in St. Petersburg but in some cases revised for export. The enormous success of that first 1909 season, followed by the equally highly acclaimed one in 1910, led Diaghilev not to rely on dancers he borrowed from the Imperial Theaters in St. Petersburg and Moscow but to form his own company in 1911, Ballets Russes de Serge Diaghilev. Signalling his total commitment to ballet, this decision must have been reinforced by his personal alliance with Vaslav Nijinsky, whom he first met in 1908 and who became the object of his most intense emotional involvement since his break with Filosofov.

The early Paris seasons were a triumph for Diaghilev's dancers, his designers (especially the friends of his youth, Benois and Bakst), and for Fokine's choreography. But in a larger sense, they were also a vindication of the positions for which the World of Art group had fought so hard during the 1890s. In *Les Sylphides* Fokine went back to the *ballets blancs* of the age of Marie Taglioni, showing to what extent his reform was a return to the dance concepts of the age of romanticism. Both *Les Sylphides* and Schumann's *Carnaval* were rehabilitations of that very romanticism that generations of Russian critics had rejected and reviled, beginning with Vissarion Belinsky in the 1840s.

The spectacular productions about love punished by death in an exotic setting (*Egyptian Nights*, renamed *Cleopatra* by Diaghilev, *Scheherazade*, and the later *Thamar*) all used this favorite theme of Russian romantic poets such as Pushkin and Lermontov, a theme that was taken up in a big way by the senior Russian Symbolists Valery Briusov and Feodor Sologub, both of them valued contributors to *World of Art* around the turn of the century. The ballets that depicted ancient Greece perceived through a prism of modernist sensibility (*Narcissus, Daphnis et Chloë, L'Après-midi d'un Faune*) represented another bridge between Russian romantic poetry (ballads of Vasily Zhukovsky in the second decade of the nineteenth century) and the Symbolists (the plays of Innokenty Annensky in the first decade of the twentieth). And of course each of these Fokine ballets was a *Gesamtkunstwerk* of the kind that Diaghilev had dreamed of for years, with the harmony of all contributing elements. The exceptions were the divertissement ballets (*Le Festin* and *Les Orientales*), which were medleys of composers and choreographers. But they were an aberration, not encountered in Diaghilev's subsequent seasons.

With *The Firebird* (1910) Diaghilev revealed to the world the genius of Igor Stravinsky, the composer closely associated with him for the rest of his life. Still in the repertory of many companies, the ballet is a masterpiece, but it also betrays the eclecticism inherent in the World of Art mentality. Fokine's choreography employs both the classical ballet techniques (the role of the Firebird) and a freer interpretive style (the Enchanted Princesses). Stravinsky's music draws on authentic folksongs from Rimsky-Korsakov's collection but they are harmonized and orchestrated in the manner of French Impressionism. The libretto uses motifs from Russian folklore, but also includes elements taken from the symbolist writers Alexei Remizov and Sologub, and possibly even from *Swan Lake*.

In Russia, in the meantime, the Symbolism that inspired the early Diaghilev ballets was receding. The gates opened by *World of Art* had admitted a host of new schools of painting, which paralleled the rise of Cubism in the West. In literature the symbolist movement was being challenged by such futurist poets as Vladimir Mayakovsky and

Velimir Khlebnikov, the latter specializing in ultramodernist and primitivist portrayals of the Slavic Stone Age. Stravinsky's score for his next ballet for Diaghilev, *Petrushka* (1911), was, in its raucous modernity, a musical equivalent of these new developments, just as the theme of that ballet had clear analogies with Vsevolod Meierkhold's 1906 production of Alexander Blok's lyrical comedy *The Puppet Booth* (the play in which that great poet bid farewell to the symbolist excesses of his youth). The angular beauty of Nijinsky's choreography for Debussy's *L'Apres-midi d'un Faune*, one year after *Petrushka*, was likewise a step into the future and away from the World of Art aesthetics. So was Nijinsky's *Jeux* (1913), the first Diaghilev ballet on a modern theme danced in modern dress.

The collaboration between Stravinsky and Nijinsky on *The Rite of Spring*, despite its archaic theme, was very much of a piece with the most recent advances in Russian literature and art of the time. Western audiences and critics, accustomed to the retrospective idealizations of the past in Fokine's ballets, were not ready for this breakthrough into Russian futurism and they reacted with hostility. Stravinsky's music, initially rejected as vehemently as Nijinsky's choreography, went on to an independent career as a concert work and eventually won recognition as a great masterpiece in the history of music. But Nijinsky's choreography of *The Rite of Spring* was seen only a total of nine times and was never given the opportunity to win audiences through further exposure and greater familiarity.

Some contemporaries, including Benois and Fokine, have dismissed Nijinsky's choreography as inept and ugly, an opinion to which Stravinsky added a cachet by his utterances of the 1930s. But as Nijinsky's biographers Vera Krasovskaya and Richard Buckle have eloquently argued, as his sister Bronislava tried to demonstrate in her memoirs, and as Stravinsky himself came to recognize shortly before his death,[18] Vaslav Nijinsky was not only a great dancer, but also an innovative choreographer of remarkable vision and power. A study of photographs, drawings, and eyewitness accounts of his ballets will bear this out. But for once in his life, Diaghilev listened to the critics and the public. Influenced by them and, no doubt, by his rancor about Nijinsky's sudden marriage, which Diaghilev felt as a personal betrayal, he let both *Jeux* and *The Rite of Spring* lapse from the repertory.

Nijinsky's departure plunged Diaghilev into a period of uncertainty. After *Petrushka*, Fokine seems somehow to have lost his innovative touch. From about 1911 on, he could only repeat himself. Diaghilev had to learn that while he could go on presenting Fokine's earlier World of Art-style ballets (in the case of *Les Sylphides* and *Scheherazade* almost ad infinitum), creating new specimens of this genre in the second decade of the twentieth century was much harder. Not even all the glories of Ravel's music, which Diaghilev had commissioned, could save Fokine's *Daphnis et Chloë* (1912) from failure. Fokine's *The Legend of Joseph* and *Midas* (both 1914) were retreads of his earlier spectaculars, although *Le Coq d'Or* (1914) did contain some innovations dictated by its staging as a ballet-opera. Diaghilev was forced to turn to second-rate choreographers such as Boris Romanov and Adolph Bolm, and from 1915 on he fostered the choreographic abilities of his new discovery, Léonide Massine (in Russian, Leonid Myasin). A prolific dance maker, Massine never quite reached the level of originality and invention of Diaghilev's other major choreographers.

The liberal-democratic revolution of February 1917, which overthrew the Romanov monarchy, was greeted ecstatically by the entire World of Art circle. This was the coming of the free and just society that Diaghilev had predicted and hailed in his oft-cited banquet speech at the time of the revolution of 1905. He had Ivan Tsarevich carry a red flag in the

18 On Stravinsky's changing attitude to Nijinsky's RITE OF SPRING *choreography, see Pieter C. van den Toorn,* STRAVINSKY AND THE RITE OF SPRING *(Berkeley and Los Angeles, 1987), 2, 6-8, 16. Millicent Hodson's reconstruction of that choreography, danced in 1987-1988 by the Joffrey Ballet, confirms the unfairness of Fokine's and Stravinsky's hostile evaluations.*

19 *The text of Diaghilev's speech welcoming the 1905 revolution is reproduced in Buckle's* DIAGHILEV, *87. Eyewitness accounts of the red flag in* THE FIREBIRD *are also cited in Buckle, 328-329. Like many people in the West, Buckle confuses and conflates the liberal-democratic revolution of February 1917 with the Bolshevik-led October Revolution of the same year.*

20 *For more details about Diaghilev's reasons for staging* THE SLEEPING BEAUTY *and for the production's financial failure, see Boris Kochno,* DIAGHILEV AND THE BALLETS RUSSES *(New York, 1970), 168-175; and Nancy Van Norman Baer,* BRONISLAVA NIJINSKA: A DANCER'S LEGACY, *exh. cat., The Fine Arts Museums of San Francisco (1986), 27-28.*

21 *See the section "His Legacy" in John Percival,* THE WORLD OF DIAGHILEV *(New York, 1979), 125-140, on the fate of individual Diaghilev ballets in later decades.*

finale of *The Firebird*, much to the consternation of the Parisian public, and he commissioned from Stravinsky an orchestration of "The Song of the Volga Boatmen" as a replacement for the old imperial anthem that used to be played at the beginning of performances.[19] But the establishment of the Bolshevik dictatorship in October of the same year spelled the end of these sanguine hopes. Within a decade, the new regime began to impose on the arts the very restrictions that its nineteenth-century utilitarian precursors had advocated and which *World of Art* had struggled to depose. With very few exceptions (such as the dancers Alexei Bulgakov and Maria Piltz), almost everyone connected with the Diaghilev ballet and with his earlier enterprises joined the great exodus of 1918-1922 and found themselves in the West.

The production in 1917 of Jean Cocteau's ballet *Parade* with choreography by Massine, music by Satie, and sets and costumes by Picasso marked the arrival of the international orientation that would become a hallmark of the Diaghilev ballets. He had used music by non-Russian composers almost from the beginning of his seasons, but after 1917 his composers and designers were as likely as not to be foreigners. So were many of his dancers, even if they were given Russian-style stage names. Only his choreographers remained Russian-bred and trained until the very end. Post-1917 Diaghilev repertory regularly included ballets on contemporary subjects. But he also kept alive many of the ballets from his early seasons and he occasionally presented a nineteenth-century classic, such as a two-act version of *Swan Lake*.

In 1921 Diaghilev presented Europe with its first full-length Petipa ballet, *The Sleeping Beauty*, in which four exiled Russian ballerinas alternated in the leading part. But the production's English audience was not as enthusiastic for full-length ballets as it would be a half-century later. Financially, the production was a disaster.[20] Many commentators saw the presentation of the Tchaikovsky classic by the same Diaghilev who had earlier given the world *The Rite of Spring* and *Parade* as a betrayal of his artistic principles, but in fact the production was very much in line with his usual practice of presenting innovative new ballets, while retaining in his repertory such earlier classics as *Swan Lake*.

After 1917 Diaghilev's umbilical connection to the World of Art aesthetics faded away. His principal Russian designers from 1914 on were the advanced modernists Natalia Gontcharova and Mikhail Larionov, although he was to turn a few more times, for sentimental reasons, to his old associates Benois and Bakst. Beginning in 1917, he relied on Picasso, Braque, Matisse, Derain, Gris, and other painters from the School of Paris for his sets and costumes. The one World of Art trait that remained with Diaghilev until the very end was his devotion to ballets on eighteenth-century subjects, which began with *Le Pavillon d'Armide* and continued through *The Good-Humored Ladies* (1917), *Pulcinella* (1920) and all the way to the visually arresting Massine-Nicholas Nabokov-Pavel Tchelichev *Ode* of 1928.

In the 1920s Diaghilev discovered and promoted the talents of two strong and resourceful choreographers, Bronislava Nijinska and George Balanchine. They rewarded him with a half-dozen important ballets, four of which, Nijinska's *Les Noces* and *Les Biches* and Balanchine's *Apollo* and *The Prodigal Son*, are still in the repertory of various companies today.[21] While continuing his association with Stravinsky in the 1920s, Diaghilev also had ballets composed by his other Russian "musical sons," as he called them —Sergei Prokofiev (on three occasions), and also Nicholas Nabokov and Vladimir Dukelsky, later known as Vernon Duke of Broadway fame (on one occasion each). But he also relied on English, Italian, and especially French composers for his scores during this decade. In

Mikhail Larionov, *Caricature of Diaghilev's Circle*, ca. 1920, cat. no. 64. Clockwise from lower left: "Impressario," Jean Cocteau, Ernest Ansermet, Igor Stravinsky, Léonide (Léla) Massine, Diaghilev.

the last few years of his life Diaghilev watched closely the artistic developments in the Soviet Union and found some of them intriguing. The result of this interest was the ballet about Soviet life, *The Steel Leap* (this is a far closer translation of *Stal'noi skok* than the usual French *Le Pas d'Acier*), with a score by Prokofiev and design by the Soviet artist Georgii Iakulov.

Considering the various aspects of Diaghilev's heritage, one common denominator emerges—he was a cultural educator of genius. He brought his native culture out of narrow provincialism and taught his fellow-countrymen to see and understand art, to broaden their literary and philosophical horizons, to publish beautiful journals, and to arrange art exhibitions. From the 1930s on, the Soviet regime did its best to undo his work, but an astounding amount of it survived and managed to prosper in post-Stalinist times. Outside of Russia Diaghilev revealed to the Western world the importance and beauty of Russian art and music. Ballet, when he turned his attention to it, was in a state of greater and lesser decline everywhere. He brought it to unprecedented new heights, re-established its prestige as a major art form, and was ultimately responsible for its huge popularity in this century in many countries where it was not previously known, such as Japan. In his last years, Diaghilev became a bibliophile and amassed an important collection of rare books and manuscripts, many of which have found their ways into the major university libraries of the Western world.

But if Diaghilev educated countries and societies, he was also a master educator of individual artists. Without his influence it would be hard to imagine the careers of Igor Stravinsky, Tamara Karsavina, Vaslav Nijinsky, Léonide Massine, Bronislava Nijinska, Alexandra Danilova, George Balanchine, and Alicia Markova—a by-no-means exhaustive list. But even artists who were fully formed when they began working with Diaghilev, such as Benois and Fokine, nonetheless had the finest moments of their careers during their association with him, moments that could not be duplicated after they had parted ways.

On a more personal level, there were his pedagogical relationships with the three young men with whom he was intimately involved during the 1920s–the dancer and choreographer Serge Lifar; the English dancer Patrick Healey Kay, better known as Anton Dolin; and the composer and conductor Igor Markevich, who was Diaghilev's last love. All three were unknown and unformed artistically when they came to Diaghilev and all went on to major careers in their respective fields.

Diaghilev was not an easy man to deal with, and the memoirs left by his associates reflect this. Alongside the intelligence and loyalty of Karsavina's recollections, we find hidden animosity (Benois), open hostility (Fokine), self-glorification (Lifar), and evasions combined with forgetfulness (Massine). But even the inexact memoirs add to the sum of our knowledge. The vast literature on Diaghilev and his era testifies that his life and achievement are of universal interest.

The publication in the Soviet Union of the two-volume collection of writings by and about Sergei Diaghilev, *Sergei Diaghilev i russkoe iskusstvo* (Sergei Diaghilev and Russian Art) in 1982, edited *con amore* by Ilya Zilbershtein and Vladimir Samkov, marks, despite certain evasions and distortions, the final rehabilitation of Diaghilev and his cause in the Soviet Union. In the current atmosphere of greater openness and relaxation of censorship, there is hope for publication of invaluable Diaghilev materials that are known to exist in heretofore inaccessible Soviet archives. Among them are private journals of Dima Filosofov, Filosofov's book-length manuscript on Alexander Benois, and the memoirs of Diaghilev's stepmother, Elena, and of Walter Nouvel.[22] Publication of these documents should make possible the future study of Diaghilev and his times with a depth of understanding and on a scale that has not been possible until now.

22 *These archival holdings were used by Natalia Lapshina (see note 5 above) and by Zilbershtein and Samkov.*

MIR ISKUSSTVA

Origins of the

Ballets Russes

Elena Bridgman

▼

NOTE:
All translations from the Russian in this article are by the author.

1 *Sergei Diaghilev, "In Memory of Levitan,"* MIR ISKUSSTVA 3 (1900):29.

"WE RUSSIANS HAVE TWO HOMELANDS: RUSSIA AND EUROPE" – Diaghilev quoted Dostoyevsky in an essay in memory of the artist Isaac Levitan that he wrote in 1900 for the art journal *World of Art* (Mir iskusstva).[1] This statement could have served as an appropriate motto to any of Diaghilev's great enterprises—the journal, art exhibitions, the Ballets Russes. It would also be a fitting characterization of Diaghilev himself: he was Russian to the core, yet much of his life was spent in Europe in a kind of self-imposed exile. That part of Diaghilev's career–officially as the impresario, but more as the "tsar" and the guiding genius of the Ballets Russes–is well remembered in the West. However, the younger Diaghilev, the publisher and chief editor of *World of Art*, unfortunately has been known only to a limited scholarly circle, for that first, formative part of Diaghilev's life in and around *World of Art* was in its own way no less exciting than his years with the Ballets Russes. But most important, the Ballets Russes could not have happened without *World of Art*.

Even if eighteen-year-old Sergei Diaghilev had not arrived in St. Petersburg in 1890, ostensibly to study law, the art journal *World of Art* would have eventually come into existence without him. The prerequisite conditions for such a publication made its emergence in fin-de-siècle Russia almost a necessity. Familial ties brought Diaghilev into the orbit of the so-called Nevsky Pickwickians, a select group of well-educated young men among St. Petersburg's literati. They shared a passion for fine arts, music, and literature; most of them were dilettantes, many of them quite brilliant. They also shared a conviction that Russian art had entered a period of stagnation and lagged far behind European developments. The Pickwickians regarded the self-absorbed quality of their native art as one of the chief reasons for its decline and saw the need to do for Russian art what Peter the Great had done for Russia itself–as Pushkin put it, "to hack a window through to Europe." But unlike the eccentric tsar, the Pickwickians armed themselves with pens, not axes, heeding the old Russian proverb that "what is written with a pen cannot be chopped out with an axe."

Although Diaghilev was brought up as an aristocrat, he was initially condescended to by the St. Petersburg Brahmins, who found his provincial tastes and adolescent exuberance hard to bear. Nonetheless, Dmitry Filosofov and Alexandre Benois–perhaps the two most influential members of the Pickwickians—undertook the refinement of his sensibilities. Their efforts paid off in 1898; although the others had discussed an art magazine for years, it took twenty-seven-year-old Diaghilev's ambition and energy to bring their dreams to reality.

It would be impossible to gain a true insight into the development of the Ballets Russes without first understanding the historical and intellectual significance of World of Art as a phenomenon with three distinct manifestations. First, by the late 1880s the Pickwickians renamed their group World of Art and, although their association was quite informal, established a recognized presence in Russian art criticism. Second, as the group's influence grew, it attracted new members, sympathizers, and disciples. And finally, the journal bearing their name, published and edited by Diaghilev, became the voice of the Russian avant-garde, dedicated to the fine arts, including architecture, literature, music, and theater (figure 1). Chief among its aims was to disseminate European art in Russia and educate both Russian artists and the public. It also intended to bring Russian art into the mainstream of European art. At the same time, the journal promoted traditional Russian folk arts and crafts which, it was hoped, would rejuvenate the visual arts and help to create a new style that would be not only modern but also truly Russian in spirit. *World of Art* succeeded to such an extent that roughly a decade after its founding, Russian painting was among the most progressive in Europe.

figure 1
Mir iskusstva (World of Art) 5-6 (1902). Cover design by Léon Bakst.

1902
№ 5—6.

The journal's aesthetic manifesto, broadcast by Diaghilev in four introductory essays in its first issue, proved to be of remarkable longevity, for the Ballets Russes followed this aesthetic program years after the journal ceased to exist. These essays, gathered under the title "Complicated Questions," have already been thoroughly researched. However, in addition to "Complicated Questions," *World of Art* offers a plethora of information about the group's aesthetic and ideology which is buried in minor essays, notes, and reviews that have not received much attention, in part because an English translation of the journal has never been published. This essay will discuss the portion of this material that is pertinent to the subsequent conception of the Ballets Russes.

A brief digression into Russian history might explain why Diaghilev's aesthetic manifesto referred to "complicated questions." Since the 1860s, Russian art had been dominated by two schools: the Academy of Fine Arts on the right, and the Society for Traveling Exhibitions, also known as the Wanderers, on the left. With characteristic sarcasm, *World of Art* described a typical painting in the "academic" style as "Fulvia reposing on carpets, before Cicero's head on a platter."[2] Yet the Wanderers pursued social realism to such a startling degree that the peasants, as Diaghilev put it, "virtually climbed out of the picture frames."[3] Although the Wanderers started as a progressive, anti-academic movement, by the 1890s both academic art and social realism became equally exhausted and so interchangeable that they even were exhibited together, and certain members of the Wanderers had been accepted into the Academy. Dogmatic and powerful, both movements tolerated no divergence from the course they had chosen for Russian art, and they dominated art education at all levels.

2 "Notes" in "Art Chronicles," MIR ISKUSSTVA 2 (1899):82.

3 Sergei Diaghilev, "Art Criticism" in "Art Chronicles," MIR ISKUSSTVA 3 (1900):148.

Behind *World of Art*'s supercilious jabbing lay serious concern about the future of new generations of artists. But, while the journal ridiculed academic interpretations of "classical" art and disagreed in principle with social realism, it recognized their right to exist even though these schools produced, in its opinion, inferior art. Diaghilev wrote in 1900 that "all art styles have an equal right to exist," rather grudgingly suggesting that if academicians and the Wanderers must exhibit, they at least should do so in a well-organized manner.[4]

4 Sergei Diaghilev, "Exhibitions" in "Art Chronicles" and "Art Criticism," MIR ISKUSSTVA 3 (1900):105, 145.

5 Diaghilev, "Exhibitions," 105.

Although *World of Art* dismissed academic art as toothless and tiresome and likened academy exhibitions to monasteries where venerable academicians gather to pray for their sins, Diaghilev and his colleagues revered true classicism, particularly that of ancient Greek art, as well as French rococo and eighteenth-century Russian painting.[5] In one of the first issues of the journal Diaghilev declared that although objective criteria cannot be applied to art, indisputable masterpieces do exist, and these "highest expressions of genius" should serve as points of departure in evaluating art.[6] Diaghilev's respect for classicism, or the enduring values in art, resurfaced years later in his insistence on classical ballet training for the dancers of the Ballets Russes.

6 Sergei Diaghilev, "On Exhibitions" in "Art Chronicles," MIR ISKUSSTVA 2 (1899):98.

Although the World of Art group admired classical art, they realized that blind following of established canons and narrow-minded definitions of classicism inevitably lead art toward stagnation. In his 1900 essay "Art Criticism," Diaghilev remarked with relief that no one believed any more in the idea of a single, "correct" kind of art: "paintings either have merit or they don't, regardless of what style they belong to."[7] Taking an artist's "sincerity of feeling" as one of its chief guiding criteria, *World of Art* opened its pages and its exhibition halls to an eclectic assortment of artists—James McNeill Whistler, Valentin Serov, the Nabis, Philip Maliavin, Ilya Repin, Aubrey Beardsley, Paul Gauguin, John Singer Sargent, Goya, Konstantin Somov, Auguste Rodin—whose art works often resisted

7 Diaghilev, "Art Criticism," 144.

strict classification and contained elements of realism, Impressionism, Art Nouveau, or neoclassicism. Incidentally, certain academicians and the Wanderers, such as Ilya Repin and Victor Vasnetsov, were regularly invited to exhibit with *World of Art* in spite of the journal's animosity toward the Russian art establishment. Indeed, the group's major point of contention with the Wanderers was not over realism as such but over the fact that the social realists sacrificed form to content and insisted that art serve society's needs. In its sterile pretensions toward classicism, "academic" painting had poor form and worse content and therefore was regarded by *World of Art*–which had been branded "decadent" by the Russian art establishment–as the repository of what was truly decadent in Russian art.

However, for all the accusations of decadence, *World of Art* never advocated "art for art's sake"; in fact, Diaghilev explained in "Complicated Questions" that "art cannot be without ideas any more than it can be without form or without color, but no one of these elements can be deliberately introduced into it without destroying the harmony of its parts."[8] Not surprisingly, *World of Art* had a distinct bias in regard to the genres that, in their opinion, expressed a harmonious balance of form and content. In their choice of images, landscapes seem to predominate, with portraits following–in other words, they preferred non-narrative genres that were inherently decorative and appealed more to emotion than to thought. Indeed, decorativeness was the principal concern of page illumination in *World of Art*.

In sum, *World of Art* regarded a certain amount of realism as indispensable, but not its disturbing or unpleasant aspects. Thus, they praised Finnish artists for expressing "the poetry of the people," and ridiculed the Wanderers who painted raw truth.[9] Their hero was Whistler, whose painting they saw as realistic yet "so intimate that it crosses over into the realm of dreams and fantasy."[10] They looked for that ideal in other arts as well, as illustrated by Benois's statement that "theater does not need either absolute realism or absolute fantasy."[11] *World of Art* did not offer any ironclad formulas, only observations and suggestions as to the desirable proportion of realism to fantasy.

However, *World of Art*'s rather complicated attitude toward realism took an unequivocally hostile form as far as social realism was concerned, because the Wanderers had come to monopolize art as the Russian "national" school. In his first issue Diaghilev denounced the Wanderers' brand of "nationalism" as forced and closeminded.[12]

At the same time, another art current in Russia was also challenging the Wanderers' monopoly on nationalism. The so-called neonationalist movement started in the 1870s by the millionaire Savva Mamontov and Princess Tenisheva regarded folklore and peasant crafts as repositories of true native spirit. The neonationalists cultivated a distinctly anti-realist bias and drew their inspiration from Russian fairytales and legends. Their art works emulated traditional peasant styles, which were simple in terms of form and space, yet highly decorative and often striking in color. Unconstrained by theories and dogma, the neonationalist movement attracted many gifted artists–Konstantin Korovin, Mikhail Vroubel, Alexander Golovin, Elena Polenova, Maria Yakuntchikova–who eventually became closely associated with *World of Art*.

Another characteristic of the neonationalists that endeared them to *World of Art* was their belief in the equality of all arts. In Europe, Art Nouveau had succeeded in breaking down the barrier between "decorative" and "fine" arts, and *World of Art* sought to accomplish as much in Russia. To them, every work of art–a monumental painting, a minute ceramic vessel, or an ornamental vignette on a book cover–was equally interesting and valid, to be judged according to the degree of expressed artistic individuality.[13]

8 Sergei Diaghilev, "Our Imaginary Decadence," MIR ISKUSSTVA 1 (1898):15.

9 Sergei Diaghilev, "Exhibition of Helsingfors" in "Art Chronicles," MIR ISKUSSTVA 1 (1898):3.

10 "Whistler," MIR ISKUSSTVA 2 (1899):63.

11 Alexandre Benois, "The Magic Mirror" in "Chronicles," MIR ISKUSSTVA 11 (1904):3.

12 Sergei Diaghilev, "The Bases of Artistic Evaluation," MIR ISKUSSTVA 1 (1898):58.

13 "Notes" in "Chronicles," MIR ISKUSSTVA 7 (1902):42.

In the first years of its existence, especially since Mamontov and Princess Tenisheva subsidized it, the periodical assigned considerable space to the works of neonationalist painters, although their presence was diminished in later issues. In 1902 Benois summarized this shift in a review in which he described the state of applied arts as one of "degeneration, depression, tastelessness, the most pathetic, slavish imitation of the West or, if possible, the even more pathetic and vulgar attempt to create in the native spirit. . . . This is a picture of the decline of an entire people . . . next to which the decadence of the educated circles is sheer nonsense." Benois went on to state that although he had been sympathetic to the efforts to return to native values, he knew now that Vasnetsov, Polenova, and others had been merely indulging in "paysannerie" and dilettantism. He ended on a pessimistic note: "The people are in a state of complete degeneration, and . . . it is a frightening business."[14] The reasons for the decline—that neonationalist art was too self-contained and backward-looking—was diagnosed by Igor Grabar, a painter and an art critic, who stated that although the neonationalists diligently set out to create "in the Russian spirit," they were "guided more by imitation than assimilation."[15]

In the judgment of the World of Art group, "assimilation" could only occur when all human culture was, as Diaghilev put it, "soaked in," because "only in comparison can an

14 Alexandre Benois, "Applied Arts Exhibition" in "Chronicles," MIR ISKUSSTVA 7 (1902):47-50.

15 Igor Grabar, "Thoughts on the State of Applied Arts in Russia" in "Chronicles," MIR ISKUSSTVA 7 (1902):56.

artist appreciate his own individuality, his own strength." Diaghilev called attention to the fact that the best of the Wanderers—Vasnetsov, Surikov, Repin—"challenged the West" by the quality of their painting, but they could not have done so without first acquainting themselves with Western art.[16] Likewise, the landscapist Isaac Levitan, whom Diaghilev regarded above all as "profoundly Russian," admired European art, especially Whistler's paintings, and was not afraid that he might lose his "Russianness" in contact with it.[17] In the end, argued Diaghilev, shutting the door on the "contaminating" West would not safeguard the purity of Russian art. However, *World of Art* did acknowledge the possibility of negative influences from Europe by complaining on several occasions about the inundation of Russian graphic arts by secessionist styles from Germany.

As most graphic artists operated from St. Petersburg, it is hardly surprising that by 1901 the World of Art group came to believe that the hope of Russian art was to be found in the "commercial" Moscow rather than the "aristocratic" northern capital. They felt that because of Moscow's relative "provinciality," it was closer to the indigenous Russian culture and that "somewhere in Moscow there is a deep, eternal stream of life."[18] It is no coincidence that the neonationalist painters were primarily associated with Moscow. The two cities, whose historic rivalry was described by Leo Tolstoy in *War and Peace*, jealously

16 *Sergei Diaghilev, "The Bases of Artistic Evaluation" and "On the Exhibition of V. M. Vasnetsov" in "Art Chronicles,"* MIR ISKUSSTVA 2 *(1899):59, 66.*

17 *Diaghilev, "In Memory of Levitan,"* 29.

18 *P. Pertsov, "Three Sisters," in "Art Chronicles,"* MIR ISKUSSTVA 5 *(1901):96.*

figure 2
Paneling and door by Alexander Golovin, cupboard by Viktor Vasnetsov. *Mir iskusstva* 3 (1900): 69.

figure 3
Woodcut of a small Russian church, signed *I. Bilibin*. *Mir iskusstva* 5 (1901): 27.

figure 4
The World of Art symbol designed
by Léon Bakst for the first issue of
the journal in 1898.

19 Diaghilev, "Art Criticism," 147.

20 Joan Ross Acocella, "The
Reception of Diaghilev's Ballets
Russes by Artists and Intellectuals
in Paris and London, 1909-1914"
(Ph.D. diss., Rutgers, 1984).

21 Diaghilev, "The Bases of
Artistic Evaluation," 60.

22 Acocella, 170.

23 Diaghilev, "Exhibitions," 104.

24 Diaghilev, "Art Criticism," 149.

cultivated their respective reputations—the conservative, cosmopolitan St. Petersburg versus the warm, informal Moscow—that symbolized Diaghilev's "two homelands." Among the neonationalist Moscow artists, the "assimilators," unlike the "imitators," were the ones who not only survived the decline of that movement but even prospered. In other words, where mindless imitation of either European or old Russian styles did not work, the fusion of the best elements that both traditions had to offer resulted in what *World of Art* defined as "new art." Operating in a variety of styles, this new art tended to reflect the "painterly" tendencies of Moscow versus the linear emphasis of St. Petersburg. This distinction becomes especially apparent if we compare the bold and colorful designs by Golovin and Vasnetsov (figure 2) with the restrained, elegant line of the St. Petersburg Slavophile Bilibin (figure 3).

Although, as Diaghilev stated, it was hard to characterize "new art" because it lacked theory, *World of Art* had a strong affinity with Symbolism.[19] In view of the journal's animosity toward social realism, it is understandable why Symbolism—a European movement in literature and art that originated in France as a reaction to naturalism—would appeal to Diaghilev's circle. Realism, a vigorously extroverted movement, demanded active participation in life and objective representation of the concrete world. In contrast, Symbolism relied on intuition and evocation in seeking and expressing profound meanings behind mere appearances of the physical world. Symbolist art had a strongly introverted character and concerned itself with subjects descriptive of psychological states, moods, eroticism, and mysticism. To Diaghilev's fin-de-siècle generation, who were obsessed with beauty, the highly decorative and emotional symbolist aesthetic represented an expression of that elusive ideal.[20]

World of Art's aesthetic views, articulated by Diaghilev in "Complicated Questions," derived from symbolist theory and may be distilled to the following principles. First, Diaghilev's circle saw art as the foremost expression of individuality: an artist, blessed with a spark of genius, has the capacity to grasp and communicate higher truths which otherwise would remain concealed from ordinary minds. Second, because expressions of individuality are subjective, *World of Art* defended artistic freedom: "Beauty in art is temperament expressed in images, and we do not care where these images came from." Bakst's logo for the first issue represented an eagle, proud in its lofty isolation among the stars, and was supposed to symbolize art's disassociation from earthly concerns (figure 4). Finally, *World of Art* regarded beauty as the ultimate, if rarely definable, ideal: "We are a generation thirsting for Beauty. And we find it everywhere, both in Good and in Evil."[21]

The exhibitions organized by the journal put symbolist theories to practice. The symbolist concept of synthesism derived from a Platonic aesthetic that regarded all arts as components of a single divine truth, and integration of all arts as a means of attaining it. Consequently, all aspects of a work of art had to conform to a unifying idea, and in this respect *World of Art* itself was a synthesist endeavor.[22] Diaghilev also applied the concept of synthesism to the exhibitions. Proclaiming that "in every work of art all parts must be unified by some kind of inherent logic," he denounced traditional academic and realist exhibitions as chaos, where paintings were lumped together regardless of their merit, style, or even period, and compared them to eating soup, entrée, and dessert off the same plate.[23] *World of Art*'s reviews of the "establishment" exhibitions were often merciless and witty, as for example in their description of an exhibition organized by the Society of St. Petersburg Artists who "assembled everything in Russian art that is trite and inept, so in this sense the exhibition possessed a definite style."[24]

In decisive contrast, World of Art exhibitions were meticulously selected and organized, and elegantly displayed (see figures 5, 6, and 7). A profusion of plants and flowers created a festive air and special attention was paid to the shape and color of picture frames.[25] Certain ideas that originated in connection to these displays of art may have subsequently been applied by Diaghilev to ballet. For instance, just as Diaghilev regarded large exhibitions as "sores on the body of art," he saw the traditional ballets *à grand spectacle* as "ponderous and tasteless" and lacking in unity. Consequently, the Ballets Russes presented short, one-act ballets, turning away from the classical *ballets-féeries*, that, in Diaghilev's view, were nothing more than "tricks, window-dressing, posing, false paints, and glitter."[26] Moreover, Diaghilev's belief that the same criteria should be applied to displays of art as to works of art prompted him to completely overhaul the shabby Théâtre du Châtelet in order to make it a fitting setting for his company's first Paris season in 1909. Incidentally, it was through World of Art exhibitions that Diaghilev arrived at another principle that he never failed to apply with the Ballets Russes, that is, the more controversy, pomp, and scandal created by the event, the better the publicity.

Although the visual arts were the focus of Diaghilev's activities within World of Art, he was also a lover of music and at an early age had even entertained the notion of becoming a composer. Dissuaded by the eminent composer Rimsky-Korsakov, Diaghilev nevertheless remained a passionate connoisseur of music, especially opera. Like all Symbolists, the World of Art group worshipped Wagner, not only for his genius as a composer but also for his concept of *Gesamtkunstwerk*, namely, a theatrical performance

25 *As described by John Bowlt in* THE SILVER AGE: RUSSIAN ART OF THE EARLY TWENTIETH CENTURY AND THE WORLD OF ART GROUP *(Newtonville, Me., 1979), 170-171, quoted in Acocella, 211.*

26 Diaghilev, "Exhibitions," 104; and "Art Criticism," 146.

figures 5-7
Photographs of World of Art exhibitions. *Mir iskusstva* 5 (1901): 102-103.

figure 8
The Stars, by Léon Bakst.
Mir iskusstva 6 (1901): 69.

in which all the constituent parts—music, singing, acting, scenery—were integrated into a perfect unity. *Gesamtkunstwerk* represented the theatrical equivalent of synthesism in the visual arts, and was closely related to the symbolist theory of *correspondances*, which maintained that musical tones found analogues in colors, while colors and color combinations, like music, were capable of inducing psychological states.

World of Art assiduously reviewed performances of Wagner's operas—usually negatively—both in Europe and in Russia. Those reviews rarely offered any practical solutions as to how Wagner should be produced, but they did invoke symbolist theories by stating that Wagner must never be staged verbatim and that the effects must be stylized, i.e., rendered in a "poetic code."[27]

27 Alexandre Benois, "A Performance of THE VALKYRIES" in "Art Chronicles," MIR ISKUSSTVA 4 (1900):240.

Ironically, Wagner discounted ballet as proper material for *Gesamtkunstwerk*, for he did not consider it "serious" theater. However, the French Symbolists regarded dance as an essential element in theatrical art because movements and gestures are inherently suggestive. While European ballet by the late nineteenth century had degenerated to vulgar acrobatics, in Russia the classical tradition was preserved in its pristine form by dedicated artists like Marius Petipa. Russian intellectuals did not realize what a "rare pearl" they had in Russian ballet until the St. Petersburg premiere of *The Sleeping Beauty*, staged to Tchaikovsky's score in 1890.

In their discovery of ballet, the Symbolist-oriented World of Art group at last found a perfect art, as Benois attested to in his *Reminiscences of Russian Ballet*:

The ballet is one of the most consistent and complete expressions of the GESAMTKUNSTWERK, *the idea for which our circle was ready to give its soul. . . . Everything followed from the common desire of several painters and musicians to see the fulfillment of the theatrical dreams which haunted them. . . .*[28]

28 Alexandre Benois, REMINISCENCES OF THE RUSSIAN BALLET (London, 1941), 370-371, quoted in Acocella, 212.

While opera relied on the word as a chief vehicle of expression and therefore had to be fairly concrete in order to be intelligible, ballet represented the ultimate symbolist spectacle because of the inherent suggestiveness of dance, its principal element. Just as Wagner had revolutionized opera, so was the ever-ambitious Diaghilev prepared to revolutionize ballet. He may have had virtually no one to emulate, but he knew what paths *not* to follow.

Diaghilev's growing preoccupation with the stage, and especially ballet, expressed itself in an increasing number of theater reviews in the later issues of *World of Art*. Diaghilev and Benois, who believed that Russian ballet had entered a phase of stasis, in their comments began to express more concrete criticism about specific aspects of Maryinsky productions. Diaghilev constantly complained about the poor quality of the ballet scores, while the orchestra performances, in his opinion, ranged from "indifferent" to "wilted." He was particularly incensed when the administration of the Imperial Theaters committed the "barbarism" of hiring students to reorchestrate Léo Delibes's score for the ballet *La Source*—an act he described as Delibes's castration by St. Petersburg bureaucrats.[29] Marius Petipa, the celebrated Maryinsky choreographer, was regarded by *World of Art* as a competent, but spent, academic whose choreography had become tiresome and unimaginative. To *World of Art*, true ballet should make the viewer "sob in rapture, as our grandfathers did" in the day of the legendary ballerina Marie Taglioni, who had personified classical perfection.[30]

29 Sergei Diaghilev, "To the Theater" in "Art Chronicles," MIR ISKUSSTVA 8 (1902):32.

30 Alexandre Benois, "New Performances" in "Art Chronicles," MIR ISKUSSTVA 7 (1902):25.

World of Art considered the entire conception of the Maryinsky ballet productions as the antithesis of *Gesamtkunstwerk*. Benois complained in his 1904 review of the *Magic Mirror* that not only were Golovin's decors, Koreschenko's music, and Petipa's choreography

ЗВѢЗДЫ.

31 Benois, "The Magic Mirror," 3.

32 Benois, "New Performances," 25.

33 Benois, "The Magic Mirror," 2.

incompatible, but also Golovin's scenery overwhelmed everything else. Moreover, Golovin's decors, although wonderful in parts, did not present a coherent whole and therefore failed to create an illusion despite the beauty of their colors.[31] For a similar reason—the absence of a unifying idea—Benois likened the 1902 Maryinsky production of the ballet *Don Quixote* to an "animated kaleidoscope."[32]

In his review of the *Magic Mirror*, Benois also expressed the wisdom that Diaghilev would rely on in years to come: that a ballet audience readily forgives all sorts of inadequacies as long as the music is good, for then it creates an illusion, which is the essence of theater.[33] Throughout the history of the Ballets Russes, Diaghilev hired only first-rate composers, conductors, and musicians. Neither did he economize on a ballet's decors and costumes, having observed the Maryinsky's shabby decorations and frayed dresses. In fact, Diaghilev was more likely to fall victim to the other extreme, lavishing extravagant sums of money as long as he thought it could get him what he wanted.

Just as with his composers, Diaghilev always commissioned scenery and costumes from leading artists, whose long list included both Russian and European names. By hiring easel painters to create theatrical decors, Diaghilev not only ensured originality and the high quality of his productions but also exercised his genius for spotting and cultivating talent. For example, Lev (Léon) Bakst, a minor society painter, through his association with the journal was introduced to theater design and eventually gained considerable recognition in St. Petersburg. However, it was with Diaghilev and the Ballets Russes, who offered him much greater opportunities for expression and more appreciative audiences, that Bakst's art reached its true efflorescence and international acclaim. That Bakst possessed an innate feeling for spatial arrangement, particularly well suited to dramatic action, is already evident in his drawing *The Stars*, which appeared in the 1901 *World of Art* as an accompaniment to a selection of poetry (figure 8). Several of its salient features— the dramatic view from far above, the tendency toward heavy framing of the central space, the proliferation of hanging ornament, such as vines, boughs, and even snakes—would reappear in sets for *Schéhérazade* (Plate 12), *L'Après-midi d'un Faune, Le Dieu Bleu* (see Misler, figure 9), and other ballets. Dramatically amplified by the scale and the infusion of color in stage design, these devices contributed to the overwhelming effect of Bakst's art on European audiences. Similarly, the painters Benois, Golovin, and Nicholas Roerich did their best work for the theater. Having started with Mamontov's private opera, they were praised, guided, scolded, prodded, and eventually brought to the Maryinsky, and ultimately to the Ballets Russes, by Diaghilev. If in all other respects Russian art lagged behind European, by the turn of the century Russian stage design evolved into one of the most progressive in Europe. Until the World of Art movement the participation of leading easel painters in major theatrical productions was virtually unprecedented in Europe, for even though the Nabis had painted sets for the experimental Théâtre de l'Oeuvre, they remained unknown outside of a narrow avant-garde milieu.

In addition to the Maryinsky productions, *World of Art* diligently monitored the events at the progressive Moscow Arts Theater. Despite the fact that the Moscow Arts Theater advocated stage realism, World of Art often encouraged them in their experimentation and then learned from their mistakes. For instance, the journal acknowledged that the Moscow Arts Theater achieved near perfection in persuading the audience that the stage is reality. Having attained that perfection, however, there was nowhere for the theater to go. Thus, wrote Filosofov, the only way out of this state of imminent "degeneration" was to get away from realism.[34]

For Diaghilev and Benois, the issue of synthesism was directly related to the problem

34 Vladimir Filosofov, "Uncle Vanya" in "Art Chronicles," MIR ISKUSSTVA 5 (1901):103.

figure 9
Photograph of a wooden church in Vyterg, Russia. *Mir iskusstva* I (1899): 91.

figure 10
A wooden church in northern Russia, signed *I. Bilibin*. *Mir iskusstva* I (1899): 92.

35 Benois, "The Magic Mirror," 5.

36 P. Gnedich, "Ibsen's DR. STOCKMAN *at the Moscow Arts Theater*" in "Art Chronicles," MIR ISKUSSTVA 5 (1901):102.

37 "Notes" in "Art Chronicles," MIR ISKUSSTVA 4 (1900):214.

38 Diaghilev's title at the Tauride Exhibition, as reported in "Notes" in "Chronicles," MIR ISKUSSTVA 11 (1904):113. See Simon Karlinsky's essay in this catalogue for additional discussion.

of suggestiveness versus realism. Writing in defense of suggestiveness, Benois stated that obsession with realism and trompe l'oeil in details is not art, for it is more important to sacrifice details in favor of the whole. Moreover, "fantastic" in art does not necessarily mean something amorphous or approximate. In fact, he found that the best practitioners of the "fantastic" in painting, such as Vroubel and Somov, were quite concrete and lucid, even when they dealt with imaginary worlds.[35]

In another 1901 review, *World of Art* again noted that the meticulous attention to details, so typical of realist theater, was perfect to a fault. That is, by relentlessly imposing a certain mood on the audience, the Moscow Arts Theater only succeeded in monotony.[36] According to *World of Art*, where the Moscow Arts Theater failed, Golovin succeeded with his designs for the Maryinsky production of the opera *Ice House*, which were distinguished by their veracity and convincing effects based on contrast.[37] In sum, while the Moscow Arts Theater strove for a convincing realism, *World of Art*, and later Diaghilev's Ballets Russes, aimed at a convincing illusion—a unity of mood created through suggestiveness.

The final year of *World of Art*'s publication was 1904. The mission of linking Russian and European art having been accomplished, its members went separate ways. Diaghilev had spent a good portion of the previous three years darting all over Russia in search of half-forgotten works of art for his 1905 exhibition of Russian historical portraits. Focusing on works from the eighteenth and early nineteenth centuries by such brilliant Russian artists as Levitsky and Borovikovsky, the show opened at the Tauride Palace and was the crowning achievement of the "General-Komissar" Diaghilev's unceasing labors to restore and preserve Russian artistic heritage.[38] If *World of Art* had not initiated a campaign aimed at the preservation of indigenous art and architecture, many art treasures would have been lost and the exquisite wooden churches of northern Russia (figure 9) would exist only as glimpses in Bilibin's graphics (figure 10) or Gontcharova's theatrical designs.

Having achieved triumphal success in Russia, Diaghilev then set his eyes on Europe.

The exhibition he organized for the 1906 Salon d'Automne in Paris offered the European public their first opportunity to view Russian art of all periods, thus fulfilling one of World of Art's principal ambitions. The success of this venture was also a portent of Diaghilev's gradual moving away from Russia toward Europe, and especially Paris, the art capital of the world. The motivations behind Diaghilev's decision were, no doubt, varied and complex, and were already at work in 1900 when he wrote in an article in memory of Levitan that "not much is understood in Russia."[39] Throughout its existence, World of Art had regularly aired grievances regarding the obstinate ignorance of the Russian public. For instance, an exasperated note in the 1900 issue addressed the fact that in Russia excellent paintings at auctions brought less money than candelabras and furniture—a sad reflection on the society's attitudes toward art. Moreover, foreign collectors were aware of that fact and every year took away from Russia "the most precious, the most wonderful of what our forefathers had gathered."[40] With characteristic irony, World of Art commented that awarding the gold medal to the painter Konstantin Korovin at the 1900 Paris Exposition Universelle was construed by the Russian public as a symptom of incompetence on the part of the French jury.[41]

By the end of the first decade of the new century Diaghilev realized that he must go to Europe if he wanted an enlightened and appreciative audience for his artistic enterprises. By 1909, things Russian had become quite the vogue in Paris, not exactly supplanting but rather reinforcing the persistent European fascination with the exotic and mysterious East, of which, from the Western European point of view, distant Russia was a part. At the same time, there were indications that Europe was tiring of the Wagnerian "Viking world of bearded warriors drinking blood out of skulls" and was restless for something new.[42]

The year after his Salon d'Automne exhibition, Diaghilev had brought to Paris a season of Russian music consisting of five concerts, which proved to be a great success and further stirred curiosity about Russia. In the next year, relentless Diaghilev delivered the best of Russian opera, interspersed with short ballet segments. These performances created a tremendous impression on Parisian audiences, who were quickly acquiring a taste for that distant, enigmatic culture, perceived as a land of untamed nature and unbridled passions. At the same time, to a public who equated ballet with music-hall revues, the dancing sequences gave a hint of what true ballet could become. Diaghilev had misgivings about an entire season of ballet in Paris, but finally in 1909 he took that risk, though he wisely still included a few operas in the repertory—just in case.

Descriptions by Diaghilev's contemporaries of the reception of the Ballets Russes in Paris abounded in adjectives like "marvelous," "overwhelming," and "intoxicating" and referred to the effect on the audiences in terms of "shock" and even "mass delirium."[43] The Parisians were astonished not only by the superb technical mastery of the dancers, but also by their ability to express dramatic nuances not so much through miming, as was the case with European ballet, but primarily through dance itself. The musical scores were exquisite: Chopin and Tchaikovsky, as well as the virtually unknown Borodin, Tcherepnine, and Arensky, whose unusual Slavic harmonies Europeans found spellbinding. But unquestionably it was the decors that created the biggest sensation— highly stylized, in fantastic hues and shocking color combinations, they were a world apart from either traditional theater with its trompe l'oeil or the somber, austere air of the European avant-garde stage. The designers for the first Parisian season, whose names and works were a familiar sight on the pages of World of Art, included Benois, Roerich, Korovin, Golovin, and, of course, Bakst, for it was primarily Bakst's colors and ornamentation that "intoxicated" by their blatant sensuality and originality bordering on

39 Diaghilev, "In Memory of Levitan," 4.

40 "Notes" in "Art Chronicles," MIR ISKUSSTVA 3 (1900):116.

41 "Notes" in "Art Chronicles," MIR ISKUSSTVA 4 (1900):161.

42 "Notes" in "Art Chronicles," MIR ISKUSSTVA 3 (1900): 116.

43 Based in part on the recollections of Diaghilev's lover and collaborator Serge Lifar, in SERGE DIAGHILEV, HIS LIFE, HIS WORK, HIS LEGEND: AN INTIMATE BIOGRAPHY (1940; rept. New York, 1976), 158.

L'Echange des Favorites

heresy. What a revelation they must have been if even the modern eye—jaded by an unprecedented exposure to styles ranging from cave paintings to Abstract Expressionism—still responds with wonder to Bakst's bizarre harmonies—or riots—of color and pattern.

The Ballets Russes not only resurrected classical ballet at its purest, but served it to Europe in novel, exciting ways. The first season in 1909 presented a rich program of ballets inspired by the historical periods favored by *World of Art*: *Le Pavillon d'Armide*—the eighteenth century, *Cléopâtre*—Egyptian, *Polovtsian Dances*—ancient Russia, while *Le Festin* and *Les Sylphides* were classical divertissements. *World of Art's* enthusiasm for Greek arts and theater resulted in *Narcisse* in 1911, followed by *L'Après-midi d'un Faune* and *Daphnis et Chloë* in 1912. Just as the journal had maintained a careful distance between the aesthetic and the cerebral, that is, the visual arts versus religion and philosophy, so did Diaghilev, at least in the early years, regard ballet as entertainment, primarily an emotional and aesthetic experience. And just as Benois criticized the whole premise of the Maryinsky production of *Don Quixote* as a subject inappropriate for ballet—because "it made a travesty of a tragic story"—so did Diaghilev, especially in the pre-war ballets, choose themes of fairytale or allegorical quality, which primarily engaged the viewers' fantasies by transporting them to a make-believe world or situation.

Diaghilev's early ballets were symbolist experimentations, in which the constituent parts—movement, costumes, decor, and music—worked *en ensemble* to induce specific emotional states. As the Ballets Russes leaned toward what Wagner termed "semi-subterranean convulsion" (the varieties of eros), eroticism—an important ingredient of symbolist art—played a part in virtually all early ballets. Whether an element of narrative ballets, such as *Cléopâtre*, or divertissements like the *Polovtsian Dances*, eroticism in Diaghilev's productions had a remarkably expressive range, from the poetic lightness of *Les Sylphides* to the orgiastic maelstrom of *Schéhérazade*. However, eros at its darkest manifested itself in only three ballets: *Cléopâtre*, *Schéhérazade*, and *Thamar*, which explored the symbolist obsession with the duality of love and death. All other early ballets,

figure 12
Illustration with a nude figure,
signed *L. Bakst. Mir iskusstva* 5
(1901): 207.

44 *Konstantin Balmont, "The
Poetry of Horror,"* MIR ISKUSSTVA 1
(1898):175.

figure 13
Reproduction of T. T. Heine's
painting *The Vestal* from the Berlin
Secession exhibition of 1902.
Mir iskusstva 8 (1902): 204.

even the most flamboyant and sensuous, eschewed the "poetry of horror"–that strain of Symbolism that sought beauty in the darker, lower currents of life.[44]

Similarly, *World of Art* may have enthusiastically reproduced the "decadent" art of Beardsley and the Secessionists and emulated their superb technique, but in content the decorative graphics by Lancerey, Somov, Benois, Bilibin and others reflected their essential Russianness, that "unconscious nationalism of blood" that Diaghilev spoke about in "Complicated Questions." This "unconscious nationalism" had traditionally tended toward the spiritual rather than the physical. At times, it could be sensuous, passionate, and playful, but it was always lyrical and hardly ever sinister. In Russian folklore and literature, even the devil is just another creature among their pantheon of Russian bugaboos, such as Baba Yagas, changelings, and vampire bats, as opposed to sinister Lucifer, the Prince of Darkness. Bakst was the only contributor of outright naughtiness to the illustrations of *World of Art*, with one or two exceptions, such as Benois's uncharacteristic lapse into eroticism (figure 11). But even here the tone is lighthearted and tongue-in-cheek or, as with Bakst's nudes (figure 12), provocative but completely lacking in the disturbing, almost obscene implications of some of Beardsley's works or of T. T. Heine's painting of a woman embraced by the Devil (figure 13). *World of Art* Symbolists may have paid their respects to the more outré currents of European aestheticism, but they did so from a safe distance.

Although Diaghilev in his ballets made every effort to capitalize on the untamed, passionate aspects of the Russian spirit, he was particularly conscious of that "other" view of Russia which, in his opinion, had been best visually articulated by Levitan–the "eternal lyricism," "love for small (but not insignificant) things," and "a strange, romantic sadness."[45] These qualities had also been noted by European critics, one of whom commented that "Roerich's melancholy, meditatively sad landscapes and Somov's intoxicating dreaminess reveal yet another side of Russia."[46] At the same time, Diaghilev understood that the "intimate, gray, northern" nature of Levitan's Russia would not have been appreciated in fin-de-siècle Paris, because it was "in love with the opulence and glitter of Impressionism."[47] In 1909, the French capital was infatuated with glitter of a different kind, so Diaghilev gave them what they craved–novelty, passion, and exotica.

To the symbolist "poetry of horror" and the Wagnerian recipe for "sex and violence," Diaghilev's answer was passion à la Russe. He may have consciously catered to that vague European suspicion that the "primitive" people, whose senses have not been dulled by civilization, might possibly feel more than the jaded Europeans. Because Russia was associated with something unrepressed and instinctive, Diaghilev gave them *Cléopâtre*, *Schéhérazade*, and *Thamar*, but he suppressed the morbid meanings in favor of the idea that sexual ecstasy at its highest is worth dying for. With unerring instinct, Diaghilev understood that Parisians wished to be transported rather than punished. Just as Diaghilev discussed in "Complicated Questions" the unique ability of an artist to communicate to ordinary minds what would otherwise be unattainable to them, so too did the Ballets Russes allow Parisian audiences to feel "through" them, to expand and free their senses.

The subject of sensuality as a necessary ingredient of art had often been discussed by *World of Art*. Artistic freedom, a chief principle of symbolist aesthetics, presupposed no taboos. In reality, however, *World of Art* had its prejudices: for instance, Diaghilev found Gustav Klimt's *Medicine* "repelling" because its provocative description of the human body was too graphic, therefore "unbeautiful." Yet, the journal was quick to denounce a proposed censorhip law in Germany that would have automatically made the art of Correggio and Michelangelo a "threat to society's morals." *World of Art* argued that art must inspire passion, and that sensuality should be dealt with in the open, as in the Bible– always candid yet never crude.[48] Taking pains to distinguish between sensuality and prurience, they ridiculed the St. Petersburg "Society for the Encouragement of the Arts," who "bashfully covered Rodin's *Eve* with flower pots," while Diaghilev fumed about "nude wenches" on the ceiling of the Musical Society, saying that such "murals would be a fitting decor for a Moscow tavern but not for what considers itself to be a 'temple of art.'"[49]

Eroticism and nationalism had been characteristic themes of Diaghilev's ballet productions. With *Le Sacre du Printemps*, Diaghilev not only desired to show Europe yet another aspect of Russia–its pagan past, with its own primitive passions–but also to explore the concept of eros as the moving force of all creation. In its inspiration, the ballet could be traced back to the Nietzschean view of modern civilization and its art as hopelessly fragmented, whereas he saw art in its cradle as pure and whole. *Le Sacre du Printemps* revealed a vision of a world at the dawn of civilization, when man was still an inextricable part of nature's wholeness. The human senses, in their primitive purity, still retained their intimate connection with the chthonic forces, which could be set into motion in early spring by the passionate, abandoned dance of the sacrificial virgin.

45 Diaghilev, "In Memory of Levitan," 29.

46 "Notes" in "Chronicles," MIR ISKUSSTVA 7 (1902):14-16.

47 Diaghilev, "In Memory of Levitan," 30.

48 "Notes" in "Art Chronicles," MIR ISKUSSTVA 3 (1900):120.

49 "Notes" in "Art Chronicles," MIR ISKUSSTVA 2 (1899):81.

Certain portions of Nietzsche's philosophy, and especially his relationship to Wagner, were discussed in *World of Art*, and *Le Sacre du Printemps* may well be one of the more successful attempts at *Gesamtkunstwerk*, for the ballet's decors, music, and choreography effectively collaborated at evoking a vision of awakening nature and awakening humanity. Roerich's costumes were designed after the original peasant dresses he had seen in Princess Tenisheva's collection, and with their spare forms and a simple geometricized trim they constituted a perfect accompaniment to Nijinsky's deliberately awkward choreography and Stravinsky's dissonant, angular music. However, if Roerich's decors could still be qualified as symbolist, the atonal musical score and the emphatically unclassical choreography were modernist, and with *Le Sacre* the symbolist period of Ballets Russes came to a close. The ballet may have almost caused a riot, but the process of making it in itself almost constituted allegorical "rites of spring": the birth of a new form was painful for everyone. Diaghilev himself initially had misgivings about Nijinsky's radical choreography, which Stravinsky did not approve of and most of the dancers hated.

The paths of Diaghilev's enterprises were, in fact, rarely smooth. Diaghilev's Western contemporaries often commented on the emotionally charged world of the Ballets Russes: the high-strung, impulsive Russians constantly argued, fought, stormed in and out, and engaged in tearful reconciliations. However, Diaghilev clearly thrived on conflict and controversy, as had the members of World of Art, who believed that division and sectionism among artists is natural and is a symptom of viability.[50] The World of Art group lived in a state of perpetual disagreement, often contradicting one another. Yet, in equating artistic freedom with agony, they gladly embraced it, for they regarded freedom as "the crowning glory of all-encompassing art."[51] In their anxiety to avoid dogmatism, the group tried to keep an open mind toward styles they did not quite approve of, such as Impressionism, which, they said, "must not be ignored, otherwise it would be a symptom of a superficial attitude toward art."[52] However, in their proud dilettantism one can perhaps detect a pang of insecurity: a note in the 1900 issue, somewhat defensive in tone, argued that dilettantes are necessary to art, for they are often erudite, altruistic, helpful and, most important, they "reflect the brilliance of others."[53] If Diaghilev fell prey to that insecurity, he resolved it by becoming a benevolent dictator of the Ballets Russes. An anonymous note in the same issue of *World of Art*, which could have been Diaghilev's, questioned the usefulness of committees and panels and concluded that deciding matters by majority vote is not for art—logic dictates that "there must be absolute, unrestricted power in the hands of one man."[54]

Thus, Diaghilev did not object to chaos as long as he presided over it. Neither did he mind mistakes, provided there was progress, for, as he announced in *World of Art*, "there is no life without movement."[55] In his review of Alexandre Benois's book, *The History of Russian Painting of the Nineteenth Century*, Diaghilev wrote that without mistakes, the book would be lifeless.[56] Likewise, in his theatrical experiments, Diaghilev strove for perfection, but in the absence of that elusive ideal, he was willing to overlook flaws if the result was fresh and interesting. As he wrote in a review of a concert given by young musicians in 1899, unevenness and a certain weakness are expected of those "who have not yet reduced their art to a dispassionate automatism by endless repetition."[57] In his praise of the artist Vroubel, Diaghilev wrote in 1900 that "attempts to transcend the ugliness of reality are often risky"—a statement that acquired a special meaning with the Ballets Russes productions that occasionally went awry.[58]

50 "Notes" in "Art Chronicles," MIR ISKUSSTVA 3 (1900):116.

51 Diaghilev, "The Bases of Artistic Evaluation," 61.

52 "Notes" in "Art Chronicles," MIR ISKUSSTVA 2 (1899):118.

53 "Notes" in "Art Chronicles," MIR ISKUSSTVA 4 (1900):116.

54 "Notes" in "Art Chronicles," MIR ISKUSSTVA 3 (1900):79.

55 "Notes" in "Art Chronicles," MIR ISKUSSTVA 4 (1900):162.

56 Sergei Diaghilev, "Alexandre Benois's THE HISTORY OF RUSSIAN PAINTING OF THE NINETEENTH CENTURY," MIR ISKUSSTVA 7 (1902):39.

57 "Notes" in "Art Chronicles," MIR ISKUSSTVA 1 (1898):63.

58 "Notes" in "Art Chronicles," MIR ISKUSSTVA 3 (1900):79.

Diaghilev's unquenchable thirst for novelty prompted rapid evolvement of the Ballet Russes. As the company grew more experimental, Diaghilev engaged leading European avant-garde painters as his collaborators, who introduced Cubism, Futurism, Orphism, and Constructivism to the theatrical stage. The later productions, unlike the earlier history-oriented symbolist ballets, frequently addressed contemporary issues and concepts and in their form tended to reflect the abstract concerns of the twentieth-century art. Musical scores by such modernist composers as Eric Satie, Sergei Prokofiev, Francis Poulenc, and George Auric enhanced the innovative decors and costumes. The Ballets Russes, as a logical extention of *World of Art's* aesthetic ideology, had given Symbolism a new lease on life, if only for a few years. Now the advent of Modernism infused new life into the Ballets Russes.

FROM STUDIO

TO STAGE

The Painters

of the

Ballets Russes

━━━━━

John E. Bowlt

▼

1 Y. Annenkov, untitled, undated manuscript in TsGALI (Central State Archive of Literature and Art), Moscow, f. 2618, op.1, ed. khr. 15, 1.147.

2 This article repeats some of the information included in my article "Stage Design and the Ballets Russes" in THE JOURNAL OF DECORATIVE AND PROPAGANDA ART (Miami) 5 (Summer 1987): 28-45.

Plate 1
Léon Bakst, Costume design for a Dancer and Slave, 1921, based on the original design for Diaghilev's production of Cléopâtre in 1909, cat. no. 25.

ONE OF THE PRIMARY AREAS in which the Ballets Russes excelled, leaving an indelible impression on the development of twentieth-century theater as a whole, was stage design. The sets and costumes that artists such as Léon Bakst, Alexandre Benois, Natalia Gontcharova, Mikhail Larionov, Nicholas Roerich, Pavel Tchelitchev, and Georgii Yakulov designed for the famous productions of the Diaghilev era–Cléopâtre (1909, Plate 1), Le Pavillon d'Armide (1909), Schéhérazade (1910), Petrouchka (1911), Le Sacre du Printemps (1913), Jeux (1913), Le Coq d'Or (1914), Chout (1921), Les Noces (1923), and Le Pas d'Acier (1927)–still dazzle us with their colors and forms.

There are many reasons why this magic persists. One is a very practical one, for the sets and costumes that have come down to us are the most tangible components of those fabulous spectacles of the Ballets Russes that, as the artist Yurii Annenkov once observed, were "like a butterfly. They come to life one evening and within three or four hours vanish forever."[1] Bakst's costume for Tamara Karsavina as L'Oiseau de Feu in 1910 or Larionov's buffoons for Chout still generate some of the excitement and dynamism of their time and help us to understand why such artists achieved recognition precisely as stage designers for the Ballets Russes. The aim of this essay is to examine their contributions to key productions of the Diaghilev era and to pinpoint some of the formal innovations that were assimilated by modern ballet and that to this day continue to be practiced and elaborated.[2]

It was not only a question of understanding and evoking the essential spirit of a historical epoch, national character, or plot line that distinguished Diaghilev's designers. His twenty-two Russian-born artists also introduced new formal resolutions within the scenic space, often–directly or indirectly–incorporating ideas that we tend to associate with the Russian avant-garde. Indeed, in some cases the Ballets Russes served as a practical extension of theoretical ideas that the radical artists of the 1910s (Larionov, Kazimir Malevich, Vladimir Tatlin, et al.) entertained in their studios. Ever open to new aesthetic concepts, Diaghilev used his company as a laboratory for testing Neo-Primitivism, Cubism, Futurism, Simultanism, and Constructivism, that is, most of the movements that determined the course of twentieth-century art. We think of Jeux in Paris in 1913 with its strange parallels with the "transrational" opera Victory over the Sun produced in St. Petersburg the same year; of Larionov's geometric references to his own abstract system of painting, Rayonism, in his sets and costumes for Le Soleil de Nuit in 1915 (see cover and Garafola essay, figures 1 and 2); of Naum Gabo's and Antoine Pevsner's application of Constructivism to La Chatte (see figure 7) in Monte Carlo in 1927. The relationship between the Ballets Russes and the Russian avant-garde is complex, but there is one important aspect that deserves special emphasis, namely that the real experiments and innovations in sets and costumes were made by Russian rather than by Western artists. Of course, Balla, Braque, Ernst, Matisse, Picasso, de Chirico, and other Western painters also contributed to the success of the Ballets Russes, but ultimately the styles that they applied (for example, Cubism and Surrealism) were pictorial systems appropriate to the intimate space of the studio, and not always operative within the public space of the theater. Primary exceptions are Picasso's creations for Parade (1917) and Balla's for Feu d'Artifice (1917), but Braque's resolutions for Zéphire et Flore (1925) or de Chirico's for Le Bal (1929), while visually appealing, hardly relate to the dynamic, constructive demands of the ballet in action.

During what is known as Russia's Silver Age (ca. 1895-ca. 1920), poets, painters, and musicians brought about a veritable renaissance of Russian culture. Sergei Diaghilev was one of the principal contributors to this spiritual awakening and, through his many

3 *"Na khudozhestvennykh
vystavkakh" in* KULISY *(Moscow)* 1
(January 1917): 11.

enterprises, not least the Ballets Russes, helped bring his country into the European mainstream. True, well before the first Paris productions of the Ballets Russes in 1909, European audiences had already been primed for the "exotic barbarism" of Russia. Both Savva Mamontov and Princess Maria Tenisheva, for example, the two great maecenates of Russia's fin de siècle, ensured that the Russian arts and crafts were well represented at the Exposition Universelle of 1900 in Paris. Moreover, it was the artists who designed the productions for Mamontov's private opera (some of them, such as Konstantin Korovin, later worked for Diaghilev) who masterminded a "revolt in stage design";[3] and thanks to Princess Tenisheva, Roerich and Igor Stravinsky located essential materials for the elaboration of *Le Sacre du Printemps*. The princess also organized an enormous exhibition, *Objets d'Arts Russes Anciens Faisant Partie des Collections de la Princess Marie Ténichév*, at the Musée des Arts Décoratifs in Paris in 1907, which she hoped would overshadow Diaghilev's rival efforts to export Russian culture.

But it was hard to outwit Diaghilev. From the very beginning, he was convinced of the need to promote Russian art abroad and that he was the person to do this. He wrote in 1897,

At the moment Russian art is in a state of transition. History places any nascent movement in this position when the principles of the older generation clash and struggle with the newly emergent demands of youth. . . .

Our art has not only collapsed—on the contrary, I feel that this is the best moment to unite and, as one, to assume our place in the life of European art.[4]

4 Letter from Diaghilev to Apollinarii Vasnetsov of 20 May 1897, quoted in V. Lapshin, SOIUZ RUSSKIKH KHUDOZHNIKOV *(Leningrad, 1974), 18-19.*

Diaghilev's *World of Art* (Mir iskusstva) magazine and exhibitions, his critical publications, and then his ballet troupe helped make this wish come true. Following the precedent of the Exposition in 1900, he organized the Russian section for the Salon d'Automne in Paris in 1906, including Russia's newest and most talented artists (Bakst, Benois, Viktor Borisov-Musatov, Konstantin Somov, Mikhail Vrubel, etc.). The following year he arranged the Cinq Concerts Historiques Russes which, perhaps more than any other event, can be regarded as the direct precursor to the Saisons Russes of 1909 onward. With music by Glinka, Musorgsky, Rimsky-Korsakov, Scriabin, Tchaikovsky, among others, and with operatic excerpts (*Boris Godunov, Ruslan and Ludmilla, Sadko, Snegurochka*, etc.) sung by Feodor Chaliapin, Vladimir Kastorsky, and Evgeniia Zbrueva, the concerts were an immediate success. The handsome program carried not only biographical notes on the composers, commentary on the operas, and musical notations, but also portraits of the composers by Bakst, Valentin Serov, Ilia Repin, and Evgenii Zak, and designs of the St. Petersburg and Moscow productions. In other words, even in this comparatively simple context (a concert brochure), Diaghilev made sure that the arts were integrated, implying that the success of an opera or ballet depended as much on the visual component as on the music and the libretto.

There is no question that Diaghilev and his early associates (Bakst, Benois, Ivan Bilibin, Mstislav Dobujinsky, Alexander Golovin, Korovin) came to their particular understanding of the stage—and stage design—thanks to their "apprenticeship" within the World of Art. The group's principal achievements (see Bridgman essay) and their ancillary activities, such as Benois's editorship of the magazine *Khudozhestvennye sokrovishcha Rossii* (Art Treasures of Russia, 1901-1903) and Diaghilev's organization of the *Exhibition of Historic Russian Portraits* at the Tauride Palace in 1905, determined the predilections of the Ballets Russes. The aspiration toward artistic synthesism, the fascination with past cultures (especially Greece, Egypt, and Versailles), the emphasis on the individual artist's creative expression (Diaghilev welcomed the most varied styles to his exhibitions and ballet productions), the search for new methods of design (the book ornament or stage costume as an integral and equal part of the organic whole)—all these principles were later expressed and interpreted by the Ballets Russes.

Actually, during the period 1898-1906 the World of Art members, including Diaghilev, were not particularly interested in the ballet, and the discipline was rarely discussed on the pages of their journal. However, as Benois maintained, their "mania for the theater"[5] prompted them to visit all manner of productions in St. Petersburg and abroad, even though they seemed to prefer opera to drama and the ballet. Their general attitude towards the function of theater in its widest sense was closely connected to the aesthetic demands that they made of all artistic activity—that it should be outside of social and political "usefulness," that it should reflect the artist's free spirit, and that it should disclose the higher reality beyond the world of tawdry appearances. Because neither Diaghilev nor Benois evinced a particular enthusiasm for the ballet at this time, their attitude towards the Imperial Ballet was, to say the least, restrained. Diaghilev made this

5 A. Benois, MEMOIRS *(London, 1964), 2:26.*

6 S. Diaghilev, "V teatre. 1. Balety Deliba" in "Art Chronicles," MIR ISKUSSTVA 8 (1902): 32.

clear in a 1902 review entitled "In the Theater. I. The Ballets of Delibes" in which he described a performance at the Maryinsky Theater: "Here we saw how the eternal Petipa stormed around so clumsily, how the corps de ballet idly went through its tedious 'pas.'"[6] Of course, Diaghilev's negative attitude was prompted by his direct and unsavory experience with the cumbersome apparatus of the Imperial Ballet: the Imperial Theaters had invited him to produce the ballet *Sylvia*, but because of his innovative approach supported by Bakst, Benois, and other modern artists, he was forced to resign from this position in 1901. It should be remembered, however, that a number of Diaghilev's experimental ballets had their premieres (albeit in tamer versions) on the Imperial stage. *Egyptian Nights*, for example, which became *Cléopâtre* in Paris, was first produced by Michel Fokine at the Maryinsky Theater in St. Petersburg (1908), as was *Le Pavillon d'Armide* (1907). Of course, it would have been impossible for the Imperial Ballet to have staged the innovative productions that Diaghilev realized in Paris such as *Schéhérazade* and *Jeux*, but as far as dancing and choreographic technique were concerned Diaghilev and his colleagues maintained and propagated, rather than destroyed, the Imperial tradition.

7 F. Syrkina, RUSSKOE TEATRALNO-DEKORATSIONNOE ISKUSSTVO VTOROI POLOVINY XIX VEKA (Moscow, 1956), 24.

Furthermore, we should not underestimate the achievements of late nineteenth-century Russian stage design, for, in spite of Diaghilev's hostility to the Imperial theaters and the intransigent bureaucracy and self-satisfaction they represented, there were capable artists who worked in the St. Petersburg and Moscow theaters. The romantic extravaganzas concocted by Mikhail Bocharov, Anatolii Geltser, Andrei Roller, and Matvei Shishkov evoked "flights, magic transformations, fires, destructions,"[7] changing any ballet, opera, or play—whether Alexander Pushkin's *Ruslan and Ludmilla* or Johann von Schiller's *Jungfrau von Orleans*—into a celebration of the picturesque. But a direct consequence of these flamboyant productions of the late nineteenth-century was a marked tendency towards eclecticism. The unscrupulous mixing of styles resulted in the most curious combinations, for example, of dancers in tights with moustaches à la Wilhelm dancing the ballet *Pharoah's Daughter*. Fokine was especially disturbed by this laxity:

In their attempts to add variety to the performance, [authors] neglected integrity of style, forgetting completely the character of the ballet. . . . on the bottom of the Nile, in Ancient Egypt, the Neva River danced in the costume of a Moscow Boyar. . . . mazurkas and csardases were used in almost all ballets.[8]

8 M. Fokine, MEMOIRS OF A BALLET MASTER (London, 1961), 109.

A striking characteristic of the designers of Russia's Silver Age, whether in the Ballets Russes, Alexander Tairov's Chamber Theater, or Vsevolod Meierkhold's Theater of the Revolution, was their avoidance of these defects. Artists such as Bakst, Benois, Alexandra Exter, Liubov Popova, and Yakulov manifested a remarkable cohesion and consistency of style, whatever the national or historical background, for they were willing to investigate and analyze the ethnographical content of a given theme. Bakst's serious study of ancient Greece and Siam which influenced his designs for *Hélène de Sparte* and *Le Dieu Bleu* of 1912, Benois's vast knowledge of seventeenth- and eighteenth-century France evident in his designs for *Le Pavillon d'Armide*, Gontcharova's and Larionov's deep appreciation of Russian folk art—these qualities were symptomatic of the modern Russian designer's readiness to provide interpretations that, while imaginative, retained historical credibility.

Still, within the specific context of stage design, the World of Art made scant reference to particular principles or even productions. In fact, commentary was limited to a few appraisals of spectacles undertaken by members of the group—Bakst, Benois, Golovin. Evidently, in those early years the World of Art artists had little understanding of the revolution that was already occurring in Western European stage design thanks to the scenographic experiments of Adolf Appia, Edward Gordon Craig, and Max Reinhardt. But by 1909 the Russian artists were themselves at the forefront of this revolution, for it was their sets and costumes as much as, if not more than, Nijinsky's leap and Stravinsky's brave discordance that astounded, angered, or perplexed the Edwardian audience.

The immediate success of Diaghilev's designers in Paris in 1909 onward is all the more surprising when we recall that not one of them was actually trained as a designer or decorator, and all of them came to the stage by way of studio painting. Moreover, most of the artists were graduates not of the St. Petersburg Academy of Arts, but of less prestigious private schools such as those of Princess Tenisheva and Elizaveta Zvantseva in St. Petersburg. Some, such as Benois, were simply brilliant amateurs. Far from hindering them, the absence of a strict, academic mentality provided them with a necessary flexibility. Perhaps ultimately their training as studio painters also stood them in good stead, and all of them were especially fond of nature painting and the outdoors, something that sharpened their powers of observation and adaptability. They delighted in the malleability of pencil drawing and watercolor, and they regarded the sketch and the study as independent works, self-contained and intrinsically valid. Naturally, Boris Anisfeld, Bakst, Benois, Gontcharova, Larionov, and others maintained recognizable styles, often repeating points of view, color combinations, and thematic motifs. But their initial training as studio artists contributed to their stylistic vitality and facilitated their automatic suspension of disbelief each time they were confronted with a new design commission. Undoubtedly, this spontaneity and freshness added much to the distinctive collective psychology of the Ballets Russes.

One of the attractions that the stage presented to artists of the fin de siècle was the possibility of exploring a large decorative space, i.e. a pictorial area that traditionally fresco and wallpainting had provided. Since there were few opportunities to decorate public spaces at the time, artists such as Bakst, Benois, Roerich, Nikolai Sapunov, Soudeikine, and Vrubel welcomed the theater as an environment for the wider display of pictorial ideas. By and large, this approach benefited the stage, although, as the critic Raymond Cogniat pointed out, in the context of the Ballets Russes,

Serge de Diaghilev imposed something that, through excess, would become a mistake: the painter in the theater. This mistake would be discovered later on: the easel canvas enlarged out of all proportion to the scale of the stage.[9]

9 R. Cogniat, DECORS DE THEATRE *(Paris, 1930)*, 12.

10 A. Boll, DU DECOR DE THEATRE: SES TENDANCES MODERNES *(Paris, 1926)*, 55.

In varying degrees, perhaps even Benois and Bakst, Diaghilev's primary designers, were guilty of this mistake. Both contributed to the "transports of admiration"[10] that the Ballets Russes elicited among the Paris audiences, but both of them gained their initial recognition as studio painters, and something of the pictorial, narrative emphasis remained in their sets and costumes. In any case, as the supporters of two different, often conflicting approaches to stage design, Benois and Bakst deserve particular attention and, by their very differences, illustrate the richness and diversity of early twentieth-century stage design.

Benois did not possess the unbridled imagination of Bakst, but he was able to tackle very different subjects, whether French (*Le Pavillon d'Armide*, figure 1), Russian (*Petrouchka*, figure 2), or Chinese (*Le Rossignol*, 1914, figure 3), and his enthusiasm for the theater never waned. As he wrote to Walter Nouvel in 1905, "I'm dreaming of having just one enduring cause in the future. And insofar as I know myself, I would do best of all in the theater."[11] Benois always tried to be consistent in his historical recreations and was

11 *Letter from Alexandre Benois to Walter Nouvel dated 20 October 1905, in TsGALI, f. 938, op. 1, ed. khr. 46, 1.197.*

upset whenever a designer preferred "irrelevant" luxury of ornament to an ethnographically correct reconstruction. On the other hand, Benois's sense of history was so acute that he knew exactly when and how to enliven a certain set or costume and how to invest it with the spirit of its time. Consequently, with his encyclopedic knowledge of the era of the Sun King and his personal passion for Versailles, Benois was an ideal interpreter of the ballet *Le Pavillon d'Armide* staged by Fokine in 1907 and then taken to Paris in modified form by Diaghilev in 1909. With the exception of a few designs for an unrealized production of his own ballet, *Le Fils Prodigue* (spring 1907), *Le Pavillon* was Benois's first professional theatrical engagement since 1903 (when he had designed the Maryinsky production of *Die Götterdämmerung*), and it was one of his most successful. As Fokine recalled:

*Alexandre Nikolaevich seemed to be—immediately and exclusively—a theatrical artist.
All his colors, his lines related directly and obviously to the particular juncture on stage.
The costumes, the sets, the lighting—everything was aimed at expressing the content of
the piece.*[12]

12 *Fokine,* 188.

13 C. *Beaumont,* DESIGN FOR THE BALLET *(New York, 1937),* 9.

Benois's interpretation of *Le Pavillon* was a striking one, expressing the "fantasy of Berain allied to a delicate colour sense of Bocquet."[13] He demonstrated clearly how well he understood the historical epoch—especially in his celebrated decor for Scenes I and III and his numerous costumes such as those for the Vicomte and Armide's Favorite Slave. True, Benois's art sometimes fell victim to pedantic compilation of historical detail, but this failing was not too evident in *Le Pavillon* or in any early production such as *Le Festin* (1909), *Giselle* (1910), *Petrouchka,* or *Le Rossignol.* For example, his designs for *Giselle* were so well received at the Paris premiere that this original version was repeated many

14 A. Benois, REMINISCENCES OF
THE RUSSIAN BALLET *(London,
1941), v.*

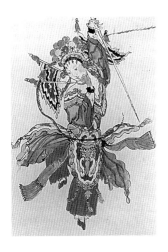

times thereafter. Benois's lyrical evocation of Giselle, his fantastic castle and romantic cemetery of the Wilis, became images enjoyed by many audiences, in spite of Diaghilev's initial unwillingness to allow a Russian company to present this famous French ballet to a French audience.

Diaghilev knew very well that the French also expected a measure of "barbarism" from the Russians, and, of course, he satisfied this desire with the productions of *Petrouchka* and *Le Sacre du Printemps*, presenting Stravinsky's "pagan" music to audiences still unaccustomed even to the mellifluous Impressionism of Debussy. *Petrouchka* was especially close to Benois's heart since he associated it with fond childhood memories when the bazaars, fairs, and *balagany* (Punch and Judy booths) were still part of St. Petersburg folk life. In his resolution for the Paris *Petrouchka*, Benois managed not only to express the simple charm of a childhood souvenir, but also to enhance Stravinsky's music in an especially appropriate manner. Benois's stylization and emphasis on the angular character of the decor was an ideal visual parallel to the discordant syncopations of Stravinsky's music and to the rigid, abrupt patterns of Fokine's choreographic system danced by Karsavina and Nijinsky.

Obviously, Benois contributed much to the global success of the Ballets Russes, but it is important to realize that at heart he was an illustrator and a studio painter and gave his first attention to the "picture." He even asserted that he was *not* a devotee of the ballet.[14] A man of extraordinary erudition, Benois was a traditionalist and, with Fokine, represented the conservative faction of Diaghilev's enterprise. At heart, he was perhaps suited more to the academy than to the riotous living of the St. Petersburg and Paris bohemia–and he did not take lightly to the aesthetic and sensual vagaries of his rival Bakst or, for that matter, of Diaghilev himself.

Bakst understood that the set and costume designer, the dancer, the actor, the singer were of equal importance within the spectacle, and he tried to perceive the stage in three dimensions rather than as the mere extension of the easel, something that is immediately apparent from his major achievements such as *Schéhérazade* (see Plate 12). In contrast, some of the designers such as Dobujinsky (*Papillons*, 1914) and Léopold Survage (*Mavra*, 1922) still regarded the stage as a series of decorated surfaces, creating elegant *belle prospettive* that served, however, merely as passive backdrops for the action. True, Bakst did not believe in audience participation and distinguished between proscenium and auditorium, but his concentration on elements such as diagonal axis, asymmetry, and rhythmicality of the body broke the pictorial, illustrative convention of nineteenth-century stage design and built a solid bridge between *artiste* and public–for both parties came to share in a real, constructive space.

Bakst's conception of stage design was an exciting one because his sets and costumes relied on the maximum interaction of decor and the human figure. Like the Constructivist designers of the 1920s, especially Exter, Popova, and Varvara Stepanova, Bakst regarded the body as a kinetic force that was to be exposed and amplified in its movements, not enveloped and disguised. Instead of the constrained, static unit that the body tended to represent on the academic stage (a tradition that Benois never finally rejected), Bakst tried to make the body itself as expressive as possible. He also supplemented the physical motions of the body either by attaching appendages such as veils, feathers, and jewelry (see the costumes for *Cléopâtre*, Plate 1, and *Schéhérazade*, in Garafola essay, figures 3-5) or by creating intricate abstract patterns of dress (as in the costumes for *L'Après-midi d'un Faune*, 1912; see Acocella essay, figures 7-9)–so as to extend and emphasize the body's movement.

figure 4
Varvara Stepanova,
Designs for *sportodezhda*
(sports clothes), 1923, from T.
Strizhenova, *Iz istroii sovetskogo
kostiuma* (Moscow, 1972), 96.

15 *Letter from Alexandre Benois
to Walter Nouvel dated
3 November 1897, in TsGALI,
f. 938, op. 1, ed. khr. 46, 1. 66.*

16 *"Gowns of the Sexes,"* DAILY
MIRROR *(London), 3 April 1913.*

17 *A. E. Johnson,* THE RUSSIAN
BALLET *(New York, 1913), 195-196.*

While Bakst liberated the body from its traditional uniform on stage, he did not expose it merely for erotic appeal, and he did not sympathize with the trend towards nudity on stage that Nikolai Evreinov and other St. Petersburg theater producers were trying to promote in the 1910s. However much Bakst loved the human anatomy, he saw its beauty to lie in the tension between the seen and the unseen–hence his simultaneous application of transparent and opaque materials in, for example, *Cléopâtre* and *Schéhérazade*.

Bakst's gravitation toward exotic ballets–*Cléopâtre, Schéhérazade, La Péri, Narcisse, Le Dieu Bleu*–coincided with a fashion for the Orient that affected Moscow and St. Petersburg almost as much as it did Paris and London. Nevertheless, Bakst should not be identified exclusively with this trend, even though he was fascinated by the sex and violence of the East, for he also possessed a shy, "Magdalenian" character[15] that sometimes dictated restrained and sober artistic forms–a case in point is *Jeux*, one of Diaghilev's most experimental ballets of the early phase. Presented to the Paris public in May 1913, *Jeux* (music by Debussy, choreography by Nijinsky, decor by Bakst) carried a schematic, "modern" narrative about a flirtation during a game of tennis "placed in the year 1925."[16] Against a set of stylized trees, rambling villa, and electric lanterns, Bakst placed his tennis players, clothing them in simple, utilitarian costumes (see Harris essay, figure 6) that anticipated Constructivist dress designs, i.e. the so called *prozodezhda* of the 1920s by Popova and Stepanova (figure 4).

There is one visual element in particular that connects *Jeux* to the productions of the avant-garde in the 1910s and 1920s, and that is the restrained use of color and the consistent application of contrast between white and black (or white, black, and red). The critic A. E. Johnson even referred to the cinematographic quality of *Jeux*, although he was thinking in terms of the sequence of stills that go to make up a film rather than the particular formal resolutions in each still.[17] This, together with Nijinsky's reliance on geometric movements in his choreography and performance, brings to mind parallel developments in the visual arts–Tatlin's uncolored reliefs of 1914 onward, Malevich's *Black Square* of 1915, Alexander Rodchenko's black-on-black paintings of ca. 1918, and his photographs of 1923 onward, even Gabo's translucent constructions of the 1920s and 1930s. Fascination with black and white, mechanical accuracy, economy of form, urban civilization (the game of tennis takes place in a London garden), and the exposition of the intrinsic elements of the medium itself were the main stimuli to the establishment of Constructivism and the International Style of the 1920s–and all these ideas were already part of *Jeux* in 1913.

In our search for those designers who really made a determined effort to construct rather than to paint the sets and costumes for the Ballets Russes, we must give particular attention to the work of Gontcharova and Larionov, even though some of their key commissions for Diaghilev (for instance, *Liturgie* of 1915 and *Histoires Naturelles* of 1917) were not realized. Drawing on their knowledge of indigenous art forms such as the *lubok* (cheap, handcolored print), the peasant toy, and the icon, Gontcharova and Larionov transformed the Russian stage into a buffoonery. With their bright colors, distorted perspectives, and love of play, they imbued the theater with an effervescence and vitality that reminded spectators of the *balagany*, the fairground, and the circus.

Bright colors, crude forms, "wrong proportions," and a wonderful joviality and optimism–such are the qualities of Gontcharova's designs for her first undertaking for the Ballets Russes, *Le Coq d'Or* in 1914 (Plates 3-5). Accepting Benois's suggestion that this opera be staged as a ballet-opera, Diaghilev and Gontcharova arranged for the action

18 C. Beaumont, FIVE CENTURIES OF BALLET DESIGN (London, 1939), 127.

19 A. Benois, "Vospominaniia o balete" in RUSSKIE ZAPISKI (Paris) 18 (1939): 101.

20 S. Golynets (compiler): IVAN YAKOVLEVICH BILIBIN (Leningrad, 1970), 12.

to be mimed by the dancers while choirs sang on steep ramps either side of the stage. Gontcharova turned the stage into a three-dimensional *lubok*, and critics who saw the premiere agreed that the "setting inaugurated a new phase of stage decoration."[18] Even so, the moderate Benois was rather taken aback: "Least of all did I like the protrusion of her scenery which seemed to impede the action."[19] No doubt, Benois preferred the restrained, stylized designs that his World of Art colleague Bilibin had made for the 1909 production of *Le Coq d'Or* in Moscow–"looking like a book illustration."[20]

After her debut with the Ballets Russes, Gontcharova set to work on four other ballets (through the end of 1916), not one of which, unfortunately, was realized–*Liturgie*, *España*, *Triana*, and *Foire Espagnole*. This intense activity produced not only numerous designs for sets and costumes, but also three portfolios of *pochoirs*–*Liturgie* (Lausanne, 1915), *Album de 14 Portraits Théâtraux* (Paris, 1916), and *L'Art Théâtral Décoratif Moderne* (Paris, 1919), the last two created jointly by Gontcharova and Larionov. During the 1920s Gontcharova continued to work for Diaghilev, integrating her visual ideas with the daring choreographies of Bronislava Nijinska (for instance, *Les Noces* of 1923). Perhaps

Plate 3
Natalia Gontcharova, Project for the front curtain for *Le Coq d'Or*, 1914, cat. no. 47.

Coq d'Or. 1914.
Projet de tableau

N Gontcharova

because of her initial training as a sculptor, Gontcharova was able to adjust readily from two dimensions to three and to transfer her vivid colors and lapidary forms to the stage, eliciting constant surprise and delight, but rarely indignation. Larionov, however, seems sometimes to have disturbed even the most emancipated viewer.

Larionov restored the element of farce to the professional stage, achieving this not through a confirmation of historical or ethnographical fact, but rather through a contradiction of it. Borrowing much from the circus, he operated like a clown perpetrating all manner of practical jokes, poking fun at his audiences, and then laughing with them. Indeed, Larionov was drawing directly on the traditions of the circus and other forms of "magic" that were enjoying tremendous popularity in Russia at the turn of the century. As the *skomorokhi* (mountebanks) and *balagany* receded into history (Benois records that the last *balagany* closed in St. Petersburg ca. 1900),[21] so new forms of mass entertainment developed, including the professional circus and, beginning in 1896, the movie industry. Catering to an eager public, these recreations concocted and proffered "illusions" (the Russian word for "conjuror" is *illiuzionist*, and the early cinemas in Russia were called *illiuziony*) that became ever more complex and spellbinding as technological possibilities advanced. In fact, we should remember that the making of these factories of dreams just before and after 1900 paralleled the development of more practical wizardries, such as the telephone, the phonograph, the telegraph, and various other mechanical and electrical apparatuses that could also create miracles. Conjurors and clowns—and also stage designers —relied increasingly on such machines to enhance their acts. Larionov's costume for a Peacock in *Histoires Naturelles*, for example, was supposed to have been operated by a sophisticated vocal mechanism regulating the actual movements of the costume. Furthermore, Larionov was not averse to combining these tricks with ideas advocated by the Italian Futurists on "polydimensional Futurist spatio-stage" and "electro-dynamic architecture . . . plastic, luminous elements moving at the center of the theater pit."[22]

21 *Benois*, REMINISCENCES, 325.

22 F. Marinetti, "La scenografia futurista," LA BIENNALE, *Venice* (June 1928): 14-15.

23 An undated prospectus by Depero for LE CHANT DU ROSSIGNOL (IL CANTO DELL'USIGNUOLO) on display at the Galleria Museo Depero, Rovereto, Italy, carries clear indications that Depero was highly incensed by Larionov's apparent plagiarism.

24 D. Kobiakov, "Sovremennaia zhivopis. Larionov," ZEMLIA (Paris) 2 (1949): 16.

25 Memoir by C. P. Cochran, quoted in N. MacDonald, DIAGHILEV OBSERVED BY CRITICS IN ENGLAND AND THE US 1911- 1920 (New York, 1975), 263.

figure 6
Mikhail Larionov, Design for decor for *Chout*, Scene I, 1921. Gouache on paper, 19½×27½ in. Collection Mr. and Mrs. Nikita D. Lobanov-Rostovsky.

26 Interview given by Diaghilev to the OBSERVER (London), 5 June 1921, quoted in MacDonald, 262.

27 Review from the OBSERVER for 12 June 1921, quoted in MacDonald, 263.

28 A. Maslovsky, "Balety S. Diaghileva i russkie khudozhniki," TEATR (Berlin) 9 (1922): 6.

We remember, for example, his vigorous costume for a Lady with Fans created probably for Catherine Devillier (Devilliers) who, in the company of Diaghilev, Gontcharova, Larionov, and Léonide Massine, rehearsed *España* and *Histoires Naturelles* in San Sebastián and Rome in 1916-1917. Larionov's dynamic composition brings to mind the contemporary work of the Italians, especially Fortunato Depero's dance themes, namely *Ballerina* and *Futurista–Movimento d'Uccello*. Highly indignant, Depero himself noted the apparent borrowing.[23]

Larionov's projects for *Le Soleil de Nuit* (1915, see cover), *Contes Russes* (1917), and, in 1922, *Histoires Naturelles* (figure 5), *Chout* (Plate 2 and figure 6), and *Le Renard* rely for their effect precisely on this tension between the believable and the unbelievable, the expected narrative or choreographic sequence and the unexpected visual displacement. Larionov was well disposed to low taste, fooling around, eclecticism, and plagiarism, but he combined these qualities in a vivid, clever manner that was very distant from the staid elegance of *Le Pavillon d'Armide* and *Giselle*. Promoting both primitive art and his abstract system of Rayonism, Larionov produced sets and costumes that were at once vulgar and sophisticated, "popular art in a renewed and vigorous form."[24] The result, as some observers implied, was hilarious, if somewhat unwieldy:

I think CHOUT *came a little too early, and I, for one, should like to see it again. . . . I recall one moment when seven suitors, after shaking their cardboard swords at seven fathers, spun round on their heels to express their devotion to seven red-haired daughters, who poised passionately on their fourteen big toes.*[25]

Diaghilev was even forced to threaten the dancers with penalties in order to make them dance in clothes that interfered with the very movements of their dancing. Even though Diaghilev spoke of *Chout* in laudatory terms, referring to its "new principle" and "highest modernity,"[26] it had a cool reception in Paris and London, causing the critic of the *Observer* to remark that the "new art-form, as represented by *Chout*, has not yet learned to walk. It can scream very piercingly while waiting for its bottle."[27]

However, *Chout* and *Le Renard* marked a new departure in Diaghilev's ballet endeavor, for thereafter his productions became increasingly experimental as he gave attention to new composers, new dancers, untried choreographic systems, and radical styles of art. For Larionov, this period was a happy one, a mood reflected in the "exclusive vitality and saturation of color, in the distinctive dynamism"[28] of his designs. But his days were numbered. Even though Serge Lifar rechoreographed *Le Renard* for a new production in 1929, Larionov, with his Russian ingenuousness and boisterous behavior, seems to have appealed less and less to Diaghilev after 1922. The change coincided with Diaghilev's orientation towards a more complex, cerebral, and mechanical conception of ballet and stage design, prompting him to draw on the expertise of a new group of artists, among them Gabo, Tchelitchev, and Yakulov.

It is a tribute to Diaghilev's unfailing curiosity about the new in art and to his instant recognition of authentic innovation that his most experimental productions were staged at the end of his life–*La Chatte* (1927), *Le Pas d'Acier* (1927), and *Ode* (1928). These ballets integrated new concepts of music, choreography, and visual resolution, and actually have more in common with developments in ballet today than they do with the heyday of Bakst and Benois.

La Chatte, choreographed by George Balanchine, premiered in Monte Carlo in April 1927 and then in Paris the following month. Telling the story of a young man in love with

figure 7
Naum Gabo and Antoine Pevsner,
Design for decor for *La Chatte*,
1927. Photograph of the
reconstruction at the Tate
Gallery, London.

figure 8
Alexandra Exter,
Costume design for the Queen of
the Martians in Yakov Protazanov's
movie *Aelita*, 1924. Gouache on
paper, 27 × 18 in. Collection Mr. and
Mrs. Nikita D. Lobanov-Rostovsky.

29 *Quoted in the exhibition
catalogue* LES BALLETS RUSSES DE
SERGE DE DIAGHILEV 1909-1929
(Strasbourg, 1969), 227.

30 *L.* Massine, MY LIFE IN
BALLET *(London, 1968), 172.*

a cat who becomes a woman only to change back into a cat, *La Chatte* deals with the central theme of instability and metamorphosis. In order to emphasize these qualities, the designers—Gabo and his brother Pevsner—applied their abstract principles of Constructivism. By building transparent and refractive surfaces from mica, talc, celluloid, black oilcloth, etc., they created a plastic, variable decor and costumes that reflected and magnified the movements of the dancers, who, clothed in these weird science-fiction costumes, danced on a revolving stage. The result was something like a "radio or gymnastic apparatus."[29]

La Chatte was one of several "industrial" spectacles inside and outside Russia that relied for their scenic effect on modern, technologically sophisticated materials and streamlined actions (see figure 7). Meierkhold's constructivist presentations such as *The Magnanimous Cuckold* (1922), the movie *Aelita* (1924, with designs by Exter and Isaak Rabinovich, figures 8 and 9), Nijinska's *Le Train Bleu* (1924, with designs by Henri Laurens), and, of course, Massine's *Le Pas d'Acier* were other expressions of this aesthetic. The latter, in particular, symbolized Diaghilev's wish to relate ballet, still regarded by many as a "classical" art, to twentieth-century concerns. Produced in Paris in June 1927 with music by Serge Prokofiev and sets and costumes by Yakulov, *Le Pas d'Acier* portrayed the new Socialist Russia with her glorification of the factory and the machine. As Massine recalled,

The wheels and pistons on the rostrums moved in time to the hammering movements of the young factory workers, and by strengthening the tableau with a large ensemble group in front of the rostrums, so evolving a multi-level composition which welded together the scenic and the bodily movements, I was able to create a climax of overwhelming power.[30]

Actually, neither Massine, Yakulov, nor Diaghilev seemed especially interested in the "socialist" dimension of *Le Pas d'Acier*, and for Yakulov, at least, it provided an opportunity to emphasize what he regarded as the basic ingredient of theater—"the principle of

31 *Quoted in the exhibition catalogue* TEATRALNO-DEKORATSIONNOE ISKUSSTVO ZA 5 LET (*Kazan, 1924*), 45.

32 A. *Efros,* KAMERNYI TEATR I EGO KHUDOZHNIKI 1914-1934 (*Moscow, 1934*), xxxvi.

perpetual action, the kaleidoscope of forms and colors."[31] Yakulov conveyed this through his involved system of kinetic machines that "moved forward some parts, removed others, rolled out platforms, let down ladders, opened up traps, constructed passageways."[32] There was something of the circus and the happening in all this, although what provoked good humor and amusement in proletarian Moscow did not find quite the same sympathy in bourgeois Paris.

The last of Diaghilev's truly innovative ballets was Nicolai Nabokov's *Ode* produced in Paris in June 1928 with designs by Tchelitchev (see figure 10) and choreography by

figure 9
Frame from Yakov Protazanov's movie *Aelita*, 1924. Institute of Modern Russian Culture.

33 *P. Tyler*, THE DIVINE COMEDY
OF PAVEL TCHELITCHEW
(London, 1967), 331.

34 *Tyler, 331.*

35 *L. Moussinac*, TENDANCES
NOUVELLES DU THEATRE
(Paris, 1931), 21.

figure 10
Pavel Tchelitchev,
Design for a group of figures in
Ode, 1928. India ink on paper,
16¾ × 14 in. Collection of Mr. and
Mrs. Nikita D. Lobanov-Rostovsky.

Massine. Although relying on occult and alchemical sources, specifically on the hermetic schemes of the universe that Tchelitchev was exploring avidly at the time, *Ode* (telling the story of Nature and one of her pupils) was also "modern" and "technological." In fact, some of Tchelitchev's requests were so audacious—movie cameras and neon lights representing a "galaxy of celestial manifestations"[33] and a spotlight to be beamed at the audience—that Diaghilev had to reject them, although he seems not to have been unduly perturbed by the "unadorned white all-over tights" worn by the dancers.[34] Unfortunately, this was Tchelitchev's only contribution to the Ballets Russes, although he had been involved in many stage productions since his initial training with Exter in Kiev in 1918-1919. He returned to the ballet only after Diaghilev's death, working with Balanchine, for example, on the 1936 production of *Orfeo*.

While paying homage to their rich legacy of local myth and ritual, the Russian artists explored visual concepts that became part and parcel of international scenography. Bakst's view of the body as a kinetic construction, Gontcharova's and Larionov's deliberate vulgarization of style, Yakulov's and Tchelitchev's reliance on sophisticated machinery—such ideas helped transform the ballet into total living theater. For them the stage was a living entity that provided the dancer with an organic, architectonic space that was neither subservient to, nor dominant over, the other ingredients of the performance. Remembering the splendor of the Ballets Russes, the critic and historian Léon Moussinac noted in 1931 that "the theatrical realizations of the Russians have had an enormous influence in Europe and America."[35] But the success of the Ballets Russes and not least of its designers depended fundamentally on the inspiration of Diaghilev, and with his passing in 1929 the company disbanded and an era ended. The direct heir to the Diaghilev legacy, Colonel Wassily de Basil's Ballets Russes (1931-1952), never attained the synthetic and experimental level of the Diaghilev enterprise, even though it boasted many famous names and was well organized. Of course, numerous individuals and companies sought appropriation of the Diaghilev legacy, claiming right of ownership, and the spoils were divided among many parties. Ultimately, Balanchine was perhaps the greatest disciple, but Marie Rambert in England, and even Martha Graham, also owed much to the genius of Diaghilev. Furthermore, as the recent reconstructions of *Petrouchka* and *Le Sacre du Printemps* have demonstrated so clearly, the innovations in choreography, dance technique, and scenography that Diaghilev advocated continued to serve as a primary source of artistic inspiration.

●

DESIGN

AND

CHOREOGRAPHY

Cross-influences

in the

Theatrical Art

of the

Ballets Russes

───────

Nancy

Van Norman Baer

▼

IN 1909 PARISIAN AUDIENCES seeking *le dernier cri* in art gathered at the Théâtre du Châtelet for the electrifying performances of Serge Diaghilev's first dance season—a forerunner of his celebrated Ballets Russes. The technical perfection and daring abandon of the Russian dancers, the brilliant colors of the costumes and painted decors, and the music of new Russian composers astonished the sophisticated public. During the next five years, the Ballets Russes presented extraordinary visions of classical antiquity, pagan Russia, and the exotic, mysterious Orient never before seen on a ballet stage.

In creating their spectacles, like moving, three-dimensional paintings, Diaghilev's designers understood that a dancer's continual movement onstage leads the viewer's eye into, out of, and across the background or scenic decor. During a performance, a series of visual impressions unfolds, and their cumulative effect conveys the story and emotion of a ballet. The American dance critic Edwin Denby, discussing the tasks of costume and decor, noted that

a ballet set has to stand up under steady scrutiny almost as an easel painting does. At first sight it tells a story, it has local color or period interest or shock value. But then it starts to change the way a picture in a museum does as you look at it attentively for five or ten minutes. The shapes and colors, lines and textures in the set and costumes will act as they would in a picture, they will seem to push and pull, rise and fall, advance and retreat with or against their representational weight. The backdrop may tie up with a costume so that the dancer's figure seems to belong in it like a native, or it may set him plainly forward where he has a floor to dance on. A good ballet decor, like a good painting, does different and opposite things decisively; like a painting, it presents a bold equilibrium of pictorial forces.[1]

For his Ballets Russes productions Diaghilev commissioned easel painters as designers instead of relying on professional scenic craftsmen whose methods derived from stale theatrical formulas. Painters brought fresh ideas to the stage as well as a concern for what keeps pictures "active," or pictorially alive for years on end, let alone for the duration of a performance. In return, artists working for the ballet gained wide exposure and new patronage, as well as an opportunity to explore different period styles, three-dimensional space, and the human figure in motion.

During his company's early seasons (1909-1914), Diaghilev exclusively engaged Russian artists to design the operas and ballets that established the Ballets Russes's reputation. All had been members of the World of Art group (Mir iskusstva) and shared its progressive ideas about art, music, literature, and theatrical production.[2] Diaghilev was not the first to engage independent easel artists in the service of the theater, but he did place their work before a broad (versus a limited avant-garde) audience.[3] He thus made popular the results of the revolution in scenographic design that had begun sixty years earlier with the publication of Richard Wagner's dramatic theories. Wagner's ideal, which he himself never realized on the opera stage, centered on the concept of *Gesamtkunstwerk*, the total work of art in which decor, drama, music, and movement were united into a single, organic whole. It was this same unity of vision that Diaghilev and his collaborators brought to the Ballets Russes stage.

▲   ▲   ▲

Léon Bakst is the best-known of Diaghilev's Russian designers, and his sensuous, exotic art was regarded as an essential ingredient of early Ballets Russes performances.

1 Edwin Denby, "About Ballet Decoration," NEW YORK HERALD TRIBUNE, 26 November 1944.

2 For a full discussion of MIR ISKUSSTVA see Elena Bridgman's essay in this catalogue.

3 In the 1890s, many Parisian avant-garde theaters commissioned stage sets from artists, in particular the Nabis Paul Serusier, Maurice Denis, and Edouard Vuillard. For a listing of their work see Joan Ross Acocella, "The Reception of Diaghilev's Ballets Russes by Artists and Intellectuals in Paris and London, 1909-1914" (Ph. D. diss., Rutgers, 1984), 4-5.

Plate 6
Léon Bakst,
Costume design for a Negro
Dancer in *Le Dieu Bleu*, 1912, cat.
no. 11.

4 Mary Fanton Roberts, "The New Russian Stage, A Blaze of Color," THE CRAFTSMAN 29 (1915): 265.

5 Letter from Léon Bakst to Diaghilev dated 28 April 1911. Quoted from Irina Pruzhan [Proujan], LEV SAMOILOVICH BAKST (Moscow, 1975), 130, by John Bowlt in a forthcoming catalogue of the collection of Mr. and Mrs. Nikita D. Lobanov-Rostovsky.

6 Arsène Alexandre, THE DECORATIVE ART OF LEON BAKST (London, 1913), 2.

7 Lynn Garafola, ART AND ENTERPRISE IN DIAGHILEV'S BALLETS RUSSES, forthcoming in 1989 by Oxford University Press.

Bakst viewed ballet as a continually changing sequence of picture frames, and he equated the designing of a production with the painting of a series of thematically related tableaux.[4] His sumptuous and provocative theatrical designs were also carefully organized drawings, and their detailed draftsmanship revealed a technical mastery of color and line. As Bakst wrote to Diaghilev in 1911, "My mises-en-scène are the result of a very calculated distribution of paint spots against the background of the decor."[5]

Bakst designed four major ballets (*Cléopâtre* in 1909, *Schéhérazade* in 1910, and, in 1912, *Le Dieu Bleu* and *Thamar*) as well as several minor productions for the Ballets Russes with costumes and sets inspired by the Far East. Prior to Bakst, costumes for ballets with oriental themes such as *Le Bayadère* and *La Fille du Pharaon* consisted of tutus with fitted bodices and billowing skirts decorated with exotic motifs. Bakst dressed his oriental dancers in loose-fitting garments—tunics, boleros, harem pants, and split skirts—that were closer to the attire of the historical period represented, and that allowed the dancers a wider range of movement, especially in the torso. The audience's fascination with these productions was due in large part to their exotic and sado-erotic themes, heightened by Bakst through a "strange blending of rich and sensuous beauty with a note of something sinister and menacing."[6]

Bakst's unconventional costumes supported the equally unconventional dances of Michel Fokine, the choreographer of most of Diaghilev's prewar repertory. Fokine sought to extend the line of the dancer's body and to increase its plasticity and expressiveness through fluid, more natural movement. The bare torsos and midriffs of Bakst's costumes for *Le Dieu Bleu* allowed dancers to bend freely at the waist, arching backward or curving forward in phrases of dynamic, uninhibited movement (Plate 6). This liberation of body and dress brought a greater psychological naturalism to the ballet stage, creating an expressive picture rather than a stilted, conventional reality.

Stylistically, the sinuous line, rich embroidery, and decoratively woven fabrics of Bakst's oriental costumes reflected Art Nouveau and Jugendstil from the late nineteenth century. So, too, did Fokine's choreography, which emphasized fluidity and a lengthened body line, especially in the use of the arms "not to frame the body but to sculpt it three-dimensionally."[7] Even in *Le Dieu Bleu*, where the choreography was strongly influenced by the angular poses of Hindu sculpture, Fokine conveyed—through supple arms and torso—the illusion of spontaneous, flowing form within a rigorously disciplined order. His movements for the corps de ballet in *Le Dieu Bleu* again made reference—perhaps unconsciously—to Art Nouveau. The constant circling and interlacing patterns of the ensemble traced graceful, curvilinear forms in space, as did the loose garments, draperies, and veils that swirled around them.

Bakst's settings for the oriental ballets invoked the opulent, decadent world of the legendary East (Plate 12). Their vivid colors, voluptuous interiors, and steamy groves evoked a fantastic world of sensual pleasure and dizzying opium-induced sensations. Oriental themes were not new to European art and literature: they had appeared, with frequency, in the works of such nineteenth-century painters as Eugène Delacroix, Gustave Moreau, and Jean-Léon Gérôme, as well as in the writings of Gustave Flaubert and Théophile Gautier. The orientalism of the Ballets Russes served much the same purpose that it had in art and literature. In addition to providing an escape from everyday reality, it also supported the symbolist aesthetic that sought to expand the mind and senses and intensify emotions in the quest of a heightened, superior reality.

In his desire to stimulate the audience's emotions and fantasies, Bakst relied on color

Plate 7
Léon Bakst,
Nijinska and Fokina in "Narcisse."
Pencil, watercolor, gouache, and gold and silver on paper, 27 1/8 × 19 5/8 in. Dance Collection, The New York Public Library.

8 For an explanation of nineteenth-century theories regarding the affinity among color, musical tones, and emotions, see Charles S. Mayer, "The Theatrical Designs of Léon Bakst" (Ph. D. diss., Columbia University, 1977), 183-186.

9 Roberts, 265.

as well as exotic, sensual themes. Like many European theosophists at the turn of the century, he believed in the consonance of specific emotions and colors. He was also familiar with the theories of Russian composer Alexander Scriabin, who believed that each musical note had a corresponding color equivalent.[8] Bakst expressed his views in the subtle and metaphysical power of color in a 1915 interview:

I have often noticed that in each color of the prism there exists a gradation which sometimes expresses frankness and chastity, sometimes sensuality and even bestiality, sometimes pride, sometimes despair. . . . The painter who knows how to make use of this, the director of the orchestra who can with one movement of his baton put all this in motion, without crossing them, who can let flow the thousand tones from the end of his stick without making a mistake, can draw from the spectator the exact emotion which he wants him to feel.[9]

Like a conductor, Bakst "orchestrated" the constantly changing color sequences created by dancers in motion. The tonal relationships between costumes and sets and the striking chromatic chords that he consciously achieved required a close working relationship with a ballet's choreographer.

In addition to evoking a specific emotional response, Bakst's strident, sometimes violent color combinations heightened the passions of the stage drama. The juxtaposition of his intense oranges, blues, purples, reds, and greens imparted energy and abandon to the choreography, echoing and reinforcing Fokine's intent. Color and movement worked together to suggest, rather than literally depict, scenes of passionate, uninhibited sex and violence. In *Schéhérazade*, for example, the orgy that forms the climax of the ballet draws the entire cast into a circling, swirling vortex of color in the midst of which the Golden Slave leaps relentlessly up and down.[10]

10 Acocella, 231-232.

The bold use of color and the simplified, flattened forms of Bakst's painted decors reveal his awareness of fauvist art. Although Fauvism culminated in 1905-1906, it was still an important avant-garde movement in Paris in 1910. Bakst's experiments on the Ballets Russes stage thus reflected various artistic currents in contemporary European painting– Symbolism, Art Nouveau, proto-Expressionism, and Fauvism. In fact, the select, highly publicized world of Ballets Russes performances–in which Bakst's radical use of color was so evident–may have encouraged broad acceptance of fauvist theories. Unlike the Fauves, however, Bakst maintained, "It is in line as well as in color that I make my emotions."[11]

11 Roberts, 265.

As has been suggested, Bakst did not merely supply the costumes and decors for numerous Ballets Russes productions, but he also contributed ideas about staging and choreography. Dancer/choreographer Bronislava Nijinska explained,

Léon Bakst often worked with Fokine and inspired us during the rehearsals; from time to time he would correct us, showing us the proper position of a hand or the movement of an arm, sometimes even demonstrating an oriental pose for us and explaining the way we should move our bodies during the dance.[12]

12 Bronislava Nijinska, BRONISLAVA NIJINSKA: EARLY MEMOIRS, trans. and ed. Irina Nijinska and Jean Rawlinson (New York, 1981), 292.

This is not to suggest that Bakst should receive choreographic credit for a given ballet. But the extent to which his designs and stage visions *influenced* a production's choreography should certainly be acknowledged. This role is most clearly documented in what are known as Bakst's "Greek" ballets–*Narcisse* (1911), *L'Après-midi d'un Faune* (1912), and *Daphnis et Chloë* (1912).

▲   ▲   ▲

13 In Paris, Bakst studied with the Finnish painter Albert Edelfelt (b. 1854) and occasionally worked at the Académie Jullian. For complete documentation of Bakst's activities in Paris in the 1890s see Mayer, 15-22.

14 DAPHNIS ET CHLOE was commissioned by Diaghilev in 1909 and scheduled to premiere in 1911. Because Ravel did not produce the music on time, Diaghilev asked Nicolas Tcherepnine to compose the score for another Greek ballet, NARCISSE, to replace the postponed DAPHNIS, eventually performed in spring 1912.

15 Serge Lifar, SERGE DE DIAGHILEV (London, 1940), 140.

16 André Levinson, BALLET OLD AND NEW, trans. Susan Cook Summer (New York, 1982), 66-67.

Bakst's interest in ancient Greece dated to the 1890s when, as a student in Paris, he often visited the city's museums, particularly the Musée du Louvre.[13] Bakst was also familiar with the antiquities collection at the Hermitage museum in St. Petersburg, and, as a member of World of Art, knew Vasily Rozanov's essays on ancient civilization published in the group's magazine. In 1907 Bakst spent a summer in Greece with fellow artist Valentin Serov and returned anxious to incorporate his vivid impressions into a theatrical production. He had already designed three Greek tragedies for the Imperial Theaters, but these—by necessity—were more researched than inspired.

The most salient feature of Bakst's designs for *Daphnis et Chloë*, the first Greek ballet commissioned by Diaghilev but the second actually to be produced,[14] was their stylized, highly organized nature. This element of classical restraint was consistent with prevailing artistic views of ancient Greece, a culture traditionally regarded as a Golden Age—rational, ordered, and pleasantly pastoral. In *Narcisse*, however, his second Greek project for the Ballets Russes, Bakst revealed an entirely different side of Hellenic society—its tendency toward passionate excess. His costume designs for the Bacchantes, for example, blatantly call attention to female breasts, thighs, and calves through the use of painted decoration and draperies (Plate 7). At the same time, the figures are rendered in such a forthright manner that their eroticism could also be seen as an expression of pagan innocence—that elemental state of being that existed before society was constrained by Western civilization.

Fokine's choreography for these two Greek ballets emphasized qualities similar to those found in Bakst's designs. The movement for *Daphnis et Chloë* has been described as poetic, lyrical, and tender, while *Narcisse* contained dances of wild frenzy and intoxicating joy. Like the costumes and decor, the choreography reflected more than one aspect of ancient Greece: with the pastoral and picturesque, it evoked a land of passionate temperament. Because these ballets were worked on simultaneously, similarities of movement and design are apparent. *Narcisse* was even presented with the backdrop originally intended for *Daphnis et Chloë*, and several of the costumes for the corps were used in both productions. Similar movements appeared in both ballets, although they were performed with a different rhythmic and emotional emphasis.

Because of Bakst's knowledge of ancient art and culture, Fokine naturally deferred to him in staging the Greek ballets. As Bakst explained: "I had to show [Fokine] scene by scene what needed to be done. Then finally he worked out the dance steps."[15] In this process Bakst guided Fokine to the figural poses and groupings found in ancient art, particularly in Greek vase painting and sculpture.

The existence of poses and movements common to classical ballet and ancient orchestic (Greek choral) dance has been pointed out by many critics, including the Russian André Levinson.[16] In Greek vase painting, in particular, one finds many examples of attitude (where a dancer stands on one leg with the other leg bent at the knee and extending behind), grand battement (a high kick), and jeté (a jump on one leg). The principle of opposition, by which opposing limbs are cross-associated to achieve the utmost stability and harmony, is also fundamental to both ancient dance and classical ballet. Such similarities of form provided Fokine with a highly accessible movement vocabulary. By either recreating these poses or finding their equivalents in academic technique, he could invent the appropriate motions and critical movement transitions that would in turn produce a fluid dance sequence. In so doing, Fokine—like Bakst—created a modern interpretation instead of a historical reconstruction of ancient Greece.

Bakst's Greek costumes and decors extended the effect of the choreography that he had so directly stimulated. Their symmetrical design enhanced the natural symmetry and contour of the body and underscored the asymmetry of Fokine's groupings and poses. Simply cut and made of lightweight fabric, his pleated tunics permitted complete freedom of movement while their soft flowing lines emphasized the dancer's natural grace. At the same time, the movements, gestures, and pairings of the dancers initiated a subtle, sometimes complicated, play of drapery that added significantly to the costume's visual interest. It is not a coincidence that Bakst and Fokine saw the 1904, 1905, 1907, and 1909 performances of Isadora Duncan in St. Petersburg, and that both acknowledged her influence. In Duncan's dances, simple, natural movements took precedence over virtuoso technique, and loose flowing tunics replaced conventional stage dress. By rejecting the "artificial" positions and tightly corseted costumes of classical ballet, Duncan increased the expressive possibilities of dance and emphasized qualities of pictorial harmony and balance.

Many of the motifs that appeared on Bakst's costumes were taken directly from Greek vase painting. In *Daphnis et Chloë*, for example, he decorated the costumes for the Brigands with chevrons, triangles, checkerboard motifs, and stylized vine and leopard-spot patterns (figure 1), all of which appear on Attic black figureware. The yoke of a Bakst costume, in fact, can be seen as the neck of a Greek amphora—which is decorated with highly sophisticated, geometric patterns (Plates 8 and 9). Equally noteworthy is the bold polychromatic style of the Brigand costumes. Although their pure color tones and complete absence of shading have a historical source, Bakst mixed his brilliant yellows, greens, purples, oranges, and blues in completely new, often harsh combinations. The aggressive nature of Bakst's color harmonies heightened the effect of the Brigands' boisterous, pyrrhic dance. Their circling bounds and leaps created a kaleidoscope of color that underscored the most exhilarating moment of the ballet's action.

The third, and last, Greek ballet produced by the Ballets Russes was also directly influenced by Bakst. Not only did he design the costumes and decor for *L'Après-midi d'un Faune*, choreographed by Vaslav Nijinsky, but he also instructed Nijinsky on the movements and gestures of Greek dance.[17] The angular poses, rigid stance, and two-dimensional movement that created the ballet's frieze-like effect were largely inspired by ancient art, as were the soft, pale, hand-pleated chiffon tunics worn by the female dancers. The composer Igor Stravinsky described the ballet as an "animated bas-relief" and explained that "Bakst dominated this production. Besides creating the decorative setting and the beautiful costumes, he inspired the slightest gesture and choreographic movement."[18]

Nijinsky's *Faune* revealed certain striking similarities to Fokine's Greek ballets, particularly *Daphnis et Chloë*. Both portrayed an Arcadian vision under which lurked the unpredictable human instinct. Because of their disparate choreographic styles, however, Nijinsky and Fokine interpreted their Grecian source material differently. Fokine's treatment was lighter and more natural; his lyricism softened the archaic poses that he blended with movements derived from academic technique. Nijinsky, on the other hand, emphasized the angularity and two-dimensionality of the flattened figure. By deliberately fracturing the dancer's classical line, he eliminated virtually all references to the traditional ballet lexicon and invoked the geometricized forms of Cubism.

The excitement of the Ballets Russes's exoticism, symbolized by the designs of Bakst, could not be sustained indefinitely, particularly in a society thirsting for novelty and innovation. Ironically, it was Bakst's immense popularity that led to his loss of favor, for as audiences grew accustomed to "audacious" colors and a "decadent" aesthetic, Diaghilev looked elsewhere for a new source of pictorial intoxication.

figure 1
Léon Bakst,
Costume design for the Brigands
in *Daphnis et Chloë*, 1912,
cat. no. 14.

17 Although Nijinska (315) saw her brother as the sole creator of L'APRES-MIDI D'UN FAUNE, Arnold Haskell (DIAGHILEFF: HIS ARTISTIC AND PRIVATE LIFE [London, 1935], 268-269) attributes the ballet's conception to Diaghilev and Bakst. For a description of L'APRES-MIDI D'UN FAUNE see essay by Joan Acocella in this catalogue.

18 Igor Stravinsky, AN AUTOBIOGRAPHY (New York, 1936), 56. For a discussion of Bakst's source material, including Vsevolod Meierkhold's 1905-1907 experiments in "static theater," see Lynn Garafola, "Vaslav Nijinsky," RARITAN 8, no. 1 (Summer 1988): 2-6

Plate 8
Léon Bakst,
Costume for a Brigand in *Daphnis et Chloë*, 1912, cat. no. 120.

▲　　　▲　　　▲

19 *Alexandre Benois claims that he recommended Gontcharova to Diaghilev because he was too busy to design the production himself. Arnold Haskell states that the commission came about because of a chance meeting between Diaghilev and Gontcharova's companion, Mikhail Larionov. See Alexandre Benois,* REMINISCENCES OF THE RUSSIAN BALLET *(London, 1947), 356, and Arnold Haskell,* BALLETOMANIA *(London, 1934), 308.*

20 *Nathalie Gontcharova, "Le Costume Théâtral," in Michel Georges-Michel and Waldemar George,* LES BALLETS RUSSES DE SERGE DE DIAGHILEV: DECORS ET COSTUMES *(Paris, 1930), 22.*

21 *Henri Guittard, "Figaro-Théâtre,"* LE FIGARO, *26 May 1914.*

22 *Gontcharova, 22.*

In 1914, turning away from the World of Art artists (Bakst, Benois, Roerich, etc.) he had previously engaged, Diaghilev presented a startlingly original ballet-opera with costumes and sets by Natalia Gontcharova.[19] Virtually unknown in the West, Gontcharova became the first in a series of avant-garde artists, and the first woman, to design for the Ballets Russes.

The audience gasped with the curtain rose on *Le Coq d'Or* on 24 May 1914; they were stunned by the bright primary colors, distorted perspective, and stylized floral motifs of Gontcharova's neoprimitivist set (Plates 3-5). In contrast to Bakst's elaborately detailed, sophisticated designs, Gontcharova's deliberate crudeness reflected a distinctly modernist aesthetic that sought artistic truth in supposedly primitive antecedents—African masks and Byzantine icons as well as native Russian crafts and folk art. The visual impact of the opening scene was particularly dazzling because the curtain was raised during a blackout, a device that allowed the entire decor to be seen at once. This innovation had been suggested by Gontcharova who maintained that "costumes and decor create both the material aspect and the psychological atmosphere of the [stage] scene, even before the actor [dancer] has made a gesture."[20]

In addition to delighting the eye, the simplicity and naive spontaneity of Gontcharova's neoprimitive designs provided a welcome antidote to the lush orientalism and barbaric splendor that had come to symbolize the Ballets Russes and, for many, the moral decay of the prewar years. Gontcharova's outwardly innocent interpretation appealed to a society in which impending war demanded responsible thought and a conscious reassessment of values. But although it was charming and naive in appearance, *Le Coq d'Or*, in fact, was concerned with the more sensual and wicked aspects of human nature. Because of Gontcharova's stylized approach and playful interpretation, however, audiences were able to see only what they wanted—or needed—to see. By rendering festive folk art designs with a primitivizing directness, she created a childlike fantasy—pulsating with raw, vulgar energy. This duality pleased the company's symbolist-oriented audience while satisfying those who were looking for pure entertainment—"without decadent symbols or complications."[21]

Le Coq d'Or is most significant, however, because it marks a shift in the visual aspect of the Ballets Russes. Gontcharova's dynamic, semi-abstract compositions moved the company away from Symbolism and toward a modernist aesthetic. This is particularly evident in her decors where the flattening of space, altered perspective, radically stylized and geometricized forms, and repetition of ornamental motifs fragment the stage picture into blocks of pattern and color. Painted illusion gives way to abstract representation, as can be seen clearly in her project for the front curtain (Plate 3). In this unrealized design, stylized houses, animals, trees, and figures are shuffled together without a focal point to create an energetic, semi-abstract composition. By combining the dynamic colors and force lines of Futurism with the the broken lines and planes of Rayonism, Gontcharova achieved a sense of continual space in which pictorial elements are caught in a moment of flux.

Gontcharova's modernist sensibility is also evident in her use of vivid fauve chromatics. Like Bakst and the Fauves, she used color for aesthetic as well as expressive purpose. As she explained,

It is necessary . . . that the tones of the decor are sustained by the tones of the costume in order that their combination does not contradict the sense of the theatrical vision and that it creates, psychologically and visually, a unity of spectacle.[22]

Plate 9
Léon Bakst,
Costume for a Brigand in *Daphnis et Chloë*, 1912, cat. no. 121.

figure 2
Natalia Gontcharova,
Costume for a Man in *Le Coq d'Or*,
1914, cat. no. 54.

23 *Cyril Beaumont*, THE
DIAGHILEV BALLET IN LONDON
(*London*, 1940), 97.

24 *Sono Osato*, DISTANT DANCES
(*New York*, 1980), 146.

25 *Beaumont*, 95.

26 *Beaumont*, 95.

27 *Lydia Sokolova*, DANCING FOR
DIAGHILEV (*London*, 1960), 62.

28 *A. V. Coton*, A PREJUDICE FOR
THE BALLET (*London*, 1938), 194.

Gontchavora saw costumed figures as anonymous mobile units within the stage picture, as well as separate entities in the dance drama. When set in motion against a painted backdrop, her boldly colored costumes became formal design elements in the overall stage tableau. Color-coordinated ensembles faded into and out of the background by virtue of their conscious placement onstage and the dancers' carefully designed movement patterns.

Fokine's choreography for *Le Coq d'Or* lacked the invention of Gontcharova's designs, although it successfully embodied the expressive possibilities of movement. For example, the dances of the seductive Queen of Shemakhan consisted of semi-classical movements performed with supple arms whose languorous motions "could strangle as well as caress."[23] The nature of her role as temptress was dramatized by the queen's undulating retinue, moving—with slanted torsos—in sinuous, winding patterns that furthered the spell of oriental enchantment. King Dodon, on the other hand, was portrayed as a portly old man whose clumsy steps expressed his inept authority and susceptible emotional state.

Gontcharova's costumes, like Fokine's choreography, revealed the individual character of each role. The Queen of Shemakhan's loose-fitting harem pants and the lustrous gold lamé girdle that was wrapped snugly at her waist called attention to the provocative movements of her hips and pelvis. One of the dancers in the ballet's 1937 revival explained, "Between the way she looked and the way she moved, her bewitchment of Dodon seemed inevitable."[24] For the king's country folk, Gontcharova designed Russian peasant-style costumes decorated with bold appliqué patterns in primary colors (figure 2). These suited the comic, unclassical choreography that Fokine created for the dancers whose movement supported the burlesqued actions of King Dodon. The maids wore peasant dresses that were "bunched and formless despite their attractive pattern and colour."[25] With their faces "clumsily daubed with red," the dancers "resembled nothing so much as highly coloured Russian peasant toys, temporarily endowed with life."[26] These costumes were entirely consistent with the dancer's brisk, doll-like movements, however, and both enhanced the satirical element of the story that had been banned in Russia because of its political implications. As dancer Lydia Sokolova explained: "It seems easy, in the light of after events, to see in King Dodon the unfortunate spoon-fed Czar; [and] in the beautiful Queen of Shemakhan, who turns out to be an evil enchantress, the Czarina whose counsels hastened the fall of her husband's Empire."[27]

The success of *Le Coq d'Or* was due primarily to its staging, the only criticism being that Gontcharova's setting was "too overwhelming visually to permit undistracted perception of the beauties . . . of dancing."[28] This imbalance between design and choreography was partially due to Diaghilev's decision—made at the suggestion of Alexandre Benois— to present *Le Coq d'Or* as an opera-ballet with dancers miming the action of the singers who were seated in choral formation on both sides of the stage. This innovative resolution required that Fokine invent mimetic, rather than abstract, movement that conformed closely to the sung narrative. Given this limitation, it is not surprising that the dancing appeared minimal and uninspired. Although Fokine's skillful blending of movement and mime was charming, it was overshadowed by the brilliant color and primitive fantasy of Gontcharova's costumes and sets.

Le Coq d'Or's revivals and Gontcharova's continued effort to repeat and modify her designs confirm her fascination with this production. The 1937 staging for Colonel W. de Basil's Ballets Russes was presented as a straight ballet, and as a result Fokine expanded the principal dancing roles and Gontcharova redesigned several costumes. Although similar in concept to the 1914 originals, the new costumes—less constructed and made of lighter-

weight fabric—allowed a greater freedom of movement. For example, the original appliquéd satin harem pants worn by the Queen of Shemakhan were replaced by a clinging chiffon version with strategically split side seams that seductively revealed the dancer's legs while facilitating their extension.

Gontcharova designed nine productions for Diaghilev, only six of which were produced, and she assisted her lifelong companion Mikhail Larionov with the costumes for two others. Her unrealized works—*Liturgie* (1915), *Triana* (1916), and *Rhapsodie Espagnole* or *Espagna* (1916)— were created during the war years and strongly reflected the experiments then taking place in the theater of the Russian Constructivists as well as the theatrical theories of the Italian Futurists. Because of her belief in the greater expressive possibility of non-objective art, Gontcharova—like the Constructivists and Futurists—was attempting to reinvent relations between the performer and the stage space, reducing characterization and narrative in the search for a universal modernism. To various degrees, each explored the use of constructed, semi-abstract costumes and sets as well as mechanistic movement and gesture and exaggerated makeup and masks that lent anonymity to performance.

Gontcharova's *Liturgie*, a religious ballet representing seven moments in the life of Christ, embodied constructivist, futurist, and cubo-futurist ideas. The figures in her costume designs seem to have been fractured and restructured so that they become architectural supports for the all-encompassing garments (figure 3). In performance, the moving element would appear to be the cubo-futurist costume construction rather than the figure supporting it. This effect was furthered by the dancer's movement, choreographed by Léonide Massine, that existed primarily in a two-dimensional plane. Simple, angular motions were performed with a rigid torso and the use of stiff, open-hand gestures and stamping footwork. Much of Massine's stylized choreography was governed by the costumes that were not only voluminous, but also heavy, incorporating such materials as leather, wood, and metal.[29] The dancers were depersonalized by their restricted movement as well as fixed facial expressions that conveyed the impression of austere, iconic beings moving in an otherworldly dimension.

Both Gontcharova and Massine sought to communicate the ballet's liturgical theme through a series of tableaux that flowed organically from one static image to the next. Gontcharova's sixteen costume designs, conceived as a cycle and compiled in an album of *pochoirs* in 1915, illustrate this conception and her belief that "costumes can either harm or support one another."[30] By allowing the stage picture to build and evolve in front of the eyes of the audience, Gontcharova and Massine emphasized visual sensation over narrative—a further hallmark of ballet modernism.

▲   ▲   ▲

The success of the company's modernist conceptions and wartime isolation from Russia prompted Diaghilev to seek future collaborators among the painters of the European avant-garde. In late 1916 he commissioned production designs from the futurist artists Giacomo Balla and Fortunato Depero, but neither Balla's *Feu d'Artifice*, in which—with no dancing—transparent cubes and cones were lit by Diaghilev as a Stravinsky score was played, nor Depero's *Le Chant du Rossignol*, entered the Ballets Russes repertory. This was largely because of their complex design involving intricate lighting plots and constructed scenery and costumes that were too cumbersome for touring. Between 1917 and 1921 Diaghilev

29 Florence Gilliam, "Natalie Gontcharova and the New Art Décoratif," THE ARTS 5, no. 1 (January 1924): 30.

30 Gontcharova, 22.

also invited artists from the School of Paris–Pablo Picasso, André Derain, Robert and Sonia Delaunay, and Henri Matisse–to design six new ballets that premiered in the French capital and London. By placing the work of these painters at the center of his theatrical productions, Diaghilev established the Ballets Russes as a purveyor–and popularizer–of twentieth-century modernism.

Diaghilev's European artist-designers recognized that the theatrical stage provided the possibility of wide exposure as well as the opportunity for artistic experiment. According to his biographer, Alfred Barr, Matisse had no particular interest in ballet, but the success of Picasso's *Parade* (1917) and *Le Tricorne* (1919) and Derain's *La Boutique Fantasque* (1919) encouraged him to accept a commission from Diaghilev. Following an invitation in 1919 to design a new version of either *Schéhérazade* or *Le Chant du Rossignol*, Matisse listened to Stravinsky play excerpts from both ballet scores.[31] The painter elected to design the latter production, perhaps because it involved new choreography by Léonide Massine, whom he liked and admired. Matisse may also have been reluctant to tamper with Bakst's designs for *Schéhérazade* because of their popular success. It wasn't until years later that he criticized them in an article titled "The Role and Modalities of Colour":

The Russian Ballet, particularly SCHEHERAZADE *by Bakst, overflowed with colour. Profusion without moderation. One might have said that it was splashed about from a bucket. The result was gay because of the material itself, not as the result of any organization. . . . An avalanche of colour has no force. Colour attains its full expression only when it is organized, when it corresponds to the emotional intensity of the artist.*[32]

Ironically, it was the early fauve paintings by Matisse that had inspired much of Bakst's and Gontcharova's bold juxtapositions of color. But in 1920, strongly influenced by the luminous daylight on the Côte d'Azur, Matisse favored a subdued palette that he worked with intellectual rigor. Unlike his prewar odalisques and orientally inspired art, Matisse's designs for *Le Chant du Rossignol* used

very slight means–a sense of proportion, a little invention, [and] intelligent restraint . . . [to produce] something delightfully cool and fresh, and free from the oppressive opulence of conventional Western interpretations of the 'gorgeous East'[33] (Plates 10 and 11 and figure 4).

The restrained nature of Matisse's designs, however, was not in keeping with the audience's expectations. Although the painter's artistic concerns at the time were reflected in these productions (as was a broadly felt postwar need to reestablish calm and order), the public still associated the Ballets Russes with lavish spectacle. *Le Chant du Rossignol* thus appeared as a deliberate reaction to the productions of Bakst and Gontcharova, a fact that Matisse was well aware of:

Your Russians wait for violence from me? Not at all. I am going to teach them what is the measuring out of colour, according to the French tradition: two pale colours and a pure white. And that will get the better of all their bawling.[34]

The elegant simplicity of Matisse's designs influenced, and was influenced by, the ballet's streamlined choreography. Both suggested a modernist sensibility in the use of simplified form and a distancing from source material. Hans Christian Andersen's story "The Nightingale" is set in China, but the Massine/Matisse ballet, described by the choreographer as a "formalized Oriental fantasy,"[35] takes place in an unspecified exotic land–a mysteriously alluring but alien civilization. The chinoiserie that characterizes the

31 Alfred H. Barr, Jr., MATISSE, HIS ART AND HIS PUBLIC (*New York, 1951*), 207. Stravinsky's opera LE ROSSIGNOL *was first produced by Diaghilev in 1914 with sets and costumes by Alexandre Benois. The production had only six performances and in 1916 Diaghilev commissioned Stravinsky to adapt the music for a ballet with new designs by Fortunato Depero. Because Depero was late in completing the designs, which were also not suitable for touring, Diaghilev postponed the project, offering Matisse the commission in 1919.*

32 Henri Matisse, "The Role and Modalities of Colour," in Jack D. Flam, MATISSE ON ART (*London, 1973*), 99. Cited in Melissa A. McQuillan, "Painters and the Ballet, 1917-1926: An Aspect of the Relationship between Art and Theatre" (Ph. D. diss., New York University, 1979), 486.

33 R. H. W., "Matisse and Dufy as Designers," THE ATHENAEUM: A JOURNAL OF ENGLISH AND FOREIGN LITERATURE, SCIENCE, THE FINE ARTS, MUSIC AND THE DRAMA (13 August 1920): 217.

34 Michel Georges-Michel, BALLETS RUSSES: HISTOIRE ANECDOTIQUE SUIVIE D'UN APPENDICE ET DU POEME DE SHEHERAZADE (*Paris, 1923*), 31. Cited in McQuillan, 486.

35 Léonide Massine, MY LIFE IN BALLET, ed. Phyllis Hartnoll and Robert Rubens (*London, 1968*), 147.

Plate 10
Henri Matisse,
Costume for a Mourner in *Le Chant du Rossignol*, 1920, cat. no. 148.

production evokes a mood and atmosphere rather than establishing a time or place, as would a simulacrum of Chinese art.

In his biography Massine explained that his study of painted and sculpted static images taught him the rudiments of choreography. It is not surprising to read that the dances in *Le Chant du Rossignol* were as skillfully structured and harmoniously pleasing as "a porcelain or a bronze from the Ming Dynasty."[36] In creating the ballet Massine readily acknowledged his use of poses, movements, and groupings taken from Chinese art, specifically paintings on silk and lacquered screens. The dancer Sokolova noted that

36 *Jean Bernier, "Le Chant du Rossignol," in souvenir program from* LES BALLETS RUSSES A L'OPERA *(January-February 1920), n.p.*

there were some very fine and highly ingenious groupings of men in LE CHANT DU ROSSIGNOL. *They built themselves up into flat friezes, rather in the way that acrobats do, but their bodies were packed tight and knitted close together, some men on one leg, some upside down resting on a bent arm, some in a kind of hand-stand. These groups suggested to me the grotesque combinations of figures on carved ivory boxes, and I wondered if it was from these that Massine had taken his idea.*[37]

37 *Sokolova, 147.*

Massine's vertical arrangement of dancers in human pyramids belied the depth of the stage, as did the planar surfaces of the decor and–in scene two–the uptilted bed of the Emperor. These effects, with their emphasis on verticality, contributed to the impression of a three-dimensional projection of a Matisse painting rather than a splayed-out decor that leaves empty or dead space overhead. In his treatment of the stage as a pictorial surface, the artist "imagined a perspective on a very accentuated, almost vertical, inclined plane. The choreography was ordered in the same spirit to accord with this perspective."[38] The shared point of view on the part of designer and choreographer was confirmed by Massine: "I worked closely with Matisse to create a fusion of costumes, decor and choreography, and I found this ballet one of my most successful efforts at collaboration with a designer."[39]

38 *Raymond Cogniat,* CINQUANTE ANS DE SPECTACLES EN FRANCE: LES DECORATEURS DE THEATRE *(Paris, 1955), 24. Cited in McQuillan, 215.*

39 *Massine, 147-148.*

One of Matisse's concerns in designing *Le Chant du Rossignol* was the manner in which individual costumes could be made to interact and combine. The sculptural poses and ensemble movement of the uniformly clad corps de ballet allowed the artist to think in terms of volumetric modeling. Matisse designed geometrically cut costumes for the Mourners (Plate 10) and Mandarins (Plate 11) that deliberately masked the curves of the body, thereby transforming the dancers into building blocks of Massine's accumulative architectonic structures. When the costumes were isolated and placed in movement by the figures inside, they became part of an overall fluctuating pattern of stylized shape and color. The Mourners' all-encompassing white felt cloaks and hoods, appliquéd with midnight blue velvet chevrons and triangles, converted the dancer's figure into a planar surface–an abstract shape–as did the saffron yellow satin robes of the Mandarins. In scene two, matching his choreography to the spare design, Massine caused these alternately shimmering and absorbent surfaces to move "silently before the pale background . . . like spirits passing at dawn . . . [as] the pale hand of Death was outstretched over [all]."[40]

40 *Walter A. Propert,* RUSSIAN BALLET IN WESTERN EUROPE 1909-1920 *(London, 1921), 60.*

Matisse created fitted costumes for the principal dancers, Nightingale and Death, and a constructed garment for the Mechanical Nightingale, thereby separating the symbolic figures from the human characters in the ballet. In spite of their greater realism and detail, these costumes appear modern next to the elaborate 1914 versions designed by Alexandre Benois for the Ballets Russes's initial staging of the opera *Le Rossignol*. They look almost traditional, however, when compared to Depero's futurist costumes that were composed of geometrically derived forms: cones, tubes, circular masks, and disks (see note 31). Matisse was no doubt aware of the Benois and Depero designs, as well as the Maryinsky's

Plate 11
Henri Matisse,
Costume for a Mandarin in *Le Chant du Rossignol*, 1920, cat. no. 146.

figure 4
Henri Matisse,
*Le Chant du Rossignol: Sketch for
the Curtain*, 1920. Graphite and
ink on paper pasted on board,
12⅞ × 17¹⁵⁄₁₆ in. Wadsworth
Atheneum, Hartford. From the
Serge Lifar Collection. The Ella
Gallup Sumner and Mary Catlin
Sumner Collection.

1919 staging of *Le Chant du Rossignol* in Petrograd, directed by Konstantin Stanislavsky. The stylistically distinctive costumes and sets for the Maryinsky production were created by Alexander Golovin, a member of the World of Art group who designed operas and ballets for Diaghilev in 1908, 1909, and 1910. Golovin's exotic, ornate designs and emphasis on linear expressivity show his concentrated application of the aesthetic of Jugendstil (Plate 13).

▲   ▲   ▲

Massine states that after visiting the churches and museums in Florence he began "to understand that all great artists were in fact great choreographers."[41] He was referring to the painters' ability to create dynamic compositions and sculptural groupings based on the laws of perspective, architecture, and anatomy—elements that are central to design and choreography. Benois claimed that during the Diaghilev years "it was we, the painters . . .[who] helped to mold the art of dancing along new lines, and, indeed, the whole of the production."[42] But the same can be said of the dancers, choreographers, and musicians who, with Diaghilev's support, viewed the stage of the Ballets Russes as a place to reaffirm

41 *Massine, 70.*

42 *Lifar, 141.*

their own individuality and freedom from convention. What was unique about the Diaghilev enterprise was the opportunity that it provided for artists working in different disciplines–painting, choreography, and music–to inspire and learn from one another. Encouraged by Diaghilev, they took unprecedented risks, revitalizing their own art as well as that of the ballet. In 1929 Diaghilev was quoted as saying,

Our century, without halting, interests itself with new "Mouvements mécaniques," but whenever new "Mouvements artistiques" occur people seem to be more frightened of being run over by them than by a motor-car in the street. For 25 years I have endeavored to find a new "Mouvement" in the theater. Society will have to recognize that my experiments, which appear dangerous to-day, become indispensable to-morrow.[43]

43 *Letter from Serge Diaghilev to* THE TIMES, *13 July 1939, quoted in Beaumont, 324-325.*

Sixty years after his death and eighty years since the Paris premiere of the Ballets Russes, we recognize that Diaghilev was the indispensable catalyst for experiment. Just as he linked East with West, and the nineteenth century with the twentieth, he sought a fusion of design, choreography, and music that established the modern performance stage as a flexible, living vehicle for creative expression.

SIAMESE DANCING AND THE BALLETS RUSSES

Nicoletta Misler

▼

NOTE:
This article is an abbreviated version of "Ex Oriente Lux: Siamese Dancing and the Ballets Russes," ANNALI DELL'ISTITUTO UNIVERSITARIO ORIENTALE *46* (1986): 197-219.

1 N. Svetlov, "Siamskii balet," EZHEGODNIK IMPERATORSKIKH TEATROV SEZON 1900-1901, *ed. L. A. Gelmersen (St. Petersburg, n.d.), 293-298.*

2 A. Cecil Carter, M.A., ed., THE KINGDOM OF SIAM: MINISTRY OF AGRICULTURE LOUISIANA PURCHASE EXPOSITION, ST. LOUIS, MO. U.S.A. 1904, SIAMESE SECTION *(New York and London, 1904), 3, 4.*

3 *Frederic Mayer and Ferdinand W. Peck,* THE PARISIAN DREAM CITY: ILLUSTRATED WORLD EXPOSITION, *published weekly (St. Louis, 1900).*

4 *Andrei Levinson,* STARYI I NOVYI BALET *(Petrograd, 1917), 19, 52, 90.*

5 *Charles Spencer,* LEON BAKST *(London, 1973), 73.*

THE BALLET TROUPE OF THE ROYAL SIAMESE COURT (figure 1) gave two performances in the main Imperial Theaters of St. Petersburg, the Mikhailovsky and the Alexandrinsky, on Saturday, 28 October, and Sunday, 29 October 1900.[1] The Siamese ballet enjoyed considerable success with the St. Petersburg public as well as the small but important group of Buddhists there. It also provided something of a cultural shock for the local intelligentsia; it was the first time that they had been confronted with such a totally new dance form.

From the European viewpoint, at least since the time of Byzantium, Russia had been considered part of the Orient—a kind of local European Orient. This attitude was expressed both in academic and scientific circles as well as in Paris and London salons. The Siamese ballet had come to St. Petersburg in 1900 following a visit by King Chulalongkorn of Thailand. The king had toured the principal European courts, including that of Russia, in 1897 in an effort to open diplomatic relations.[2] Bringing the ballet to St. Petersburg fulfilled both a cultural and diplomatic function: Russia, bound to expand toward China and Japan, represented a useful ally for free Thailand, the only independent country in Southeast Asia.

Just as French audiences had appreciated the Siamese, Javanese, and Cambodian dance forms at the Paris Exposition Universelle in 1900, so the St. Petersburg public responded at once to the unusual rhythms of the Siamese company.[3] Among the St. Petersburg public there were two young men, the cosmopolitan and cultured Francophiles Léon Bakst and Michel Fokine, who perceived the Eastern ballet in much the same way as did their French colleagues—as an exquisite variation on a theme. In 1906, Auguste Rodin had painted various watercolor interpretations of the Cambodian ballet in Paris, and just as he had felt the need to record his impressions of this exotic, gestural art,[4] Bakst received a similar profound and immediate stimulus.[5] He recorded his reactions in the painting *A Siamese Sacred Dance* (1902, State Tretiakov Gallery, Moscow),[6] which depicted the most suggestive of the Siamese dances, the dance of the lanterns, and anticipated his later work as a designer for Diaghilev's Ballets Russes. The background in this painting actually predicts detail for detail Bakst's backdrop for *Le Dieu Bleu* (1912), relying on a diagonal composition with mysterious figures (presumably pseudo-Hindu deities) moving in front of the entrance to a cavernous temple.

The diplomatic nature of the Siamese ballet's St. Petersburg tour was made clearly evident by the selection of works performed. The aim was to present a panorama both of the Siamese theater and to emphasize the political and cultural meaning of the mission through a classical veil dance in red and white (the colors of the Siamese flag). Photographs of the spectacle document that two traditional forms of Siamese theater were featured—the Khon Theater with its masks, and the Lakon Theater with its reliance on female court dancers.

These performances had a lasting effect on Bakst and Fokine and strongly influenced their future work for the Ballets Russes. A decade later, for example, they incorporated Siamese dance motifs in their designs and choreography for *Les Orientales* (1910) and *Le Dieu Bleu* (1912), although they did so in an entirely personal and subjective manner. Their experience of the Siamese ballet, like their experience of Isadora Duncan's performances in Russia in 1904-1905,[7] constituted an important point of departure for their transformation of the traditional Russian ballet, but it also confirmed their conditioned cultural reflexes.

Bakst and Fokine regarded the scenographic and choreographic innovations of the

figure 8
Tamara Karsavina in
Le Dieu Bleu, 1910.

6 *Irina Pruzhan [Proujan]*, LEV
SAMOILOVICH BAKST (*Moscow*,
1975), 76-77.

7 *Sergei Lifar*, ISTORIA RUSSKAGO
BALETA: OT XVII VEKA DO
"RUSSKAGO BALETA" DIAGHILEVA
(*Paris*, 1945), 273.

Siamese Ballet as new technical elements to be incorporated into their own specific contexts and needs. They thereby reduced the Siamese dances to a formal language that they could use to extend the range of the classical ballet, both in terms of movement and design. They were also aware that exotic oriental themes held considerable appeal for Parisian audiences, and they were not hesitant to capitalize on the fact.

As a designer, Bakst applied Siamese motifs in specific contexts. For example, he used the short skirt with its acutely angled, petal-like folds in various costume designs for *Le Dieu Bleu* (figure 2), and the headdress for the title role brings to mind that of the *devatā* in an Angkor Wat relief (figure 3). In several instances he created geometric design patterns

figure 1
The Ballet Troupe
of the Royal Siamese Court,
in St. Petersburg, 1900.

figure 2
Léon Bakst,
Costume design for Nijinsky in the
title role, *Le Dieu Bleu*, 1911.
Collection unknown.

figure 3
Devatā headdress, detail from a
bas-relief at Angkor Wat, 1st half
of the 12th century.

such as that in the costume design for Iskander in the ballet project *La Péri* (1911) that incorporates the stylized eyes of peacock tails to suggest the exotic East. In Bakst's extraordinary artistic imagination, one decorative pattern was easily mixed with another and historical accuracy was often sacrificed to fashion. This does not mean, however, that Bakst was indifferent to the authenticity of his source material. Although he freely adapted oriental motifs in his work, his interest in Siamese ballet and in Buddhist culture in general was hardly superficial. Indeed, two 1923 photographs of Bakst's Paris studio[8] show a Thai painting hanging on the wall and a Laotian figure of a walking Buddha among other orientalia (see figures 4 and 5).

8 One undated photograph shows a long-distance view of Bakst's living room (Spencer, 190). Another photograph, dated 1923, shows Bakst evidently at the same age and in the same living room, but it is a close-up (Arnold Haskell, DIAGHILEFF: HIS ARTISTIC AND PRIVATE LIFE [London, 1955], ill. to 99).

In St. Petersburg, Vasily Rozanov, the religious philosopher, had been impressed by the authenticity of the Siamese dances and the genuine spirit of the Orient they embodied and, above all, he had appreciated the high cultural level of the dance spectacle. In his early essays published in 1901 in *World of Art* (Mir iskusstva), Rozanov called attention to the particular worldview expressed by the Siamese ballet and noted its direct contact with natural rhythms—not as some primitive inability to escape from nature, but rather as in harmony with it. He contrasted this condition with the unnatural, frenetic, accelerated speed and dynamism of the modern industrial society.

In spite of his paternalistic attitude and subtle racism vis-à-vis a people he deemed to be "children," Rozanov was able to see a global meaning in the Siamese dance, a cohesion that he felt was relevant in the contemporary world. He argued that the dancers' intense awareness of their bodies contrasted dramatically with the mute body of the Europeans

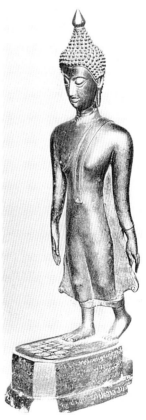

figure 4
Léon Bakst in his living room, Paris, 1923.

figure 5
Walking Buddha, 1482. Bronze, height 18 1/8 in. National Museum, Bangkok. This is the type of Buddha seen on Bakst's desk in figure 4.

9 Vasily Rozanov, "Balet ruk"
and "Zanimatelnii vecher,"
MIR ISKUSSTVA 1 (1901): 43-48.
Both essays were reprinted in V. V.
Rozanov, SREDI KHUDOZHNIKOV
(St. Petersburg, 1914),
31-45, 51-61.

10 Lincoln Kirstein, NIJINSKY
DANCING (London, 1975),
38-39, 89-93.

11 Vera Krasovskaya, NIJINSKY
(New York, 1979), 144.

12 Richard Buckle, NIJINSKY
(London, 1971), 151-152.

figure 6
Nijinsky in a "Siamese" pose,
photographed in Jacques-Emile
Blanche's garden in Paris, 1910.

figure 7
Jacques-Emile Blanche,
*Nijinsky in His Costume for "Les
Orientales."* Oil on canvas,
85¼×47 in. Private collection,
London.

who expressed themselves primarily through the head and brain. In the Siamese dance, the body alone radiated its own expressive language, not just through the legs as in classical ballet, but also in the upper torso, arms, and hands. The secondary role of the face and of facial expression contributed to the mysterious and graceful presence of the dancers who sometimes appeared to be moving in a somnambulistic state.[9]

The most striking evidence regarding Bakst's and Fokine's assimilation of the Siamese ballet is a group of photographs[10] depicting Vaslav Nijinsky in a Siamese costume designed by Bakst in poses from *Les Orientales*. A series of oriental dances rendered as solo numbers, this ballet took the form of an exotic collage.[11] One of the pieces relied on music by Christian Sinding and had Nijinsky performing steps created by Fokine that were based on classical Siamese dance. Photographs taken by Druet and Baron de Meyer in the Paris studio and garden of Jacques-Emile Blanche (figure 6) document Nijinsky's performance.[12] Blanche painted his celebrated portrait of Nijinsky based on these photographs, exploring the rapid use of brushstroke and the play of light on textured surface in his rendering of the dancer's highly ornate costume.

In performance, Nijinsky communicated an "oriental presence" through the use of hieratic pose and gesture. Nevertheless, Nijinsky's dance depended on his virile and masculine body with its dominant leg movements, related more to Russian folk dance than to the Siamese ballet. After all, Siamese dancing was an exercise in hand movements and soft, almost disarticulated, gestures. His deliberate stylization of, and even estrangement from, the original Siamese model was captured—and paralleled—in the portrait by Blanche.

13 *Krasovskaya,* NIJINSKY, *144.*

14 *Buckle,* DIAGHILEV, *222.*

15 *Charles Spencer,* THE WORLD OF DIAGHILEV *(London, 1974), ill. to 74. Vera Krasovskaya,* RUSSKII BALETNYI TEATR NACHALA XX VEKA *(Leningrad, 1972), ill. to 432-433.*

16 *Lydia Sokolova,* DANCING FOR DIAGHILEV, *ed. Richard Buckle (New York, 1961), 37.*

17 *Bronislava Nijinska,* EARLY MEMOIRS, *trans. and ed. Irina Nijinska and Jean Rawlinson (New York, 1981), 432.*

18 *Suzanne Shelton,* DIVINE DANCER: A BIOGRAPHY OF RUTH ST. DENIS *(Garden City, 1981).*

figure 9
Léon Bakst,
Design for decor for
Le Dieu Bleu, 1912, cat. no. 10.

figure 10
Towers with gigantic faces, detail,
Bayon Temple, Angkor Thom, late
12th-early 13th century.

19 *Sokolova, 37.*

20 *A. A. Ivanova, T. V. Grek, and O. F. Akimishkino,* ALBOM INDIISKIKH MINIATUR XVI-XVII VV., *ed. L. T. Giuzaliana (Moscow, 1962), ill. on 42.*

The gold Coromandel screen that Blanche used as a background for Nijinsky was as artificial as the dancer's poses (figure 7). This contrived orientalism may explain why Nijinsky's interpretation of a Siamese dance in *Les Orientales* failed to convince audiences who were confronted "with a figure looking like the statue of an ancient oriental god in the midst of an empty stage, but the statue was too small for such a big place."[13]

Despite the less than enthusiastic response to *Les Orientales,* Diaghilev staged another "oriental" ballet in 1912, again with costumes and decor by Bakst and choreography by Fokine. *Le Dieu Bleu* was set in some vaguely Indian territory and used costumes that brought to mind the original conventions of the Siamese tunic, decorated in a rather gaudy fashion. Fokine's choreography featured a "Pseudo-Indian Dance of Divine Enchantment"[14] for Nijinsky, whose otherworldly appearance was enhanced by the use of all-over blue body-paint. Tamara Karsavina also performed a solo role concentrating all the movement of her hands and feet in a series of exotic gestures (figure 8) reminiscent of Thai dance forms.[15]

The East Indian theme of *Le Dieu Bleu* could not fail to evoke associations with the highly successful *La Bayadère* staged by Marius Petipa at the Maryinsky Theater, St. Petersburg, in 1877 and then reworked by Gorsky at the Bolshoi Theater, Moscow, in 1904. The Bayadère scene in *Le Dieu Bleu* was actually one of the most impressive in the entire ballet. It was rendered by three of the tallest ballerinas in the company, Serafima Astafieva in the middle with Lubov Tchernicheva and Maria Piltz on the sides, all carrying stuffed peacocks whose luxurious tails dragged along the floor.[16] Another Bayadère role was interpreted by Nijinsky's sister, Bronislava Nijinska, and was based on a series of slow "steps and poses in pseudo-Indian-Siamese style."[17]

These dances of the Bayadère carried a cultural reference but actually had nothing to do with oriental culture. They were derived instead from the fashion for Indian dance and the dances of Southeast Asia that invaded Europe and America as a result of various professional and amateur performances.[18] The oriental dances in *Le Dieu Bleu* reflected certain aesthetic demands–spiritual, mystical, and transcendental–germane to fin-de-siècle Europe. By 1912, however, the public was growing bored with orientalism, and despite its visual and choreographic originality, *Le Dieu Bleu* was not a popular success. Bakst's artistic interpretations were criticized as fashionable gestures to orientalism whose music and image made only for banal exotic entertainment. *Le Dieu Bleu* was significant, however, from an artistic point of view, and despite the outward superficiality of the production, Bakst's designs revealed his considerable knowledge of authentic visual sources. The gigantic faces that emerged from the stone cliffs in the decor (figure 9), for example, were without doubt the same monumental sandstone faces that decorated the towers of the Bayon Temple of Angkor Thom in Cambodia (figure 10). Fokine's choreography also had historical references, seventeenth-century Indian and Persian miniatures in particular. We can infer from a description of the dervishes in *Le Dieu Bleu* in which the spinning dancers "presented an extraordinary picture of whirling white discs"[19] that Fokine may have been directly inspired by an album of Mughal miniatures in the State Russian Museum in St. Petersburg.[20]

Bakst and Fokine typify the many Russian and western European artists who paid homage to the oriental aesthetic in the early twentieth century. They are unique however in that they managed to effect a successful integration of authentic source material and an extraordinary artistic imagination. Using the Ballets Russes stage as their vehicle, they created a bridge–both visually and intellectually–between Asian and European culture that can be traced to their first experience of the Royal Siamese Ballet in St. Petersburg in 1900.

DIAGHILEV'S
BALLETS RUSSES
AND THE
VOGUE FOR
ORIENTALISM

───────

Dale Harris

▼

1 Igor Stravinsky and Robert Craft, CONVERSATIONS WITH STRAVINSKY (New York, 1959), 109.

2 Tamara Karsavina, THEATRE STREET (London, 1948), 201.

3 Karsavina, 201.

4 Harold Acton, MEMOIRS OF AN AESTHETE (London, 1984), 113.

5 Nigel Gosling, PARIS: 1900-1914 (New York, 1978), 171.

I consider Bakst's SCHEHERAZADE *to be a masterpiece . . . , perhaps the perfect achievement of the Russian Ballet from the scenic point of view. Costumes, sets, the curtain, were colorful in an indescribable way—we are so much poorer in these things now. I remember, too, that Picasso considered* SCHEHERAZADE *a masterpiece.*[1]

—IGOR STRAVINSKY

IN AN AGE LIKE THE PRESENT, when through a combination of soaring costs and changing tastes the importance and quality of ballet design have declined so precipitously, it becomes increasingly hard to understand how crucial a role in Diaghilev's initial success was played by the artists who decorated his productions: Nicholas Roerich, Alexandre Benois, and, above all, Léon Bakst. Nevertheless, their importance cannot be overestimated. In her account of the first Ballets Russes season of 1909, Tamara Karsavina speaks of Bakst—whose name, she tells us, was on everybody's lips—as *le bateau de la saison russe.*[2] More than any other of Diaghilev's designers, Bakst gave expression to the luxuriant sensuousness that in the eyes of the West was the company's most intriguing feature: "Paris," Karsavina tells us, "was captivated by the barbaric splendor of frenzied movements, the nostalgia of infinite plains, the naive spontaneity of Russia, the studied ornateness of the East.[3]

With the premiere of *Schéhérazade* the following season, the exotic appeal of the Russians was consolidated and even strengthened. For two decades after Diaghilev's death in 1929, *Schéhérazade* typified for the world at large the allure of the Ballets Russes. Harold Acton believed that "for many a young artist *Shéhérazade* [sic] had been an inspiration equivalent to Gothic architecture for the Romantics or Quattrocento frescoes for the Pre-Raphaelites."[4] Such testimony needs to be viewed with caution, even within the context of British art, which had been decisively affected by Roger Fry's great post-impressionist exhibition of 1910, the year before the Ballets Russes made its British debut. There is more truth in the cooler assessment of Nigel Gosling:

For the first time in the history of the theater a designer had won not only attention but fame. Bakst's dazzling sets and costumes [for SCHEHERAZADE; see Plate 12 and Garafola, figures 3-5], *which combined the sumptuousness of Moreau with the brilliance of the Fauves, exploded into Paris fashion and interior design, and remained an influence for years.*[5]

That the reaction to Bakst was evident less in art than in decoration is affirmed by the testimony of Jacques-Emile Blanche:

6 Quoted by Martin Battersby, ART DECO FASHION: FRENCH DESIGNERS, 1908-1925 (London, 1984), 61.

The first performance of SCHEHERAZADE *was an important event for the theatre, for dressmakers, for interior decorators, for jewelers and for all branches of decoration. It is difficult today to realise the metamorphosis which transformed the decorative arts.*[6]

7 Battersby, 66.

8 Ernestine Carter, THE CHANGING WORLD OF FASHION: 1900 TO THE PRESENT (New York, 1977), 109.

The clearest manifestation of this change was the sudden ascendancy of an all-purpose orientalism—for example, the reintroduction of the kind of heavy scent popular in the mid-nineteenth century, but now marketed with exotic names, like Guerlain's "Mitsouko," Poiret's "Nuit de Chine" and Legrand's "Balkis." The house of Bichara was explicit about the connection between its products and their supposed inspiration, claiming that "Sakountala" and "Nirvana" would convey "the voluptuous feelings of the Ballets Russes and . . . conjure in our memories the choreographic and decorative seductions of *Schéhérazade.*"[7] In the words of one fashion historian, "Scheherazade moved into the Salons not only of dress designers but of the ladies themselves on both sides of the Channel."[8]

Plate 12
Léon Bakst,
Design for decor for *Schéhérazade*,
1910, cat. no. 6.

9 André Levinson, BAKST: THE
STORY OF THE ARTIST'S LIFE
(London, 1923), 158.

10 Alison Settle, "The Birth of
Couture: 1900-1910," in
COUTURE, ed. Ruth Lynham
(New York, 1972), 66.

While the ballet's immense success must ultimately be attributed to the fusion of compatible elements (music, choreography, dancing, decor, and costumes) André Levinson suggested that its dramatic potency stemmed not simply from Bakst's designs in general, but from one particular aspect of them: "This ardent and cruel magnificence of color, this effluvium of sensuality which emanates from the setting produces an action in which the very excess of passionate ecstacy can only be satiated by the spilling of blood."[9] Certainly, the most striking result of the ballet's success was a sudden enthusiasm for brilliant colors in daily life: "What changed couture, later house decoration also, was . . . the colour which Bakst put into the background of those ballets to which he contributed décor, above all in *Schéhérazade*."[10] The wan tints characteristic of fin-de-siècle taste were suddenly overwhelmed by a flood of color:

Taste in those days [before the advent of the Ballets Russes] was dominated by . . . in-between shades and pale colors, both in the theater and in women's clothing. . . . It is easy to imagine the uproar the Russian decors created in this gentle and languid atmosphere, among this pasteboard fakery. A cat among the pigeons. A revolver-shot into the mirror.

Plate 13
Alexander Golovin,
Design for decor for *Le Chant du Rossignol*, 1919, cat. no. 42.

11 *André Warnod, "Les Peintres et les Ballets Russes," in* LES BALLETS RUSSES DE SERGE DE DIAGHILEV, *special number of* LA REVUE MUSICALE, 1 December 1930, 79-80 [present author's translation].

12 *Martin Battersby,* THE DECORATIVE TWENTIES *(New York, 1975), 117.*

13 *Richard Buckle,* DIAGHILEV *(New York, 1979), 171.*

Everything was in the style of the Russian ballet. There wasn't a middle-class woman who didn't insist on putting green and orange cushions on her black carpet. Women adorned themselves with the most garish colors and all their knickknacks were rainbow-hued. . . . Soon the decor of houses, boutiques, restaurants, cafés, followed the same trend.[11]

The Fauve-like intensity of color given widespread currency by the Ballets Russes was also reflected in the fashion that developed for vivid jewelry, such as "onyx and crystal, coral and jade."[12] The influence of *Schéhérazade* in particular was soon felt: "An unheard-of violence of peacock-green and blue was the main theme [of Bakst's designs] (which gave Cartier the idea of setting sapphires and emeralds together for the first time since the Moghul Emperors)."[13]

In England, as in France, the influence of Bakst led to a preference for brighter colors and for boldly patterned furnishing fabrics with names like "Bagdad" and "Tabdar."[14] According to Sir Osbert Sitwell,

decoration was in the air; many busied themselves with it. The currents that showed were

14 Martin Battersby, "Diaghilev's Influence on Fashion and Decoration," in Charles Spencer, THE WORLD OF DIAGHILEV (New York, 1979), 162.

15 Sir Osbert Sitwell, GREAT MORNING! (Boston, 1947), 258.

16 Richard Cork, ART BEYOND THE GALLERY IN EARLY 20TH-CENTURY ENGLAND (New Haven, 1985), 308, note 68.

17 Cork, 144.

mostly foreign, and reached life through the theatre—a new development. Every chair cover, every lampshade, every cushion, reflected the Russian Ballet, the Grecian or Oriental visions of Bakst and Benoist [sic]."[15]

The infatuation that the Ballets Russes stirred up in the younger generation in London[16] was quickly manifest in interior decoration, though at first only in advanced circles. The "Post-Impressionist Room" shown at the Ideal Home Exhibition of 1913, for example, featured a striking mural on the theme of dance. Painted by Roger Fry, Duncan Grant, and Clive Bell, it reflected the excitement aroused by "the exotic costumes and abandoned movements of Diaghilev's dancers."[17] Before long, the enthusiasm spread beyond the avant-garde. In 1919, Somerset Maugham characterized (and at the same time mocked) fashionable taste as having shifted from Aestheticism to the cosmopolitanism of the Ballets Russes:

Mrs. Strickland had moved with the times. Gone were the Morris papers and gone the severe cretonnes, gone were the Arundel prints that had adorned the walls of her drawing-room in Ashley Gardens; the room blazed with fantastic colour, and I wondered if she knew that those varied hues, which fashion imposed upon her, were due to the dreams of a poor painter in a South Sea island. She gave me the answer herself. "What wonderful cushions you have," said Mr. Van Busche Taylor.
"Do you like them?" she said, smiling. "Bakst, you know."[18]

18 Somerset Maugham, THE MOON AND SIXPENCE (New York, 1919), 277.

The force of fashion, of which Bakst, according to Maugham, was the principal representative, seems to have affected more than the colors and patterns of household furnishings. To the Russian designer, Sitwell even attributed the new vogue for slimness: "the thin woman had hardly aspired to be a *femme fatale* until Leon Bakst introduced her as a paragon into Western Europe."[19]

19 Quoted by Settle, 68.

In his witty social history of architecture, *Here, of All Places*, Osbert Lancaster designates the period from the advent of Diaghilev in London until the mid-twenties as "The First Russian Ballet Period," a time when

the pale pastel shades which had reigned supreme on the walls of Mayfair for almost two decades were replaced by a riot of barbaric hues—jade green, purple, every variety of crimson and scarlet, and, above all, orange. Gone were the Hubert Roberts and the Conder fans; their place was taken by costume designs of Bakst and theatre scenes of Benois. The Orient came once more into its own and the piano was draped with Chinese shawls, the divan replaced with the chaise longue and no mantelpiece was complete without its Buddha.[20]

20 Osbert Lancaster, HERE, OF ALL PLACES (Cambridge, Mass., 1958), 126.

One of the most important results of the Russian Ballet's success, according to Lancaster, was that it gave art a new social prestige: "Art came once more to roost among the duchesses, where it at length produced a wave of modified Bohemianism. This resulted in a tendency to regard a room not so much as a place to live in, but as a setting for a party."[21]

21 Lancaster, 126.

In his autobiography, Paul Poiret (1879-1934) corroborates the view that the decorative arts lacked vitality during the early years of the century, when, as he puts it, "all that was soft, washed-out, insipid, was held in honour."[22] Though usually cited as the first couturier to acknowledge the impact of the Ballets Russes, Poiret himself always insisted that the colorful, exotic gowns for which he became famous in the years preceding World War I were designed before the arrival of Diaghilev and thus without prior knowledge of Bakst's work.[23] In 1907, he created an evening dress, "1811" (figure 1), in mauve, red, and

22 Paul Poiret, KING OF FASHION: THE AUTOBIOGRAPHY OF PAUL POIRET, trans. Stephen Haden Guest (Philadelphia, 1931), 93.

23 Poiret, 182.

figure 1
Paul Poiret's evening dress "1811,"
at right, from *Les Robes de Paul
Poiret, racontées par Paul Iribe*,
1908, pl. 3.

figure 2
Paul Poiret's evening coat
"Hispahan," center, from *Les Robes
de Paul Poiret, racontées par Paul
Iribe*, 1908, pl. 9.

24 Yvonne Deslandres, POIRET
(New York, 1987), 101, 113-114.

25 Settle, 67.

26 Georgina Howell, IN VOGUE:
SIXTY YEARS OF INTERNATIONAL
CELEBRITIES AND FASHION FROM
BRITISH VOGUE (New York, 1976), 8.

27 Howell, 7-8.

Plate 14
Léon Bakst,
Costume design for Potiphar's
Wife in *La Légende de Joseph*,
1914, cat. no. 16.

purple, trimmed with gold braid, and with buttons in gold, red, and green. In the same year, he made the "Hispahan" (figure 2), an evening coat embroidered with Persian motifs.[24] Despite Poiret's disclaimer, one has every reason to doubt whether his success during the next few years would have been so great had his designs not echoed Bakst's work for Diaghilev.[25] Most people believe that the vogue for orientalism, which gave such distinctiveness to Poiret's dresses, and which has been called "the greatest single influence on fashion"[26] from 1910 until 1923, originated with the Ballets Russes. What the French couturier did, consciously or otherwise, was translate the achievement of Bakst from theatrical (see Plate 14) into domestic terms:

There was no fashion designer who had not been set off in a new direction by the Russian ballet, but perhaps those most influenced were Poiret, who took the whole thing in at a gulp, Callot, Doeuillet, Lucile, Redfern, Idare, and Chanel in her embroideries. . . . The modern woman in the gaiter suit turned into a beautiful barbarian in the evening, in a costume that might have been designed by Bakst. All Paris came out with evening dresses in tiers of shot tulle or silver lace and tea-rose brocade, with Turkish trousers of looped chiffon, turbans [see figure 3] and fountains of ostrich feathers.[27]

The climax of this trend occurred in 1911. At his house on the Avenue d'Antin, Poiret gave a Persian fête for three hundred guests, called the Thousand and Second Night, at which his wife wore a feather-bedecked turban, a gold-fringed lampshade skirt over silk harem pants, and silk shoes with turned-up toes.

Scarcely surprisingly, Bakst himself was soon involved in the world of couture. Though Paul Poiret refused to realize any of the sketches for non-theatrical costumes that

BAKST

figure 4
Léon Bakst,
Fashion drawing for
modern dress, 1910.

28 Poiret, 93.

29 Reproduced in Charles
Spencer, LEON BAKST (New York,
1973), 170.

30 Quoted in Alexander
Schouvaloff, SET AND COSTUME
DESIGNS FOR BALLET AND
THEATER: THE THYSSEN-
BORNEMISZA COLLECTION
(New York, 1987), 68.

31 Richard Buckle, NIJINSKY
(Harmondsworth, Middlesex,
1980), 341.

32 Alfred H. Barr, Jr., MATISSE:
HIS ART AND HIS PUBLIC, exh.
cat., The Museum of Modern Art
(New York, 1951), 207. Matisse
refused Diaghilev's offer and chose
instead to design LE CHANT DU
ROSSIGNOL.

33 Battersby, "Diaghilev's
Influence," 164.

34 Constant Lambert, MUSIC
HO!: A STUDY OF MUSIC IN
DECLINE (New York, 1967), 86.

35 Igor Stravinsky and Robert
Craft, CONVERSATIONS WITH
IGOR STRAVINSKY (New York,
1959), 47.

Plate 15
Léon Bakst,
Costume design for a Minister of
State in The Sleeping Princess,
1921, cat. no. 22.

Bakst was apparently in the habit of drawing at the request of fashionable women,[28] other dressmakers were evidently not so fastidious. For the most part, Bakst did not try to translate his oriental style into couture. A characteristic fashion drawing by him (figure 4), dated 1910, shows two dresses, both of them close-fitting and high-waisted, with only the boldly patterned fabrics betraying the influence of his most celebrated Ballets Russes mode.[29]

In the "fantasies on modern dress" which he sketched for the house of Paquin in 1912, the style is not oriental but Greek (figure 5), in the manner of his *Narcisse* and *Daphnis et Chloë*. None of the dresses realized by Paquin was considered particularly successful. A sharply worded criticism about Bakst and the fashion illustrator, Iribe (Paul Iribarnegaray), appeared in American *Vogue* in 1914:

No one denies that Iribe and Bakst are splendid artists, but neither of them understands how to dress a twentieth-century woman. They have much to contribute to modern dress, but that their ideas cannot be translated direct from sketch to gown was proved by the failure of Mme. Paquin, who, if any dressmaker could, should have been able to do so successfully.[30]

In 1913, nevertheless, it had been Mme. Paquin who had realized Bakst's designs for the contemporary, quasi-tennis costumes worn by Karsavina and Schollar in Nijinsky's *Jeux*[31] (figure 6). A ballet whose theme of polymorphous sexuality was expressed through the metaphor of twentieth-century social sports, *Jeux* portended the end of the exotic phase of the Ballets Russes. A year later, with the outbreak of World War I, Diaghilev was cut off from Russia, as it turned out, permanently. From *Parade* (1917) on, the tone of his ballets became increasingly Parisian. Typical of the change in outlook at the Ballets Russes is the fact that when in 1919 the impresario decided that *Schéhérazade* had become shabby and dated he asked Henri Matisse to redesign it.[32] The last of Diaghilev's productions with a picturesque Russian theme was Bronislava Nijinska's unsuccessful *La Nuit sur le Mont Chauve*, 1924, designed by Natalia Gontcharova. When Diaghilev returned to the subject of his homeland three years later with *Le Pas d'Acier*–choreographed by Massine, composed by Prokofiev, and designed by Yakulov–it was no longer the legendary or semi-barbarian Russian of his earlier ballets, but the newly industrialized U.S.S.R.

Though Diaghilev remained in the forefront of creative activity until the end of his career he was never again to exercise the same influence upon the decorative taste of his time. However, to say, as one commentator does, that, during the postwar years, "instead of dictating fashion Diaghilev was following it,"[33] is to confound the decorative repercussions of his ballets with their artistic substance. The most celebrated judgment of this kind is similarly wide of the mark: "Before the war [Diaghilev] created a vogue for the Russian ballet, but after the war he merely created a vogue for vogue."[34] That the impresario inclined quite naturally towards *le dernier cri* is evidence less of his superficiality than of his concurrence with the aesthetic spirit of the times, which was for a condition of perpetual metamorphosis.

In evaluating the latest cultural trends, Diaghilev exercised what Stravinsky called his "immense flair for recognizing the potentiality of success in a piece of music or work of art in general."[35] Precisely because the success to which the composer refers was artistic rather than modish, Diaghilev maintained his importance as a significant cultural force. His final production, after all, was *Le Fils Prodigue* (The Prodigal Son), with music commissioned from Prokofiev, designs from Rouault, and choreography from Balanchine. A case could be made, in fact, that during the second half of his career–the era of *Les Biches*, *Les Noces*, *Apollon Musagète*, and *Le Fils Prodigue*–he achieved more of permanent value than he did in the first.

figure 3
Georges Barbier,
Evening dress in the oriental style,
from *Journal des Dames et des
Modes*, 1913.

figure 5
Léon Bakst,
Dioné, a "fantasy on modern
dress" sketched for Paquin, 1912.

figure 6
Léon Bakst,
Costume designs for *Jeux*, 1913,
from V. Krasovskaya, *Russkii
baletnyi teatr nachala XX veka*
(Leningrad, 1971), vol. 1.

36 *Buckle, 368.*

37 *Lydia Sokolova,* DANCING FOR
DIAGHILEV *(New York, 1961), 222.*

38 *Edmonde Charles-Roux,*
CHANEL AND HER WORLD
(New York, 1979), 172.

Given this situation, it is interesting to note that during these years Coco Chanel gave the company for the first time a direct link to the world of haute couture. Paquin was sympathetic to the Russian Ballet, but Chanel, largely through her friendship with Misia Sert, Diaghilev's closest woman friend, was a member of his supportive entourage. To the ballet, she proved a generous patron, contributing 300,000 francs for the production of Massine's *Le Sacre du Printemps* in 1920,[36] and offering Stravinsky hospitality during the period when he was completing *Les Noces.* For *Le Train Bleu*—an "opérette dansée," as Diaghilev called it—set on a fashionable beach on the Riviera, she designed in 1924, not theatrical costumes, but contemporary sports outfits and knitted bathing suits (figure 7). Lydia Sokolova, who danced the role of Perlouse, wore a close-fitting bathing cap and large pearl earrings, both of which, according to the dancer, set a fashion.[37] In 1928, Chanel helped Diaghilev out by devising replacements for the unsatisfactory costumes—tutus of different lengths—which André Bauchant had come up with for the Muses in Balanchine's *Apollon Musagète.* Her design was strikingly simple: "a free adaptation of the antique tunic, whose pleats are bound with tie silk."[38] The latter actually consisted of three silk neckties from the house of Charvet.

Such excursions into couture, however, were exceptional and, despite the attention of the smart world which the collaboration of Chanel ensured, set none of the large decorative trends that the work of Bakst had once done. In the final phase of his career, moreover, Diaghilev preferred easel painters and sculptors to theatrical designers. Though

figure 7
Léon Woizikovsky, Lydia Sokolova,
Bronislava Nijinska, and Anton
Dolin in *Le Train Bleu*
(Photograph by Sasha).

in 1918 Diaghilev commissioned new costumes for *Cléopâtre* from Sonia Delaunay, later to achieve celebrity for her designs for clothes and textiles, she had at that point hardly ventured into the decorative arts. After 1917, Braque, de Chirico, Derain, Ernst, Gris, Laurencin, Matisse, Miró, Picasso, Rouault, Gabo, Laurens, and Pevsner all produced successful designs for the Ballets Russes, but their work was not easily usable for the ends of fashion. The exoticism of the early Diaghilev seasons affected the way that people saw themselves, and thus their clothing and the style in which they lived. The internationalism of the later seasons affected the way they saw art, and thus their minds and sensibilities. While there was indubitably a "First Russian Ballet Period," there was, for these reasons, no second one.

NOTE:
*This essay is adapted from an
article on Nijinsky forthcoming in
the* INTERNATIONAL ENCYCLOPEDIA
OF DANCE, *ed. Selma Jeanne Cohen
et al. Quoted by permission of
the publisher, University of
California Press.*

VASLAV FOMITCH NIJINSKY in many respects epitomizes the romantic artist. He was shy and did not do well at social gatherings. He had a faraway look in his eye. His career, in keeping with the romantic pattern, was meteoric: brilliant and short. He danced for only a decade and made only four ballets. Our only firsthand account of him is a diary he wrote when he was already half insane, and even this is heavily expurgated. Beyond that, we have accounts by his sister, his wife, his colleagues, each with his or her own parti pris. We suspect that he was one of the great modernist artists of the early twentieth century, his mind, like that of Pound or Picasso, cutting like a knife through the worn upholstery of nineteenth-century representation. But we infer this from scarce evidence.

There were three children in the family (figure 1). The eldest was Stanislav (1886-1917), who fell onto his head from a third-story window at the age of two and a half. Whether because of this or some prior defect, Stanislav was odd enough to be institutionalized by the time he reached adolescence, and he died in a sanatorium at the age of thirty-one. The youngest child was Bronislava Nijinska (1891-1972), who, taking her primary inspiration from her brother, became one of the pioneers of twentieth-century choreography. Vaslav, born in Kiev in 1889 (or 1888 or 1890—the date is disputed), was the middle child.

He received his early dance training from his parents, Foma Lavrentievitch Nijinsky (1862-1912) and Eleanora Nicolaevna Bereda (1856-1932). Both were Polish and had studied ballet at the Wielki Theater school in Warsaw. During the children's youth, they earned their living on the touring circuit, mounting and performing dances in state opera houses, summer theaters, circuses, and other enterprises throughout Russia and Poland. From them and the performers they worked with, Nijinsky learned elementary ballet and many folk and character dances at an early age. He picked up acrobatics from acrobats, and tap from Jackson and Johnson, the black American tappers, whose touring path at one point crossed the Nijinskys'. He made his first professional appearance at the age of seven, in a pantomime for children and animals staged by the celebrated Russian clown Vladimir Dourov for a circus in Vilno in 1896. Nijinsky played a chimney sweep who rescued a piglet, a rabbit, a monkey, and a dog from a burning house and then extinguished the fire. Nijinska, age five, played a bridegroom. The two children were very close.

In 1897 Foma Nijinsky left his family in order to go live with his mistress—a defection that Vaslav never forgave. With very little money, Eleanora moved to St. Petersburg with the three children. The following year, 1898, Nijinsky was admitted to the Imperial Theater School (Bronislava followed two years later). There, in the course of his nine years' training, he was taught by Mikhail Oboukhov and by the Legat brothers, Nicolas and Sergei. After graduation he studied with Pavel Gerdt, the most celebrated *danseur noble* of the period, and, in private classes, with Enrico Cecchetti, the Italian virtuoso, who was also his teacher during the years with the Diaghilev company. Nijinsky thus received at its source a pure Russian classical ballet training, the kind of training on which Marius Petipa had based his *Bayadère*, his *Sleeping Beauty*, and the other defining works of the Russian school. When, later, Nijinsky broke the rules of academic classicism, he knew the rules he was breaking.

From 1899 on, Nijinsky appeared in children's parts in the regular repertory of St. Petersburg's Imperial Ballet: in the mazurka in *Paquita*, as a page and then one of Tom Thumb's brothers in *The Sleeping Beauty*, as a mouse and then the Mouse King in *The Nutcracker*, and so on. As his remarkable virtuosity came to be noted, he was given increasingly demanding assignments in ballets mounted for student performances at the

John Singer Sargent,
Vaslav Nijinsky in *Le Pavillon
d'Armide*, 1911, cat. no. 78.

Maryinsky Theater, the home of the Imperial Ballet. In 1906, while still in school, he was already being given soloist roles at the Imperial Ballet, and when he graduated the following year (figure 2), he was made an Artist of the Imperial Theaters with the rank of coryphé, thus skipping corps de ballet, the usual starting rank.

Nijinsky's debut at the Maryinsky as a member of the Imperial Ballet (1907) was in *La Source*, where he performed in an interpolated pas de deux, *Jeux des Papillons*, one of the innumerable flower and/or butterfly dances with which the St. Petersburg repertory was stocked. He was immediately sought as a partner by the company's leading female dancers, including the famously imperious Mathilde Kchessinska, prima ballerina assoluta. He starred in *La Fille Mal Gardée* with her less than two months after the beginning of his first season with the company. Also in 1907 he danced the prized role of Bluebird in *The Sleeping Beauty*. Later during his three and a half years with the company he performed featured roles in such ballets as *The Little Humpbacked Horse*, *Giselle*, and *The Talisman* (figure 3). During the same period he created roles in the early St. Petersburg ballets of Michel Fokine, the Maryinsky's foremost choreographic reformer. Nijinsky and Fokine were soon to become even more important to each other's careers.

In 1907, Nijinsky became the companion of Prince Pavel Dmitrievitch Lvov, a wealthy court official. The following year, with what motivation we do not know, Lvov introduced Nijinsky to Sergei Pavlovitch Diaghilev. Diaghilev was an extremely important man in Russian artistic circles. He had founded and edited *World of Art*, so critical to the development of Russian painting, and had staged Russian art exhibitions, concerts, and opera in Paris. Now, for the spring of 1909, he was planning to take to Paris a mixed season of opera and ballet. Nijinsky was thus of interest to him as a dancer, and for non-professional reasons as well. They soon became lovers—Nijinsky was nineteen, Diaghilev thirty-six—and the young man's extraordinary gift was one of the features around which Diaghilev's first ballet season was built.

In St. Petersburg Nijinsky had been a locally celebrated dancer; with the Ballets Russes he became an international star. He danced in the Diaghilev seasons from 1909 to 1913 and again from 1916 to 1917. It was above all in Fokine's ballets that he became famous—as the Favorite Slave in *Le Pavillon d'Armide*, the "Poet" in *Les Sylphides*, the Golden Slave in *Schéhérazade*, Harlequin in *Carnaval*, Daphnis in *Daphnis et Chloë*, and the eponymous leads in *Le Spectre de la Rose* (figure 4), *Le Dieu Bleu*, *Narcisse* (figure 5), and *Petrouchka* (figure 6). (Of all these, the only role that was probably not created on him

figure 4
Nijinsky in *Le Spectre de la Rose*,
Paris, 1911. Photograph by Bert.
Dance Collection, The New York
Public Library.

figure 5
Nijinsky in *Narcisse*, 1911.
Dance Collection, The New York
Public Library.

was *Carnaval's* Harlequin.) Petrouchka, the great-souled puppet, was reportedly his favorite, which is interesting, as it was an atypical role. Not only did it not call upon his extraordinary technical virtuosity, it actually concealed it. Furthermore, Petrouchka was one of the few early roles that did not contain a strong suggestion of sexual morbidity. In Fokine's ballets Nijinsky spent a lot of time playing slaves or other objects of specialized sexual interest.

In 1909 and 1910 the participants in Diaghilev's ballet seasons were not a permanent troupe but a collection of Russian Imperial dancers on vacation. Then, in early 1911, Nijinsky was dismissed from the Imperial Theaters in a curious incident that, like so many episodes in the history of the Ballets Russes, has almost as many versions as there are memoirists. Nijinsky was dancing Albrecht in *Giselle* for the first time in St. Petersburg, and he chose to wear not the standard Maryinsky costume, which included trunks as well as a tunic, but rather the costume he had worn in Diaghilev's 1910 Paris production of *Giselle* and which had no trunks, only a tunic over tights. This was judged improper by the Maryinsky management, and he was told to apologize or resign. He chose the latter. Considering that Nijinsky had studied for a decade in order to join this company, was a star of it, and could expect from it an assured income for the rest of his life, this was a very bold move—his mother was utterly distraught—and it is inconceivable that he would have undertaken it without Diaghilev's support. Indeed, many believed that the entire incident was engineered by Diaghilev. In any case, he was not made unhappy by it. "Appalling scandal. Use publicity," he telegraphed to his Parisian manager, Gabriel Astruc.[1] Nor did he fail to take advantage of it. Now that his foremost male dancer was available full-time, he organized a permanent troupe, with Fokine as chief choreographer, and began seeking year-round engagements. In March 1911 Nijinsky, aged twenty-two, left Russia with Diaghilev, bound for Monte Carlo. He would never see his homeland again.

In is worth noting that Nijinska resigned from the Imperial Ballet once her brother did—a circumstance that alarmed Eleanora Nijinska even more. While Nijinsky's talent and his favored position with Diaghilev seemed to insure his success, Nijinska was more vulnerable. She was a strong and interesting dancer rather than a great one, and as reviewers never tired of noting, she was not beautiful. Nor did she have special influence. But now and in the future she cast her lot with her brother. She went where he went. Whatever his project, she sought to further it. And when, in the 1920s and 1930s, she became an internationally famous choreographer she did so, in her opinion, by filling the artistic gap left when her brother went insane. As she wrote, "I sought to realize the potential of my brother's creativity."[2] Had he remained active, would she ever have become a choreographer of note? The question must be asked. And it is quite remarkable that a person of whom such a question could be asked should have developed into such a powerful, independent, and innovative artist.[3]

Shortly before his departure from the Imperial Ballet, Nijinsky had begun choreographing his first major ballet. He had had some prior experience. In 1906, while still in school, he had arranged the dances for a privately performed children's opera, *Cinderella*, composed by Boris Asafiev. In 1907 or 1908 he created the dances for Asafiev's *The Snow Queen*, another children's opera. In 1910, according to Nijinska, he set the arm movements for her Papillon in Fokine's *Carnaval*. He may also have created his solo "Kobold" in *Les Orientales*, of the 1910 Diaghilev season. Whatever the precedents, Nijinsky in the winter of 1910, with Diaghilev's encouragement, began work on a ballet to Debussy's "Prélude à l'Après-midi d'un Faune," setting the movements on himself and his sister.

1 *Telegram of 10 February 1911, Astruc papers, Dance Collection, New York Public Library at Lincoln Center, New York.*

2 *Bronislava Nijinska,* EARLY MEMOIRS, *trans. and ed. Irina Nijinska and Jean Rawlinson (New York, 1981), 469. Most of the information that I have given here on Nijinsky's early youth, and much of the information on his later youth, is from this invaluable book.*

3 *Her career is described at length in Nancy Van Norman Baer,* BRONISLAVA NIJINSKA: A DANCER'S LEGACY, *exh. cat., The Fine Arts Museums of San Francisco (1986).*

figure 6
Nijinsky in *Petrouchka*. Photograph
by Mishkin. Dance Collection, The
New York Public Library.

figure 7
Nijinsky in *L'Après-midi d'un Faune*,
New York, 1916. Photograph by
Karl Struss. Courtesy John and
Susan Edwards Harvith.

4 *See Joan Acocella, "Photo Call with Nijinsky: The Circle and the Center,"* BALLET REVIEW 14, *no. 4 (Winter 1987): 49-71.*

First performed at the Théâtre du Châtelet in Paris on 29 May 1912, *L'Après-midi d'un Faune* is less a narrative ballet than a sort of dream vision, loosely based on Mallarmé's poem "L'Après-midi d'un Faune" (which, however, Nijinsky claimed he had not read when he made the ballet). A young faun, lazing on a rock, observes the arrival of seven nymphs, the tallest of whom takes a stylized bath. The faun tries to woo the tall nymph; she escapes, leaving a veil behind. The other nymphs attempt to reclaim the veil, but the faun will not surrender it. Carrying it up to his rock, he lovingly lays it down and then lowers his body on top of it, ending with a spasm suggestive of orgasm (figures 7-9).

The premiere of *Faune* was greeted by contending applause and booing, the latter presumably in response to the ballet's final gesture. That gesture also sparked controversy in the Parisian newspapers. In a front-page article in *Le Figaro*, Gaston Calmette, editor of the paper, accused Nijinsky of obscenity. Auguste Rodin and Odilon Redon came to the ballet's defense. It was an all-star quarrel, and excellent publicity.

Bold in its subject matter, *Faune* was even bolder in its choreography. In direct contrast to Debussy's rich and fluid music—and also to the lush backdrop, a hillside dripping greenery, created for the ballet by Léon Bakst—the movement was austere and angular. Crossing the stage in fixed lines, with their feet flexed and their limbs and heads in profile, the nymphs resembled an antique frieze—a similarity enhanced by the long pauses that broke the movement. There were no classical steps, no virtuosity, no charm, expansiveness, or "personality." The total impression, despite the flowing lines of the music, decor, and costumes, was one of true archaism: meaning compacted into mysterious, ritualistic forms.[4]

Nothing in the descriptions of Nijinsky's earlier dancing or choreography prepares one for the utterly radical break represented by this movement style. It is a break not only with classical ballet, the tradition of Petipa, but also with the anti-classical, naturalistic way of dancing that Fokine had created in reaction to Petipa. In Nijinsky's ballet the academic canon was not just adapted, as was Fokine's practice; it was truly inverted. And period style, so important to Fokine, was used not so much for decorative as for psychological value, the archaism of the movement underlining the intimate nature of the subject, the discovery of sexuality. Above all, movement was treated not as a pantomimic means, but as an end in itself; it was a mystery to be analyzed and a potent metaphor for emotion.

L'Après-midi d'un Faune precipitated a break within the troupe. Fokine was angered at the preferential treatment Diaghilev gave to Nijinsky's ballet over Fokine's own new "Greek" ballet, *Daphnis et Chloë*. *Faune*, for example, was given approximately one hundred rehearsals, a very generous allowance for a twelve-minute ballet, while *Daphnis*, far longer, had far less preparation. Furthermore, the fact that *Faune* was being created was kept secret from Fokine for a long time—a circumstance which of course encouraged him, when he finally learned about Nijinsky's ballet, to suspect the worst possible motivations on Diaghilev's part. Again, the suspicions were probably well grounded. There is evidence that Diaghilev was tired of Fokine's work and was priming Nijinsky to replace him. In any case, Fokine played his appointed role. After the premiere of *Daphnis* he resigned, and Nijinsky, age twenty-three, became the chief choreographer of the Ballets Russes.

His two new projects for the 1913 season were *Jeux*, to newly commissioned music by Debussy, and *Le Sacre du Printemps*, to a new score by Stravinsky. The two ballets were choreographed in the same stretch of time, from fall 1912 through spring 1913, a period of work on one giving way to a period of work on the other. Nijinsky was apparently less interested in *Jeux* than in *Sacre*. While the latter was to have been performed first, program

figure 8
Nijinsky in *L'Après-midi d'un Faune*,
Paris, 1912. He has captured the
nymph's veil and is taking it up to
his rock. This is one of the famous
series of *Faune* photographs by
Baron Adolf de Meyer. Dance
Collection, The New York
Public Library.

figure 9
Nijinsky in *L'Après-midi d'un Faune*,
Paris, 1912. The controversial final
gesture of the ballet. Photograph
by de Meyer. Dance Collection,
The New York Public Library.

5 GIL BLAS, 20 *May* 1913, *quoted
in Richard Buckle,* NIJINSKY
(*New York, 1971*), 290.

6 THE DIARY OF VASLAV
NIJINSKY, *ed. Romola Nijinsky*
(*1936; rept. Berkeley and Los
Angeles, 1971*), 140-141.

changes forced the rescheduling of *Jeux* for the opening night of the Paris season, so
that Nijinsky reluctantly had to set aside his work on *Sacre* and return to *Jeux*. These
circumstances, as well as artistic considerations, may help to explain the somewhat
inconclusive character of *Jeux*, in contrast to *Faune* and *Sacre*. Nijinsky referred to the
choreography as "my experiments in stylized gesture,"[5] and the ballet apparently had the
look of an experiment.

First performed on 15 May 1913 at the Théâtre des Champs-Elysées in Paris, *Jeux* was
a self-declaredly modern ballet. To begin with, it was one of the first ballets to deal with
athletics, a new enthusiasm in Europe. (The Olympic Games had been revived in 1896.)
The theme was tennis, and the cast–two young women, Tamara Karsavina and Ludmilla
Schollar, and a young man, Nijinsky–was costumed accordingly. The women wore sports
outfits designed by Bakst and realized by Maison Paquin: white knit tops and short white
skirts (see Harris, figure 6). Nijinsky carried a tennis racket and wore white stylized practice
clothes that looked vaguely sporty (figure 10). But the *jeux*, or games, of the title were
erotic as well as athletic. The characters, in their three-way courtship (figure 11), suggested
a ménage à trois. (Later, in his *Diary*, Nijinsky claimed that this grouping actually
symbolized a sexual encounter involving a man and two boys.)[6] In all, *Jeux* encapsulated a
new, light, experimental attitude to life, a recoil from the pieties of the nineteenth century.
In this it anticipated the twenties. Prophetically, Diaghilev wrote to Debussy in 1912 that
the ballet was set in 1920.

The backdrop, again the work of Bakst, showed a dense bank of trees lit by circles
of electric light and surmounted in the background by a white house. Across the green
floorcloth, painted with flower beds, a white ball comes flying. Flying after it comes a
young man with a tennis racket. Then the two women arrive, apparently seeking a private
conversation. They are interrupted by the youth, who has been spying on them. He dances

with one, then with the other, each time provoking the jealousy of the excluded one. Finally, the three dance together. Suddenly another ball falls on the stage, and the young people run away.

The movement appears to have had a shifting relationship to Debussy's symphonic poem, at times following it, at other times going its own way. The relationship to academic technique was likewise intermediate. After the great break in *Faune*, Nijinsky now reverted to some classical maneuvers. The women danced much of the time on three-quarter point and performed some basic classical steps, such as pas de bourrée. However, on the evidence of the few remaining photographs and a series of pastels by Valentine Gross, one of the company's artist-fans, Nijinsky's chief interest in *Jeux* was the mass of the bodies and their relation to one another. At this time, according the Nijinska, he was greatly excited by his recent discovery of Gauguin, and the careful sculptural groupings of the three dancers, preserved in the pictorial evidence, resemble the psychologically reverberant groupings in Gauguin's Tahitian paintings. Also Gauguin-like is the compact quality of the bodies. Presumably in emulation of sports postures, the dancers through much of the ballet held their arms bent, with the hands in a loose fist ("as one maimed from birth," wrote Karsavina,[7] who did not like *Jeux*). The result was far removed from the expansive beauties of classicism, though in its application of freer postures to the academic technique it pointed toward neoclassical ballet. Like *Faune*, *Jeux*, for its time, was a bravely unpretty work. It was an act of research, an exploration of movement, in the service of a complicated emotional truth.

7 *Tamara Karsavina*, THEATRE STREET: THE REMINISCENCES OF TAMARA KARSAVINA (*London*, *1931*), *291*.

figure 10
Nijinsky in *Jeux*, with his tennis racket, Paris, 1912. Photograph by Gerschel. Dance Collection, The New York Public Library.

figure 11
Tamara Karsavina, Ludmilla Schollar, and Nijinsky in *Jeux*, Paris, 1912. Photograph by Gerschel. Dance Collection, The New York Public Library.

The ballet was coolly received–Debussy too disliked it–and was discarded after only five performances. It is now "lost," though Kenneth MacMillan reconstructed parts of it for Herbert Ross's movie *Nijinsky* (1980).

Almost equally brief was the performance history of *Le Sacre du Printemps*, which was probably Nijinsky's masterpiece, as well as Stravinsky's. According to Stravinsky, it was he who had the original idea for the ballet. It came to him, he wrote, in 1910, in the form of a vision: "I saw in imagination a solemn pagan rite: wise elders, seated in a circle, watch a young girl dance herself to death. They were sacrificing her to propitiate the god of spring."[8] Stravinsky enlisted the collaboration of his friend Nicholas Roerich, who was both a painter and an archaeologist, in both cases specializing in ancient Slavic culture. (He had designed the sets and costumes for the "Polovtsian Dances" in Diaghilev's 1909 production of *Prince Igor*.) In summer 1911 Stravinsky and Roerich worked out a final scenario for *Sacre* and Stravinsky began to compose the music. By March 1913 the score was finished: an utterly revolutionary work whose combined innovations of rhythm and orchestration permanently altered Western music.

8 *Igor Stravinsky,* AN AUTOBIOGRAPHY *(1936; rept. New York, 1962), 31.*

Fokine was originally to have choreographed *Sacre*. Upon his departure the job fell to Nijinsky. Nijinsky began work in late 1912, first creating the ballet's one solo, the "Sacrificial Dance" of the Chosen Victim, on Nijinska. (She was to have danced this role, but became pregnant and was replaced by Maria Piltz.) In alternation with *Jeux*, *Sacre* was gradually mounted between November 1912 and May 1913, with Stravinsky often present at rehearsals.

Aside from the score, there were two important influences on Nijinsky's choreography for this ballet. One was the primitivism and incipient abstraction of contemporary painting, particularly that of Gauguin and of Roerich.[9] The second was Emile Jaques-Dalcroze's Eurhythmics, a system for inculcating musical sensitivity through the translation of rhythm into bodily movements. In 1912 Diaghilev and Nijinsky made two visits to Dalcroze's school outside Dresden. On the second, Diaghilev hired one of Dalcroze's pupils, Marie Rambert, to help Nijinsky with the complicated rhythms of Stravinsky's score.

9 *See Millicent Hodson, "Nijinsky's Choreographic Method: Visual Sources from Roerich for* LE SACRE DU PRINTEMPS," DANCE RESEARCH JOURNAL *18, no. 2 (Winter 1986-1987): 7-15, for an argument that Roerich's influence was central to Nijinsky's choreography for this ballet.*

Le Sacre du Printemps, with sets and costumes by Roerich, had its premiere at the Théâtre des Champs-Elysées on 29 May 1913. The curtain went up on what was presumably a Central Asian steppe, and the ballet consisted of the rituals enacted by the steppe's prehistoric inhabitants upon the advent of spring. It ended with the "Sacrificial Dance," in which the Chosen Victim, selected from among the maidens of the tribe to sacrifice herself for the renewal of the earth, dances herself to death in a convulsive solo while the tribe watches.

Sacre is one of the purest examples of the primitivism that so pervaded the art and thought of the early twentieth century. Superficially a portrait of precivilized society, it was also, by extension, an exploration of primitive impulses in the heart of civilized man (cf. Freud, Conrad, Lawrence). In addition, it was a tribute to the origins of dance in ancient fertility rituals. But above all, the ballet was an attempt to capture in movement the sheer, driving force of nature, irrational and amoral–nature understood as including man.

10 *From Rivière's review of the ballet: "Le Sacre du Printemps,"* LA NOUVELLE REVUE FRANCAISE *10, no. 59 (1 November 1913). This translation is quoted from Buckle, 298.*

The choreography was as drastic as the theme. Except for the solo of the Chosen Victim and the brief maneuvers of the old woman and the wise elder, *Sacre* was an ensemble ballet. But here, in violation of centuries of theatrical dance tradition, ensemble groupings were deployed asymmetrically, their movements "hatched in isolation," wrote Jacques Rivière, "like those spontaneous fires that break out in haystacks."[10] The symmetry of the individual body was also abandoned, the postures and movements, in Nijinska's

11 Nijinska, 459.

phrase, "almost bestial,"[11] with knocked knees and turned-in feet—a complete inversion of classical form. With some intervals of serene lyricism, the choreography consisted largely of shudders, jerks, stamps, and thudding runs, culminating in the hurlings of the Chosen Victim's sacrificial dance.

In keeping with Dalcroze's system, the choreography followed the music closely, Nijinsky apparently having attempted a movement-for-note correspondence and a careful synchronization of the dance with the score's shifting rhythms. Eye-witness accounts indicate that the choreography in some parts was very nearly "music visualization." Here, for example, is a description from the London *Times*'s review:

The dancers thin out into a straggling line, while the orchestra dwindles to a trill on the flutes; then a little tune begins in the woodwind two octaves apart, and two groups of three people detach themselves from either end of the line to begin a little dance.[12]

12 THE TIMES, *London, 26 July 1913, quoted in Nesta Macdonald,* DIAGHILEV OBSERVED, BY CRITICS IN ENGLAND AND THE UNITED STATES, 1911-1929 *(New York; London, 1975), 102.*

The premiere of *Sacre* appropriately provoked a riot, colorful accounts of which have been left by Jean Cocteau in his *Cock and Harlequin* and by Valentine Gross. The French reviews were generally harsh, the English reviews generally dismissive. The tumultuous premiere is now regarded by many as the final birth spasm of modernism, and Stravinsky's score has become the most celebrated musical composition of the century. Nijinsky's ballet, in the meantime, was lost, for it was dropped from repertory after only nine performances and was soon forgotten by the dancers, most of whom loathed it. In 1987, Millicent Hodson, working with Roerich specialist Kenneth Archer, mounted on the Joffrey Ballet a reconstruction based primarily on scores annotated by Rambert and Stravinsky.[13]

13 *For an account of her work on the reconstruction, see Millicent Hodson,* "SACRE: *Searching for Nijinsky's Chosen One,"* BALLET REVIEW 15, *no. 3 (Fall 1987), 53-66. For a thorough review of the production, see Robert Greskovic, "Augurs of Dance to Come,"* THE NEW DANCE REVIEW, *February-March 1988, 7-13.*

In August 1913, after the London season, the company departed by ship for a South American tour. Diaghilev did not accompany them, but someone else did: Romola de Pulszky (1891-1978), a young Hungarian woman—daughter of Emilia Markus, Hungary's foremost actress—who had attached herself to the company in the hope, she later claimed, of capturing Nijinsky. For reasons that Nijinsky's biographers have never been able to explain, she gained her object. Before the boat had reached its first port, Nijinsky had proposed. The couple were married on 10 September 1913, in Buenos Aires, and three months later the aggrieved Diaghilev dismissed Nijinsky from the Ballets Russes.

Refusing offers from other companies, Nijinsky, with the help of the loyal Nijinska, formed a seventeen-member company for an eight-week engagement at the Palace Theatre, a London music hall, during spring 1914. But because Nijinsky became ill, and because of disagreements between him and the management, the season was canceled after two weeks. Among the works shown were Fokine's *Le Spectre de la Rose*, a *Les Sylphides* rechoreographed by Nijinsky, and a few other short dances by Nijinsky.

Soon thereafter Nijinsky and Romola traveled to Vienna, where Romola gave birth to a daughter, Kyra, on 19 June 1914. (See figure 12. Kyra Nijinsky lives today in San Francisco.) From Vienna the family moved on to Budapest, and it was while they were there, staying with Romola's family, that World War I began. Because Nijinsky was a Russian, they were declared prisoners of war and placed under what was essentially house arrest until 1916. Romola bristled under this restriction, but Nijinsky used the time to work on a dance-notation system and on a new ballet, *Till Eulenspiegel*, to Richard Strauss's tone-poem. In the meantime Diaghilev, hard put to find engagements for his company in warring Europe, had succeeded in arranging an American tour, for which he had rashly promised to re-engage Nijinsky. With immense difficulty, the dancer's release was obtained, and in April 1916 Nijinsky made his American debut with the Ballets Russes at

figure 12
Romola, Kyra, and Vaslav Nijinsky,
New York, 1916. Dance
Collection, The New York
Public Library.

New York's Metropolitan Opera House, dancing his old Fokine repertory.

There followed a second American tour, coast to coast, during the fall and winter of 1916-1917. This time, at the insistence of the impresario Otto Kahn of the Metropolitan Opera Association, the company was to be directed by Nijinsky, Diaghilev meanwhile returning to Europe. Because of Nijinsky's utter lack of administrative skill, combined with his growing absorption in Tolstoyan philosophy, the tour was chaotically managed. Night after night, Nijinsky sat closeted in his train compartment with two dancers who were followers of Tolstoy, discussing the master's new, radical-Christian program for living. In the meantime, the company suffered. Programming and casting decisions were made at the last minute, with seeming capriciousness and without appeal. Nijinsky remained isolated from the dancers and most of them distrusted him.

This tour is notable, however, for its inclusion of Nijinsky's fourth and last major ballet, *Till Eulenspiegel*, which was given its premiere at New York's Manhattan Opera House in October 1916. The least discussed of Nijinsky's major works, *Till* is thought to represent a retrenchment from the modernist aesthetic that Nijinsky had advanced in the three ballets of 1912-1913. Like a Fokine ballet, it had a picturesque historico-geographical setting (medieval Brunswick, captured in handsomely stylized sets and costumes by Robert Edmond Jones), numerous character roles (portly burghers, rosy-cheeked apple-seller), a naturalistic rather than a symbolic movement style, and a fairly detailed plot: the mischief-making of the legendary Till, ending in his hanging. At the first performance the choreography was unfinished, and the company had to improvise somewhat. Nevertheless the premiere was warmly received by both audience and press. The ballet was given approximately twenty-two performances, all during the 1916-1917 American tour. Then it was dropped, making it the sole Ballets Russes production that Diaghilev never saw.

The remainder of Nijinsky's artistic history is briefly told. In summer 1917 he again joined the Diaghilev company, for a series of performances in Spain and South America. In early fall 1917, after the end of the South American tour, he arranged and danced in a Red Cross gala in Montevideo. He was twenty-nine years old, and this was his last public performance.

In December the family settled in St. Moritz to wait out the war. There, in 1918-1919, according to Romola, Nijinsky continued refining his notation system and also worked on three ballets: a tale of Sapphic love, to Debussy's *Chansons de Bilitis*; a Renaissance ballet, obviously autobiographical, about a young painter's love first for his master and then for a woman; and a ballet entitled *Les Papillons de Nuit*, set in a brothel.

Nijinsky now showed increasing signs of mental instability, evidenced in two further projects of this period, a series of drawings based on circles and arcs (figure 13), often taking the form of staring eyes, and the remarkable *Diary*, written in 1918-1919 and later published, in abridged and edited form, by Romola. One of the most direct and poignant documents of Western confessional literature, the *Diary* has as its theme the Tolstoyan dichotomy of intellect vs. feeling. It also records Nijinsky's conviction of his visionary status—"I am His present. I am God, in a present"—and, at other times, his anguished knowledge that he is going mad:

I cry . . . I cannot restrain my tears, and they fall on my left hand and on my silken tie, but I cannot and do not want to hold them back. I feel that I am doomed. I do not want to go under. I do not know what I need, and I dislike to upset my people. If they are upset, I will die.[14]

figure 13
Drawing in blue and red crayon,
by Nijinsky, 1918-1919.
Photograph courtesy Sotheby's,
Inc., New York, © 1987.

14 THE DIARY OF VASLAV
NIJINSKY, 12 ("I am His present"),
31 ("I cry").

In 1919 Nijinsky was diagnosed as schizophrenic by the eminent Swiss psychiatrist Eugen Bleuler and was institutionalized for the first time. In 1920 Romola gave birth to a second daughter, Tamara. (Tamara Nijinsky Wenninger lives today in Phoenix, Arizona.) The last thirty years of Nijinsky's life were spent partly in sanatoria and partly in the various homes that Romola was able to make for him when her work and his condition permitted. He suffered hallucinations, occasional spells of violence, and long periods of mutism. In December 1928 he was taken to see the Ballets Russes in *Petrouchka* at the Paris Opéra in the hope that the sight of this ballet, so important to his career, would give his mind a beneficial jolt. It did not. Karsavina in her memoirs describes a poignant moment backstage (figure 14) before the performance:

Nijinsky meekly let himself be led to where the photographers had set their cameras. I put my arm through his, and, requested to look straight into the camera, I could not see his movements. I noticed that the photographers were hesitating, and, looking round, I saw that Nijinsky was leaning forward and looking into my face, but on meeting my eyes he again turned his head like a child that wants to hide tears. And that pathetic, shy, helpless movement went through my heart.[15]

15 Karsavina, 299.

In 1950 in London Nijinsky died of kidney failure. He was first buried in London. Then, in 1953, his body was moved to Montmartre Cemetery in Paris, where it now rests.

In his brief time Nijinsky was the most famous male dancer in the world. This preeminence was due in part to his extraordinary virtuosity. His body was not beautiful by conventional standards. "He looked more like a factory-worker than a demi-god," wrote Alexandre Benois.[16] He was short—5′4″—with a small head, Tartar features, a long neck, and a powerfully muscled body (figure 15). His thigh muscles in particular were so heavily developed that he could not raise his leg to the front higher than 90 degrees. But owing in

16 Alexandre Benois, MEMOIRS, trans. Moura Budberg (London, 1964), 2:23.

figure 14
Backstage at the Paris Opéra before a Ballets Russes performance of *Petrouchka*, December 1928. Left to right: Nicolas Kremnev, Alexandre Benois, Serge Grigoriev, Tamara Karsavina costumed as the Ballerina Doll, Diaghilev, Nijinsky, and Serge Lifar costumed as the Moor. Dance Collection, The New York Public Library.

figure 15
Nijinsky in *Giselle*, Act II, Paris
1910. The heavily developed
thighs and the long, expressive
neck are very evident here.
Photograph by Bert. Dance
Collection, The New York
Public Library.

part to this rare endowment, he was able to achieve remarkable technical feats, such as triple tours en l'air, twelve pirouettes (onstage—in the studio, according to Nijinska, he often did fourteen and sixteen), and entrechat huit. (Nijinska reports his doing entrechat dix as well, both at the Maryinsky and in Paris.) Above all, Nijinsky was famous for his great ballon and elevation, the latter made more impressive by the fact that he took an almost imperceptible preparation for his leap and that at the apex of the leap he seemed to pause in the air. Amazing descriptions of his dancing, step by step, can be found in Nijinska's *Early Memoirs*.

These marvels were achieved, moreover, at no expense of clarity or musicality. Of his musical sensitivity, the English critic Cyril Beaumont wrote, "He did not so much dance to the music, he appeared to issue from it. His dancing was music made visible."[17]

17 Cyril W. Beaumont, BOOKSELLER AT THE BALLET: MEMOIRS 1891 TO 1929 (London, 1975), 100.

But it was not his virtuosity alone that made him such a powerful stage presence. As contemporary reports make clear, Nijinsky was a great and unusual actor. The ideal Fokine interpreter, he was able to expand a simple choreographic design into a rich dramatic portrait, using the whole body as an expressive instrument, in keeping with Fokine's dicta. Going beyond Fokine's principles, however, his acting style was not so much realistic as classical, aimed at the portrayal of a universalized state of the soul. As Beaumont remarked in 1913, "He does not seek to depict the actions and gestures of an isolated type of character he assumes; rather does he portray the spirit or essence of *all* the types of that character."[18] He thus seemed to pass through the psychological into a more elevated realm of meaning. His characters, as Dale Harris writes, were "physical consummations of fundamentally metaphysical conceptions."[19]

18 Beaumont, 135.

19 Dale Harris, "Elusive Genius," BALLET NEWS 2, no. 9 (March 1981): 20.

In this he was helped by the fact that many of the characters he depicted were something other than human: a puppet, a god, a faun, the specter of a rose. Or, if human, they were often, as noted, strange or special in some way—a slave, an androgyne, or some other object of sexual connoisseurship (figure 16). Such roles, of course, were tailor-made by Fokine for Nijinsky, who seemed strange and special to many. But Nijinsky in turn knew how to use them as a route to emblematic truth.

Such portrayals at the same time dovetailed neatly with the tastes of Nijinsky's audiences, tastes formed by the fin de siècle and specifically by literary and pictorial Symbolism. The primitivism, exoticism, mysticism, Platonism, and sexual morbidity that marked the arts of the late nineteenth century were not forgotten by Europeans of the pre-World War I period, and Nijinsky (indeed, the Ballets Russes as a whole) seemed to offer a revival of those pleasures. His androgyny was celebrated, and exaggerated, in numerous and tasteless popular drawings. His Tartar face and passionate dancing were interpreted as expressions of *l'âme slave*, the Slavic soul, mysterious and barbaric. His seemingly indeterminate nature and abstract style were seen as incarnations of symbolist metaphor—vague, radiant glimpses of a realm of noumenal truth. Such adaptability to prevailing tastes increased Nijinsky's popularity, as did the atmosphere of scandal that surrounded this modest man throughout his career.

figure 16
Jean Cocteau's caricature of Nijinsky, costumed for *Schéhérazade*, and the famously large-headed Diaghilev. The erotic use that the Ballets Russes repertory made of Nijinsky was not lost on Cocteau. Dance Collection, The New York Public Library.

The symbolic approach that Nijinsky adopted on the level of characterization in Fokine's ballets became, in his own ballets, the foundation of dance design. Nijinsky borrowed or adapted many of Fokine's innovations: costume reform, the one-act ballet, the fusion of dance and drama, the deemphasis of the academic vocabulary and particularly of virtuosity. Yet at the same time he rejected the leading points of Fokine's style: the period charm, the reliance on character dance, the fluidity of line, and, above all, the descriptive use of gesture. Like Fokine, he sought "expressiveness" in dance, but through nonrealistic means. For each of his ballets of 1912-1913, he established a general mode of movement—light, flat, and sharp in *Faune*, knotted and crossed in *Jeux*, rugged and heavy in *Sacre*—and for each mode, certain characteristic postures: the profiled limbs in *Faune*, the bunched fists in *Jeux*, the turned-in feet and generally involuted body in *Sacre*.[20] On this foundation he built his dances, largely in angular and asymmetrical patterns. Through their cumulative force such dances served to suggest emotion, but in an indirect, emblematic fashion, unlike the stylized pantomime of Fokine. They were less a story than a vision.

20 *See Marie Rambert,* QUICKSILVER: THE AUTOBIOGRAPHY OF MARIE RAMBERT *(London; New York, 1972), 55-71, passim.*

In adopting this nondiscursive, nonrealistic approach, Nijinsky brought dance into alignment with modernism in the other arts, and this was his primary achievement as a choreographer. His kinship with the framers of early modernism, such as Picasso, Joyce, and Pound, can also be read in his treatment of the medium as an absolute, a thing expressive in itself, without need of pretext; in his analytic approach to the medium; in his consequent breaking through to radically new styles, as opposed to fashioning adaptations of established styles; and in his willingness to make something that looked genuinely ugly. "Nijinsky (with Rodin, Cézanne, Picasso . . .) for his generation murdered beauty," writes Kirstein.[21] Finally, in his subject matter—above all, the exploration of sexuality as a means of self-discovery (*Faune*) and as the engine of social survival (*Sacre*)—he was at one with modernism.

21 *Lincoln Kirstein,* NIJINSKY DANCING *(New York, 1975), 42. For a recent interpretation of Nijinsky's contribution, see Lynn Garafola,* ART AND ENTERPRISE IN DIAGHILEV'S BALLETS RUSSES *(New York, forthcoming).*

Nijinsky's influence as a dancer was immediate and huge. That ballet, nearly extinguished artistically in Western Europe, was revived in this century is owing to him and the other great dancers of his generation as well as to Diaghilev. That male ballet, utterly extinguished, was also revived is owing to him preeminently. Nijinsky was the first real ballet star of the male sex that Europe had seen since the retirement of Auguste Vestris nearly a century earlier. He initiated a renaissance.

The influence of Nijinsky's choreography is harder to assess. Indeed, it was not until recently that he was accepted as a major choreographer by more than a handful of scattered voices (e.g., Kirstein, Rambert) in dance history, and by then all but one of his ballets, *L'Après-midi d'un Faune*, were lost—that is, the performance tradition was broken. (One of the great services of the Millicent Hodson reconstruction of *Sacre* is that it has reopened the discussion of Nijinsky as a choreographer.) Certain experts on his work, such as Buckle and Kirstein, claim that it had a decisive influence on early modern dance. More easily established and possibly more important is the effect his ballets had on the artistic development of his sister, Nijinska, who in turn influenced Frederick Ashton and probably George Balanchine as well. What Nijinska says of *Jeux*[22] may be true of Nijinsky's work in general: that it was the forerunner of neoclassical ballet.

22 *Nijinska, 465.*

THE
ANTILITERARY
MAN

Diaghilev

and Music

_____

Richard Taruskin

▼

NOTE:
Spellings of Russian names that are different from elsewhere in this catalogue reflect the author's preference.

1 *Vasily Vasilievich Yastrebtsev,*
NIKOLAI ANDREEVICH RIMSKII-
KORSAKOV: VOSPOMINANIIA,
1886-1908, ed. A. V. Ossovsky,
2 vols. (Leningrad,
1959-1960), 1:207.

2 *Igor Stravinsky, "The Diaghilev*
I Knew," trans. Mercedes de
Acosta, ATLANTIC MONTHLY 192,
no. 5 (November 1953), 33.

3 *Arnold Haskell, with Walter*
Nouvel, DIAGHILEFF: HIS
ARTISTIC AND PRIVATE LIFE
(New York, 1935), 51.

4 *Stravinsky, 33.*

FOR THE LAST TWO DECADES of his career Nikolai Rimsky-Korsakov was dogged by a devoted Boswell, a banker and musical dilettante named Vasily Yastrebtsev, who kept a diary of his almost daily contacts with the composer that is for historians a treasure trove of (sometimes unwittingly) revealing glimpses of the musical and cultural scene in fin-de-siècle St. Petersburg. Here is a choice item, dated 22 September (Old Style) 1894:

Rimsky-Korsakov told us about the curious visit he received from a certain young man . . . who, though he probably already considers himself a great composer, nonetheless wished to take theory lessons from Nikolai Andreyevich. His compositions turned out to be worse than nonsensical. Rimsky-Korsakov told him his opinion straight out. The other, it seems, took offense, and, leaving, said, not without arrogance, that he still believed in himself and in his powers, that he would never forget this day, and that someday Rimsky-Korsakov's opinion would occupy a place of shame in his future biography and would make him more than once regret his rashly uttered words of long ago, but that then it would be too late . . . .[1]

The young man was the twenty-two-year-old Sergei Diaghilev, not long ago arrived in St. Petersburg from his familial estate near the provincial town of Perm. Rimsky's story was the springboard, in Yastrebtsev's account, for a merry discussion of the psychiatrist Cesare Lombroso's theories, then widely accepted, which sought to explain "decadence" of all kinds, including cultural and artistic, in terms of actual genetic decay. Diaghilev, to general hilarity, was dubbed a "mattoid," Lombroso's term (derived from *matto*, Italian for insane) for what other turn-of-the-century psychologists called "borderline dwellers," especially "graphomaniacs," semi-insane persons who feel a strong impulse to write. From then on, as he began to make a name for himself in St. Petersburg cultural affairs (though not, of course, as a composer), Diaghilev would remain a figure of fun for the Rimsky-Korsakov circle. One of the intimates of this group from around 1903 was Igor Stravinsky—and what could be more ironic, given that from 1909 till Diaghilev's death Stravinsky's career would be so inextricably and symbiotically linked with that of the great impresario? But as long as Rimsky-Korsakov was alive, Stravinsky's devotion to his teacher effectively shielded him from exposure to Diaghilev. "Living in the same city," he recalled much later in a memoir ghostwritten by Walter Nouvel, Diaghilev's intimate, "I naturally had more than one occasion to meet him, but I never sought these occasions."[2] How this gulf was bridged is one of the really crucial chapters in the early history of musical modernism.

What kind of a musician was Diaghilev? To judge from the "Pièces faciles" for piano four-hands which Stravinsky composed in fun with his impresario in mind as playing partner, the latter's practical skills were meager indeed. As a singer, huffing and puffing through the tenor part of his own incoherent setting of the Fountain Scene from Pushkin's *Boris Godunov*, he made no better impression, as we learn from a memoir by Nouvel, transmitted through Arnold Haskell.[3] Though ungifted and (in the best Russian tradition) undisciplined, his ardent early efforts to excel in composition and performance at least show how important music was in Diaghilev's scheme of things artistic; and this would tell, much later, on the way he shaped the "synthesis of the arts" that was ballet. Where he showed his genius was in connoisseurship, the connoisseurship, as Stravinsky testified more than once, of "a *barin*, which means a *grand seigneur*."[4]

It was a well-chosen word. Whatever else it may have been, the Diaghilev/Benois World of Art movement (known in Russian as *Mir iskusstva*) was a vigorous reassertion of aristocratic values and taste in reaction to a prevailing *embourgeoisement* that had gradually crept over once vital and innovative tendencies in Russian art and music and ossified them.

Diaghilev and Stravinsky, Seville, Spain, 1921. Courtesy, Parmenia Migel Ekstrom.

The realist and nationalist schools that had put Russia on the artistic and musical map in the 1860s and 1870s had by the nineties turned stale, sentimental, and routine. In part this was the result of official recognition and the awarding of academic positions to their leaders (for radicals, once in power, invariably turn reactionary), and in part it was because so many leading Russian artists had been co-opted (as we would say today) by wealthy patrons from the merchant class (Pavel Tretiakov in painting, Mitrofan Beliaev in music), who, so lavishly paying the piper, began calling the tune. Artistic nationalism had turned narrowly jingoistic during the reign of Alexander III (the "bourgeois tsar") who competed with Tretiakov in acquiring "realist" (but in fact ever more idealized and sentimental) paintings, and who finally expelled the once-regnant Italian opera from the St. Petersburg stage. This left the field to a native product that, once pungent with veiled political comment (as in Musorgsky's *Boris Godunov*), was now increasingly given over to a lacquer-box folklorism that celebrated nationality per se (epitomized by Rimsky's *Sadko*, which actually glorified a legendary seafaring merchant of old Novgorod). Above all, bourgeois art purveyed *messages*: when on the offensive the messages tended to be critical; when on the defensive, celebratory. No matter what kind, messages threaten to dominate and hence debase their medium (which is precisely what Benois had in mind when he referred to Russian art of the 1860s, in a phrase that became a watchword, as "one big slap in the face of Apollo").[5]

The aristocratic view of art is one that sees it frankly as decorative—one of life's luxuries, not a moral preceptor or the agent of national self-realization. It celebrates the spirit of creative play, not the satisfaction of animal needs ("the soul, not the belly," as the composer Anatoly Liadov put it).[6] True art, in the words of Benois, sought to evoke "not laughter, not tears, but a smile."[7] And that is why among Russian musicians Diaghilev revered not Rimsky-Korsakov but Tchaikovsky, who (but for a couple of neurotically confessional symphonies that had become disproportionately popular) epitomized the decorative, cosmopolitan values Diaghilev esteemed and for whom, just as in the eighteenth century to which he was aesthetically so strongly drawn, folklore represented not "the nation," but only "the peasantry." And that is also why of all musical and theatrical genres, Diaghilev and his fellow Miriskusniki esteemed most highly not the opera—so freighted with the residue of rabble-rousing, message-mongering realism— but the ballet.

To the Rimsky-Korsakovs all this was only so much degenerate aestheticism, spelling not renewal but its very opposite, decadence. It was a throwback to an outmoded aesthetic, that of the Enlightenment, far from what the nineteenth century regarded as enlightened. Aristocratic tastes, in the eyes of a bourgeois liberal, were ethically remiss. Vladimir Stasov, the great tribune of realist and nationalist art, countered Benois's remark about a slap in the face of Apollo by branding the World of Art leadership a band of "spiritual beggars."[8] What Musorgsky called a "thinking" artist could never take seriously what the poet Apollon Grigoriev, writing for a journal edited by Dostoevsky, called "the fruits of M. Petipa's and St. Léon's nonsensical imagination," naming the two Frenchmen who had guided the fortunes of the Russian ballet from the 1840s until the end of the century.[9] Hardly a "national" art, and degraded as it was by association with empty operatic divertissement (often forcibly interpolated into otherwise serious dramatic works), ballet was regarded by most Russian composers as an entertainment for skirt-chasing snobs and tired businessmen, to be furnished by specially imported hacks in the service of the Imperial Theaters. The only exceptions were, again, Tchaikovsky, and, latterly, Glazunov. Considering that the latter had been one of Rimsky's prize pupils, the critic Semyon Kruglikov had asked the master in 1900 whether ballet had perhaps matured to the point where composers of the front rank might profitably apply themselves to it. Rimsky was intransigent:

I'm inclined to think not, probably. And therefore I myself will never write such music. In the first place, *because it is a degenerate art.* In the second place, *because miming is not a full-fledged art form but only an accompaniment to speech.* In the third place, *balletic*

5 *Alexandre Benois, "Vrubel',"* MIR ISKUSSTVA 10 *(1903): 40.*

6 *Andrei Rimsky-Korsakov, "Lichnost' Liadova,"* MUZYKAL'NY SOVREMENNIK 2 *no. 1 (September 1916): 33.*

7 *"Beseda o balete,"* TEATR *(St. Petersburg, 1908), 108.*

8 *"Nishchie dukhom" (1899), in V. V. Stasov,* IZBRANNYE SOCHINENIIA *(Moscow, 1952), 3:238.*

9 *"Russkii teatr v Peterburge,"* EPOKHA 3 *(1864): 232.*

miming is extremely elementary and leads to a naive kind of symbolism. In the fourth place, the best thing ballet has to offer—dances—are boring, since the language of dance and the whole vocabulary of movement is extremely skimpy. With the exception of character and national dance (which can also become tiring), there is only the classical, which makes up the greater part. These (that is, classical dances) are beautiful in themselves; but they are all the same, and to stare for a whole evening at one classical dance after another is impossible. In the fifth place, *there is no need for good music in ballet; the necessary rhythm and melodiousness can be found in the work of any number of able hacks today.* In the sixth place, *in view of its paltry significance in the spectacle, ballet music is usually performed in a sloppy, slapdash way which would tell sorely on the work of a highly talented composer.*[10]

10 *Letter of 2 February (O. S.) 1900.* N. A. Rimsky-Korsakov, POLNOE SOBRANIE SOCHINENII: LITERATURNYE PROIZVEDENIIA I PEREPISKA 8B *(Moscow, 1982), 105.*

History—a history Diaghilev did more than anyone else to shape—has made a mockery of this assessment, but in the context of its time and place it was entirely reasonable, if onesided. What transformed the ballet as practiced at the Maryinsky Theater under Petipa, which is all that Rimsky knew, into the art of the Ballets Russes, which contributed so many musical and choreographic masterpieces to the treasury of twentieth-century art, had a great deal to do with another major tenet of World of Art thinking. This was the movement's unprecedented creative attitude toward folklore, once again untroubled by those "cursed questions" of social value and social responsibility that had burdened an earlier generation of Russian artists (and which would come back with immeasurably greater force to burden later ones).

Approached simply for itself rather than as an expression of "the people's spirit," and apprehended directly rather than as evidence of "the people's condition," folk art in the eyes of the Miriskusniki was an aesthetically autonomous "world of art" that shared and in large part inspired ideals of exuberant fantasy, transcendence of sensory reality, and, perhaps above all, a cool, rarefied—shall we call it classical?—impersonalism. A Rimsky-Korsakov took from folk music only thematic material (as a realist painter might take his subject matter) treating it in a conventional manner decreed by the local conservatory (where Rimsky was the senior professor). By contrast, an artist in the newer tradition—art historians call it "neonationalist"—sought in folklore something far more basic to his vocabulary and technique, often employing it as an instrument of self-emancipation from that academic mainstream, even its downright subversion. One of the best assessments of neonationalism in the musical theater can be found in a review by the eminent Russian art critic Yakov Tugenhold of Diaghilev's 1910 *saison russe* in Paris, which had included the premiere of *L'Oiseau de Feu*. "The folk," he wrote, "formerly the object of the artist's pity, is becoming increasingly the source of artistic style."[11] And here is how Diaghilev himself put it several years later, when during his one visit to America he was asked by the music critic Olin Downes to explain the genesis of the Ballets Russes' aesthetic innovations: "In objects of utility (domestic implements in the country districts), in the painting on sleds, in the designs and the colors of peasant dresses, on the carving around a window frame, we found our motives, and on this foundation we built."[12]

11 *"Russkii sezon v Parizhe,"* APOLLON 10 (1910): 21.

12 NEW YORK TIMES, 19 *January 1916; quoted in Richard Buckle,* DIAGHILEV *(New York, 1979), 300.*

▲   ▲   ▲

Diaghilev's earliest professional engagement with music was a concert series he organized in Paris in spring 1907. In itself it gave little evidence of his aesthetic predilections and tastes, which is in its paradoxical way a perfect testimonial to his mastery

13 *These were the St. Petersburg composers grouped around Mily Balakivev (1837-1910) who termed themselves the "New Russian School" of self-consciously national music. The other four were Modest Musorgsky (1839-1881), Alexander Borodin (1833-1887), Nikolai Rimsky-Korsakov (1844-1908), and César Cui (1835-1918). In Russia they were usually called the "mighty little bunch"* (MOGUCHAIA KUCHKA), *whence "kuchkist," "kuchkism," etc.*

14 *"Uspekhi russkoi muzyki,"* interview in the PETERBURGSKAIA GAZETA, 1907, *no. 180 (4 June); rept. I. S. Zilbershtein and V. A. Samkov,* SERGEI DIAGILEV I RUSSKOE ISKUSSTVO *(Mosskov, 1982), 1:205.*

of the art of conquest. Whereas his Paris art exhibition the previous year had been frankly and proudly tendentious in its snubbing of realist and nationalist painting, the concerts catered conspicuously to hackneyed Parisian notions of quasi-Asiatic Slav exotica. Works by the "mighty kuchka" (a.k.a. The Five)[13] dominated the programs, along not only with Liadov and Glazunov, but also such arrant epigones as Balakirev's latter-day disciple Sergei Liapunov. Tchaikovsky, whose music was the most representative of any nineteenth-century master's of the kind of Europeanized Russia the 1906 art exhibit had so zealously, even polemically, promoted, was known to be box-office poison in Paris as he remains to this day, and so he was deliberately played down, represented only by *Francesca da Rimini* and his fairly uncharacteristic Second Symphony with its folkloristic, quasi-kuchkist finale. Diaghilev, who took enormous pride in the fact that at his concerts "literally the whole 'Faubourg' could be found in the loges of the *belle étage*,"[14] had surely taken Faubourg prejudices into account as indeed he would do for the next twenty-two years. (Even he must have savored the irony of the occasion, though, when at the last concert of the series his bejeweled and bemedaled audience rose to its feet to acclaim *Sadko*, the merchant's opera par excellence).

But if Diaghilev the showman could pander, Diaghilev the aesthete found ways of propagating his views. That, after all, is what it takes to become a "tastemaker," and it is what makes his activity, even after eighty years, such a fascinating and instructive object of study. His epochal 1908 production of *Boris Godunov*—an opera that, finally, stood for virtually everything Diaghilev hated in art—is a perfect case in point. Its selection was fore-ordained because it had been for decades a cult object among Parisian cognoscenti, ever since Debussy had brought the vocal score back from Russia in 1889 and shown it to his friends. To bring it to Paris in a spectacular production befitting the traditions of the *grand opéra*, and with the more-than-spectacular Chaliapin making his Western debut in the title role, was an opportunity no impresario with Diaghilev's instincts could resist.

Although ulterior motives are not to be discounted, the production itself possessed a fantastic and influential integrity, albeit obviously not with respect to the work itself, which was mangled and mauled to where Musorgsky himself might not have recognized it. As a synthesis of art and music over which he was able to exercise total control, Diaghilev's 1908 *Boris* represented the precise locus of confluence of the neonationalist currents described above and the aestheticizing tendencies of the World of Art. By present-day standards of textual fidelity (often mis-termed "authenticity") it was a travesty. Whole scenes were dropped, others rearranged without regard to narrative logic, Rimsky-Korsakov's gaudy orchestration was used and even augmented, and casts of thousands were unleashed on the slightest pretext. But in the context of Diaghilev's aesthetic agenda it was magnificently authentic and very much attuned to nascent modernist attitudes.

To summarize the matter, Diaghilev's *Boris* was born of and did much to foster an unliterary, even antiliterary, conception of musical theater, one the impresario made explicit some years later in an interview with a New York reporter: "Literary things one reads. It is not necessary to hear them spoken on the stage."[15] He viewed theatrical synthesis as a series of vividly projected impressions carried to the eye by the movement of bodies and by the sets, costumes, and lighting, and to the ear by the music. In its cumulation and contrasts, the sequence of images created its own coherence and logic, and that sequence could if necessary override the conventions of linear narrative. Language only made a distracting counterclaim on the faculty of hearing.

The counterclaim was eliminated, of course, in ballet, and that is just what Diaghilev

15 *"Diaghileff Talks of Soul of the Ballet,"* NEW YORK POST, 24 *January 1916.*

brought to Paris at last in 1909, although he still billed his show as a *"saison d'opéra russe."* The main vehicle would be *Le Pavillon d'Armide*, a joint creation of Benois, the choreographer Mikhail Fokine, and the composer Nikolai Tcherepnin, who was at once Diaghilev's staff conductor, Benois's nephew by marriage, and a pupil of Rimsky-Korsakov, thus neatly bridging in his person all the contending political factions that had formerly estranged the World of Art from the world of contemporary Russian music. This patently Tchaikovskian ballet, to a subject derived from a story by Théophile Gautier, at last represented World of Art tastes at full strength to the Parisian audience. Diaghilev and Benois were convinced it would usher in a new epoch in the annals of artistic synthesis. They planned a ballet evening, to run alongside several operas featuring Chaliapin, in which *Le Pavillon d'Armide* would be showcased between two other recent dance compositions of Fokine. One of the works was *Les Sylphides*, to music by Chopin (for which Diaghilev, with what still seems uncanny prescience, commissioned two orchestrations from the young Igor Stravinsky after hearing the latter's *Scherzo fantastique* on its St. Petersburg premiere in January 1909 O.S.); the other was *Cléopâtre*, which had been performed in Russia under the title *Egyptian Nights* (after Pushkin's erotic poem *Egipetskie nochi*) to music by Arensky. For Paris, Diaghilev scrapped the original score and substituted what Nouvel sneeringly called a *salade russe* consisting of fragments of Arensky preceded by the overture to Sergei Taneyev's opera *The Oresteia*, interspersed with music by Rimsky-Korsakov (the apparition of Cleopatra from *Mlada*), Glazunov (the Autumn Bacchanale from *The Seasons*), and finishing off with the Persian Dances from Musorgsky's *Khovanshchina* (Tcherepnin supplied some connective tissue). Another *salade russe* was hastily concocted under the title *Le Festin* when several of the operatic projects fell through. And one of the latter, Borodin's *Prince Igor*, was reduced to just the third act, which consists mainly of a ballet, the famous Polovtsian Dances. Thus ballet was willy-nilly far more conspicuous than opera in the programs of the 1909 *saison russe*.

The result was a triumph that led to the permanent founding of the Ballets Russes and changed the course of twentieth-century artistic history. But even as they hailed Diaghilev's spectacular achievement, all the critics agreed that music had made the poorest showing when compared with the plastic and visual components. What had been the dominant element in the Wagnerian synthesis had unaccountably become recessive in Diaghilev's. The impresario was put as it were on notice that in any future productions music would have to be brought up to the level dance and design had reached in 1909. What everyone wanted was a musical *frisson* to match those administered by Benois, Bakst, Roerich, Fokine, Nijinsky, Pavlova, and the rest. And this could only mean a neonationalist score that would provide a novel and worthy counterpart to the decorative and choreographic delights of the Polovtsian Dances and *Cléopâtre*, for these represented for the French the quintessence of Slav exotica-cum-erotica, the *raison d'être*, as far as most of them were concerned, for Diaghilev's activity in their midst.

And that is how *L'Oiseau de Feu* came about, and how Igor Stravinsky met his destiny, when first Tcherepnin, then Liadov, and who knows how many more established musicians either declined or backed out of participating in the project. The ballet's long-established status as a world classic makes it hard to see now for the anomaly it was then. For this very deliberately, in fact demonstratively "Russian" work had no antecedent in Russian art and was expressly created for a non-Russian audience. Only the circumstances of Diaghilev's "export campaign" created the need for a Russian national ballet.

These circumstances told greatly on the work's form and facture. Lacking any immediate forebear in the classical Russian ballet, *L'Oiseau de Feu* took its place rather as heir to the long line of folkloric "magic" operas that began with Glinka's *Ruslan and Ludmilla* and continued through Rimsky-Korsakov's marvelous series. In these works it was customary to differentiate the Russian folksong style associated with human characters from a colorful, recondite harmonic idiom reserved to the supernatural ones. Stravinsky remained obedient to these conventions in his inexhaustibly coloristic, transcendently decorative score, quoting or imitating folksongs (*khorovods* and "lyrical songs" of the type known in Russian as *protiazhnye*) for Ivan Tsarevich and the princesses, and resorting to artificial scales of whole tones or alternating tones and semitones to depict the Firebird and Kashchei, avatars respectively of benign and evil magic.

This strict stylistic division was maintained, as well, in *Petrouchka*, with both its aspects presented in elemental, maximalistic terms that gained the work a reputation for genuine radicalism to which *L'Oiseau de Feu* (and—it must be said—the Diaghilev enterprise as a whole) did not generally aspire. The fantastic harmonies associated with the puppets, and the title character in particular, while based securely in time-honored traditions of chromaticism *à la russe*, indulged in a few extensions of the inherited techniques that produced bitingly dissonant combinations (e.g., the so-called "Petrouchka chord," which however may be found in a few earlier European scores, such as Ravel's *Jeux d'eau* and Strauss's *Elektra*). At the same time the diatonic folkloristic element was lowered in tone from the evocatively archaic ambiance of the *khorovods* and processionals in *L'Oiseau de Feu* to the level of cacophonous street music, ca. 1830. The sheer simplicity of the crowd music in the outer tableaux was the boldest and most modernistic stroke of all, given the musical scene in the decade preceding World War I. For pages at a time the music proceeds with an absolutely unvarying pulse, with unchanging dynamics, and, almost unbelievably, without a single sharp or flat. To achieve such freshness with such simple means, and with no hint either of monotony or of lack of sophistication, was surely Stravinsky's most startling achievement and the first real earnest of his genius. But it all proceeded directly from the premises of neonationalism, in which faith he had been instructed not by Rimsky-Korsakov, who detested and despised the "neo," but by Diaghilev and Benois.

The most radical aspect of *Petrouchka*, though, was one that was only indirectly related to the music. It was the first "new" ballet for which the score had preceded, and hence controlled, the choreography. Fokine, who considered himself the creator of *L'Oiseau*, found this degrading. It was one of the reasons for his sudden departure from the Ballets Russes in 1912. But this order has become the norm, as witness Balanchine's well-publicized creative methods, and for making it so Diaghilev deserves the credit. It was in this crucial upgrading of the role of the ballet composer that Diaghilev the musician *manqué* exerted his profoundest influence on the genre, which led to its miraculous and altogether unexpected resurgence and its dramatic upgrading in the twentieth-century scale of artistic values.

Petrouchka's more immediate impact was on the young French composers who would emerge in the postwar years—the generation of Les Six—who began exploiting with a vengeance its aesthetic of the concrete and the *actuel*, turning out tours de force of chic simplicity which Diaghilev happily incorporated into his postwar repertory. His role as a catalyst for so many Franco-Russian and Slavo-Gallic cross-fertilizations was another signal Diaghilev contribution to the stylistic development of twentieth-century music, especially since so many of the ballet scores he commissioned, at least in the early part of his career as impresario, have become staples of the concert hall.

Of no other ballet is this more true than of Stravinsky's third prewar ballet, *Le Sacre du Printemps*, which has established itself far more firmly in the concert hall than on the ballet stage, recent well-publicized staged performances notwithstanding. While much has been made of its neoprimitivist harmonic and rhythmic qualities, what is less often emphasized is the way *Sacre* brought to a peak the neonationalist principles on which the aesthetic of the Ballets Russes was founded. Stravinsky limited his thematic material largely to melodies confined to a four-note scale segment found in much archaic Russian folk music (the so-called minor tetrachord), and derived his harmony largely from the tone-semitone scale (which can be constructed from two such tetrachords). In this way he succeeded for the first time in fusing the diatonic/folkloric and the chromatic/fantastic idoms of Russian art music, which till then had followed parallel lines of development, in his own works as much as in those of his predecessors. He pursued this integrated style to its apex in *Les Noces* (*Svadebka*), an extraordinary ballet accompanied by choral singing that was dedicated to Diaghilev. It was fully composed before the end of the war, but not fully orchestrated till 1923, the year of its belated and in some ways anachronistic first performance. It was another distinction of Diaghilev's export campaign to have catalyzed this unforeseen yet in retrospect inevitable and indispensable capstone to the musical traditions of the "mighty kuchka," that faction of composers to whose work the great impresario had been indifferent at home. Again, it was the paradoxical status of the Ballets Russes as a Russian company performing abroad that had brought it about.

But the neonationalist apogee was not by any means the whole Diaghilev legacy. Before the war he also produced ballets by leading French composers (and also by Richard Strauss), and in particular commissioned masterpieces from Ravel (*Daphnis et Chloë*) and Debussy (*Jeux*). The latter, though not a successful ballet and never revived after its premiere season (1913), gave an interesting–if perhaps only unwittingly prophetic–glimpse of the programmatically antiromantic direction the Ballets Russes would take after the war. Then they would shed their outmoded coat of oriental *luxus* and emerge, lithe and athletic, to celebrate with calculated frivolity what Cocteau called *choses en soi* ("things in themselves"). The "things" could be simply dance *qua* dance, perhaps the truest light in which to view all those "neoclassical" divertissements of the late wartime and immediate postwar seasons, beginning with the Scarlatti/Tommasini *Les Femmes de Bonne Humeur* in 1917 and running to seed with the Handel/Beecham *The Gods Go A-Begging* in 1928. Or, somewhat later, they could be the joys of everyday contemporary life as led, needless to say, by the carefree cynical rich who made up the Ballets Russes audience, beginning with Poulenc's *Les Biches* of 1924 and culminating in the last Diaghilev season with *Le Bal* by Vittorio Rieti, who in 1988 was the only Diaghilev composer still alive. *Jeux* had had a lawn-tennis action, but the tennis game it portrayed was metaphorical, not a *chose en soi*. It had stood, enigmatically, for the intricate maneuvering of human relationships. The mysteriously opulent Debussy score, full of veiled timbres and complex harmonies, did not accord with the ostensible concreteness of the stage action.

After the war everything was sharp-etched line and primary hue, and nothing was made to last. Today's *actualité* is tomorrow's period piece, and that has been the fate of the vast preponderance of the postwar Diaghilev repertory. Only a few Stravinsky scores from this period–*Pulcinella* (1920), *Apollon Musagète* (1928)–have stood the test of time, and even some of his have gone dowdy. A case in point is *Mavra*, an *opéra bouffe* after Pushkin that had been originally intended as a cabaret skit for Nikita Baliev's *Théâtre de la Chauve-*

Souris. Its music parodied the Italianized Russian-Gypsy idiom out of which Tchaikovsky had emerged (and which formed the main part of the Chauve-Souris repertory). It was a style associated in Russian with gentry tastes, which is to say, with tastes such as Diaghilev's. For this reason its production by the Ballets Russes in 1922 was surrounded by a huge preliminary fanfare, for it was Diaghilev's last-ditch effort to get Paris to recognize the European Russia he loved. (The year before he had tried to win London over to it with a lavish production of Tchaikovsky's *Sleeping Beauty*, and almost lost his shirt.) He preceded the premiere with a gala concert pointedly entitled "La musique russe en dehors des 'cinq,'" and gave press interviews attaching to Stravinsky's little farce an importance it could hardly justify in the event, and in which he could scarcely have believed.

In fact it is hard to know what Diaghilev really thought of the fashionable ephemera he found himself promoting after the war. He always kept up a brave front. Francis Poulenc has left us in his memoirs a vivid picture of the great impresario calling after him as Poulenc was leaving to see a revival of the prewar *Petrouchka*; "Mais quel ennui!"[16] Yet to his intimates he often expressed impatience with the "musiquette" the Faubourg now demanded. No great new Russian composer came his way after Stravinsky. Prokofiev was a half-hearted modernist who achieved his best work after returning to Soviet Russia where he could be himself without pressure from the likes of Diaghilev to keep up with Parisian taste. *Le Pas d'Acier*, his opportunistic "Soviet" ballet of 1927, was a tawdry example of "radical chic" before the term was current. On the other hand, *Le Fils Prodigue* of 1929 suffered from an incongruity that neatly reversed the one that had beset *Jeux*: great pathos on stage, sketchy *choses en soi* in the pit. The less said about Vladimir Dukelsky and Nicolas Nabokov, at this point, the better; nor did the seventeen-year-old Igor Markevitch, Diaghilev's great find in the last year of his life (but from whom he did not have time to commission a ballet), live up, as a composer, to his early promise.

Reflections of this kind point up the inevitably contingent nature of an impresario's relationship to the culture of his time, for he must be as much a reactor as an instigator, a supplier to a demand he can only do so much, finally, to create, no matter how expert his "nose" and no matter how aggressively he intervenes in the shaping of the work he catalyzes. Diaghilev was by no means the singlehanded transformer of modern taste he is sometimes made out to be. The most that can be said for him is that he managed to preserve an "enlightened" aristocratic sensibility in an age of increasing barbarism, and to guide the Franco-Italian traditions of musical theater successfully, if not quite intact, into the twentieth century. Ultimately it was a view of art as distinguished entertainment that he upheld, disdaining equally what was undistinguished and what failed to entertain. He is as easily overrated as underrated, for taking a stand on Diaghilev means taking a stand on the essence and the ends of art. If he did not lead the "quest for the Holy City," as Serge Lifar, his last premier danseur, rather fatuously insisted, neither was he just "an irascible gentleman in top-hat and silk muffler, who happened to possess a wonderful flair in the matter of dancing," which is all that Vladimir Nabokov could discern in him.[17] But then Nabokov was something of a literary man.

16 Francis Poulenc, MY FRIENDS AND MYSELF, *trans. James Harding* (London, 1978), 127.

17 "Diaghilev and a Disciple," THE NEW REPUBLIC (18 November 1940): 699.

Ernest Ansermet, Serge Diaghilev, Igor Stravinsky, and Sergei Prokofiev in Madrid, 1921. Stravinsky-Diaghilev Foundation.

ON 11 JANUARY 1916 DIAGHILEV and his Ballets Russes steamed into New York harbor for the first of two lengthy tours of the United States. Both began in New York, then crisscrossed the country, giving Americans in no fewer than fifty-one cities a taste of Diaghilev's fabled entertainment. The company that made these 1916-1917 tours was different from the one Europeans knew. There were few stars and many new faces and a repertory that gave only a hint of Diaghilev's growing experimentalism. The Ballets Russes never triumphed in the United States, as it had in Europe, nor did it immediately influence the course of American ballet. But the tours set in motion changes within the Ballets Russes itself that had lasting consequences. Thanks to American dollars, Diaghilev rebuilt the company temporarily disbanded by World War I while conducting some of the most fruitful experiments in his company's history. Those same dollars paid for the only ballet to have its premiere in the New World–Vaslav Nijinsky's *Till Eulenspiegel*. In size, personnel, and social relations, the Ballets Russes of the American tours marked the birth of Diaghilev's postwar company.

Diaghilev had long toyed with the idea of an American tour. But only in 1914, when debt threatened the very life of his enterprise, did he take steps to convert the idea into a reality. "Have had several interviews . . . Diaghileff about Ballet for New York," Addie Kahn wired her husband, Otto, chairman of the Metropolitan Opera's board of directors, from London on 18 July 1914:

[Is] most insistent troupe should go America this winter for urgent reasons too complicated to cable upon which largely depend continuance of organization. Diaghileff willing to go even for 10 New York Brooklyn performances of which several matinees and some in Philadelphia, Boston, Chicago simply to keep company together.[1]

Diaghilev did not get to America that winter. In August war began, and the company that had broken up in London for the summer holidays now found itself scattered across a divided Europe. Diaghilev himself was in Italy, and it was here on 10 October that he signed a contract with Giulio Gatti-Casazza, the Met's managing director, for the tour that began in January 1916. A man without a company, Diaghilev cajoled the Met into providing the means to create one. With a $45,000 advance, Diaghilev got what most company directors only dream of–a period of subsidized artistic freedom.[2] He spent the summer and autumn of 1915 in Switzerland, and it was there that he gradually assembled his new company. He had promised the Met forty-seven dancers and his three biggest stars –Nijinsky, Tamara Karsavina, and Michel Fokine–although at the time he signed the contract he had no idea whether he could get them. From Petrograd (as St. Petersburg had been renamed at the start of the war) he summoned Serge Grigoriev, his trusted regisseur. The purpose of the visit, Grigoriev later wrote, was "to ask [my] help in collecting a company in Russia."[3] Returning home via London (where he engaged the Polish dancer Stanislas Idzikovsky), Grigoriev went to work. He called on Karsavina and discovered she was expecting a baby. He had no better luck with Fokine, who refused to leave Russia in wartime. Nor was Olga Spessivtzeva, an up-and-coming Maryinsky ballerina, tempted to join Diaghilev. A number of old hands decided to risk the journey, such as Grigoriev's wife, Lubov Tchernicheva, and several youngsters, among them Maria and Gala Chabelska. Grigoriev next went to Moscow, where he recruited the Bolshoi ballerina Xenia Maclezova and, from Lydia Nelidova's private studio, Vera Nemchinova, her sister Lida, and Valentina Kachouba. While Griogoriev labored in the East, Diaghilev worked the Western front. Although he could not free Nijinsky from house arrest in Budapest, his

1 Addie Kahn, cable to Otto Kahn, 18 July 1914, Otto Khan papers, box 34, Princeton University.

2 Contract between Serge Diaghilev and the Metropolitan Opera Company, 10 October 1914; Otto Kahn, cable to Serge Diaghilev, 14 May 1915, "Diaghilev Correspondence 1915-1916," Metropolitan Opera Archives.

3 S. L. GRIGORIEV, THE DIAGHILEV BALLET 1909-1929, ed. and trans. Vera Bowen (London, 1953), 102.

figure 4
Adolph Bolm and
Flore Revalles in *Schéhérazade*,
New York, 1916, cat. no. 93.

figure 1
Le Soleil de Nuit, New York, 1916,
cat. no. 97.

figure 2
Le Soleil de Nuit, New York, 1916,
cat. no. 96.

agent Stanislaw Drobecki secured Léon Woizikovsky and other much-needed men from Poland. Lydia Sokolova and Nicolas Kremnev arrived from England; Flore Revalles, a strikingly attractive opera singer hired for mime roles, came from France. With the exception of Adolph Bolm, who joined in Switzerland, none of these dancers were well known. But in the postwar years, Sokolova, Woizikovsky, Tchernicheva, Idzikovsky, Vera Nemchinova, and Massine all would become Ballets Russes stars.

By autumn 1915 the company was hard at work. To whip the dancers into shape, Diaghilev reengaged Enrico Cecchetti, the Italian master teacher whose pupils included Nijinsky, Karsavina, and Anna Pavlova. Just before Christmas, the company gave its first performance—a gala matinee in Geneva—and just after the holiday, a gala benefit in Paris. On New Year's Day 1916 the company set sail from Bordeaux.

The repertory was calculated to please rather than tax local audiences. Of the fourteen works, most were by Fokine. The list included some of his best ballets—*Les Sylphides*, *Firebird* (as *L'Oiseau de Feu* was translated in the United States), *Petrouchka*, *Carnaval*, *Le Spectre de la Rose*, the *Polovtsian Dances*, and *Schéhérazade*—and also a few of his lesser ones—*Le Pavillon d'Armide*, *Cléopâtre*, *Thamar*, and *Narcisse*. From Petipa's *Sleeping Beauty* came the Bluebird pas de deux (presented as *La Princesse Enchantée*). Only Nijinsky's *L'Après-midi d'un Faune* and Massine's *Le Soleil de Nuit* (figure 1) hinted at the modernism now transforming the company's identity. In anticipation of the tour, Diaghilev had spruced up several works. Both *Schéhérazade* and *La Princesse Enchantée* arrived in America with "new decors and costumes by Léon Bakst," and the program included a similar credit for the *Polovtsian Dances*, designed by Nicholas Roerich. Bakst also created new costumes for Ivan Tsarevich and the Beautiful Tsarevna in *Firebird*.

On 17 January the company of fifty-six gave its first performance before a glittering New York audience at the Century Theatre. Although Diaghilev's dancers had taken Paris by storm, New York was cooler to the company. There was enthusiasm but little love, and for the many who knew it firsthand, not even the excitement of novelty.

Actually, one could sample many of Diaghilev's wares without going abroad. At the Met were the sets and costumes from his *Boris Godunov* and even a version of his *Polovtsian Dances*. On Broadway, in 1911 Gertrude Hoffmann's "saison des Ballets Russes" offered a program that included three of Diaghilev's most popular works—*Cléopâtre*, *Schéhérazade*, and *Les Sylphides*. Another enterprise that cashed in on the fame of the real Ballets Russes was Mikhail Mordkin's All-Star Imperial Russian Ballet, which made its debut at the Metropolitan in 1911 and carried the banner of Russian dance to no fewer than 120 towns in seven months. More longlasting was the company of Anna Pavlova, which, beginning in 1910, made extensive tours throughout the United States with a repertory that owed much of its inspiration to Fokine. If none of these troupes measured up to Diaghilev's, they exposed the American public to genres, styles, and personalities associated with the Ballets Russes. Not unexpectedly, then, reviews of the company were mixed. There was high praise for the visual aspect of the ballets, for the ensemble ("as near to perfection as is possible in this imperfect world," wrote the *New York Tribune*), and for the orchestra (described by the *Sun* as an ensemble of "uncommon excellence").[4]

4 Grenville Vernon, "Russian Ballet a Dream World," TRIBUNE, 18 January 1916; "Russian Ballet Makes its New York Debut, Revealing Beautiful Form of Dramatic Art," SUN, 18 January 1916.

The principal dancers were another story. As the Met had anticipated, Nijinsky and Karsavina were sorely missed. Nearly every critic remarked on the weakness in the upper ranks, and most had something to say about the shortcomings of specific individuals. In a rare, signed review, the *Tribune's* Grenville Vernon came down especially hard on Maclezova:

5 Vernon, "Russian Ballet."

The weak point in "The Fire-Bird" was the Bird herself. Mlle. Xénia Maclezova is an accomplished technician, but she displayed little fancy or poetry. In Tschaikowsky's "La Princesse Enchantée" her technical powers were shown to better advantage, though M. Bolm was no Mordkine, and certainly no Nijinsky.[5]

The critic had good words, however, for Massine's dancing in *Le Soleil de Nuit* (figure 2), as well as for his achievement there as a choreographer, and, later in the season, for his performance in *Petrouchka*, where he took over the title role created by Nijinsky. The *Tribune* called the performance a "remarkable creation of poetic fantasy," describing Massine's puppet as a "figure of intense pathos."[6] As the season progressed, other company members attracted notice: Flore Revalles, whose Zobeide in *Schéhérazade* (figure 3) was "an impersonation of truly splendid sensuality and abandon"; Adolph Bolm, who "displayed his really remarkable abilities" as the warrior chief in the *Polovtsian Dances*; Lubov Tchernicheva, an "alluring" Chiarina in *Carnaval*; and Lydia Sokolova, "a lovely picture" as Papillon in the same ballet.[7]

6 "Futurist Ballet of Puppet Loves," TRIBUNE, 25 January 1916.

7 Vernon, "Russian Ballet"; "Russians' 'Faune' No John Wesley," TRIBUNE, 19 January 1916; "Schumann Work Turned to Ballet," SUN, 20 January 1916.

The Met had insisted on stars. But there was one star whom the Met—or at least someone within the organization—wanted no part of. Lydia Lopokova had made her debut with the Ballets Russes in 1910, then left it (and the Maryinsky) for the vaudeville circuits of America. Plucky and unconventional, she spent the next five years in the country, working as a dancer, cabaret artist, model, vaudeville performer, and Broadway dramatic actress. Late in 1915, Otto Kahn or someone in his confidence apparently broached to Diaghilev the idea of engaging Lopokova. With no female stars in the offing, Diaghilev jumped at the chance of adding a Maryinsky graduate to his roster, one, moreover, who had actually danced with the Ballets Russes. "Delighted to engage Lopokowa," he wired Kahn (in English) on Christmas Day. "Cable her lowest terms." A week of silence followed. On 2 January he wired the Metropolitan: "No answer for Lopoukova. If you haven't already engaged her, please take an option on her until my arrival. Am counting on her."[8] Unbeknown to Diaghilev, strong objections to her engagement had been raised. The day after Christmas, Otto Kahn received a letter that presented the case against her:

8 Serge Diaghilev, cables to Otto Kahn, 25 December 1915, and to Metropolitan Opera, 2 January 1916, "Diaghilev Correspondence 1915-1916," Metropolitan Opera Archives.

I do not know whether you have suggested the engagement of Lopokowa, but I do know that the public will not accept her with this company as a five dollar artist and if we must have someone in place of Karsavina it must absolutely be someone from abroad. I can feature a new name and get the public to accept it, but please, I beg of you, do not attempt it with Lopokowa who has appeared not only at Keith's Palace [a vaudeville house] and other theatres charging dollar and a half prices, but at other theatres far below the standard set for the Ballet. Even taking her as one of the ensemble would be most inadvisable. We have advertised a complete organization from Abroad—and the public will accept nothing less.[9]

9 Letter to Otto Kahn, 26 December 1915, "Diaghilev Correspondence 1915-1916," Metropolitan Opera Archives.

Whoever wrote to Kahn (the surviving carbon copy is unsigned) was wrong. When Lopokova made her debut in *Carnaval* at the third performance (suggesting that opposition to her only ceased with the appearance of the first, critical reviews), the critics were enchanted. "Miss Lydia Lopokova did not arrive with the Diaghileff Russian Ballet," wrote the *Tribune*. "She has been with us in America for several years. The glamour of novelty does not cover her. And yet last night at the Century Theatre she won the first great personal triumph of the Diaghileff Ballet season."[10]

10 "Lopokova Achieves Triumph in Ballet," TRIBUNE, 20 January 1916.

Lopokova's triumph notwithstanding, *Carnaval* had detractors. As in Europe, music critics usually had the dance beat, and they looked upon Diaghilev's rifling of the concert repertory—in this case, Schumann's *Carnaval: Scènes mignonnes sur quatre notes*, Op. 9—

figure 3
Enrico Cecchetti and
Flore Revalles in *Schéhérazade*,
New York, 1916, cat. no. 95.

figure 5
Adolph Bolm in *Schéhérazade*,
New York, 1916, cat. no. 94.

as nothing less than sacrilege. For the company's two Stravinsky scores, on the other hand, there was only praise. For critics who knew only his quartets (first heard in America two months before the opening of the Diaghilev season), *Firebird* was a revelation. Rich in fantasy and descriptive detail, it revealed the composer as a master colorist, a bold delineator of poetic atmosphere. *Petrouchka* caused an even greater stir. Wrote W. J. Henderson in a Sunday piece for the *Sun*:

> *What is to be said of this opulent and yet marvellously simple score of "Petrouchka"? There are pages which baffle the ear, yet are perfect in their achievement of delineative purpose. The confusion of sounds which is heard in the street before the show booths is a masterpiece of orchestration. It is impossible to seize upon its constituent elements; but the result is precisely what the artist intended it should be, that of two or three musical instruments or collections of instruments, the cries and talk of the street and the fundamental roar of the city. . . . What else can we demand?*[11]

11 W. J. Henderson,
"Consummate Art, Baffling
Music," SUN, 9 April 1916, sec. 3.

Music was not alone in drawing the ire of critics. Some took offense at the "immorality" of ballets that depicted scenes of unbridled lust. *Schéhérazade* (figures 4 and 5) was not the only work to end in an orgy, but it was the one most often charged with immorality. Early twentieth-century America had more than its share of puritans, but it had an even larger number of racists, and in *Schéhérazade* the spectacle of black men embracing white women was more than many in the audience could bear. No matter that the setting of the ballet was Persia of the Arabian Nights or that the "Negroes" were actually Caucasians in dark body paint. America's ultimate racial taboo had been broken. "Even to Northern minds," wrote the *Tribune*, the spectacle was "repulsive."[12]

12 Vernon, "Russian Ballet."

Critics were not the only guardians of public morality. Members of the Catholic Theatre Movement came to a performance (*Schéhérazade* and *L'Après-midi d'un Faune*, another sexually explicit ballet, were on the bill), then circulated a bulletin against the company. Complaints, meanwhile, had been pouring into the Police Department, and Diaghilev was summoned to answer the charges. There wasn't much he could do. At the next performance of *Faune*, the end was changed: instead of lying down on the Chief Nymph's discarded scarf, Massine merely gazed at its silken folds. The orgy in *Schéhérazade* was also toned down. The censors were satisfied, but the ballet, thought the *Tribune*, was spoiled. No wonder Diaghilev found Americans crude and unsympathetic.[13]

13 "Police Are to Edit the Russian Ballet," NEW YORK TIMES, 25 January 1916; "Russian Ballet Modified," NEW YORK TIMES, 26 January 1916; Nesta Macdonald, DIAGHILEV OBSERVED BY CRITICS IN ENGLAND AND THE UNITED STATES 1911-1929 (New York, 1975), 146-147.

The critics certainly gave Diaghilev a hard time. In a way he had invited it. Long before his arrival, the press agents had gone to work. "For months," wrote the *New York Times* after the company's first performance,

the newspapers and magazines have been printing the bright-hued colors of its costume plates, or black and white reproductions of its artists and scenes. For months they have been devoting their reading columns to exposition, illustration, and argument concerning various phases of its being, until finally there seemed nothing left for pictures or printed words in their task of explaining the fame the organization had won.[14]

14 "De Diaghileff's Ballet Impressive," NEW YORK TIMES, 18 January 1916.

If critics stood ready to pounce, part of the reason lay in the massive publicity campaign orchestrated by the Met.

Heading this campaign was one of the more remarkable of the many remarkable people whose lives crossed paths with the Ballets Russes. Today, outside the business world, few know the name of Edward L. Bernays. But this nephew of Sigmund Freud was the father of modern public relations. In his early twenties, Bernays was a newcomer to the Metropolitan Musical Bureau, to which the opera company had turned over the task of promotion. In a stroke of genius, the Bureau appointed him the company's general press representative. For Bernays, the experience was eye-opening:

I learned a lot working with the Metropolitan Musical Bureau; but never more than when I handled Diaghileff's Russian Ballet in 1915, 1916 and 1917. These three years taught me more about life than I have learned from politics, books, romance, marriage and fatherhood in the years since.[15]

15 Edward L. Bernays, BIOGRAPHY OF AN IDEA: MEMOIRS OF PUBLIC RELATIONS COUNSEL EDWARD L. BERNAYS (New York, 1965), 102.

Relying on what he called "hunch and intuition," Bernays mounted a campaign that publicized the ballet, first "as a novelty in art forms, a unifying of several arts; second, in terms of its appeal to special groups of the public; third, in terms of its direct impact on American life, on design and color in American products; and fourth, through its personalities." He bombarded magazines, Sunday supplements, the music and women's page departments of daily newspapers with "reams of stories and photographs angled to their various reader groups." He persuaded manufacturers to make products "inspired by the color and design of Bakst decors and costumes, and arranged for their advertising and display in department and other retail stores through the country." Much of this "ballyhoo," as he called the months of intense, nationwide publicity, centered on the company's principals: Nijinsky, Karsavina, and Diaghilev. When neither Karsavina nor Nijinsky turned up, he prepared the ground for their replacements, on the theory that "glowing descriptions of one Russian-named dancer . . . could be applied to any other." He draped a snake from the Bronx zoo around Flore Revalles in her *Schéhérazade* costume, a stunt that brought pictures of this unknown dancer to America's breakfast tables. He planted interviews and glowing accounts of "stars" who had never performed with the Ballets Russes in Europe, and published them under a variety of pseudonyms.[16] No wonder critics felt a little miffed.

On 29 January the New York season ended. The next morning the company boarded two special trains for Boston, the first stop on a two-month tour of fifteen cities. More than two hundred people packed the trains–dancers, stagehands, supers, and musicians–along with scenery and costumes for eleven ballets. Once out of New York, Diaghilev fired Maclezova, whose roles went to Lopokova, now the company's undisputed star. (Maclezova, as Diaghilev explained to Otto Kahn, had refused to dance unless he paid her $150 more a performance. He demurred, whereupon she and her mother tried to have him arrested!)[17] In some cities houses were full. But in many others, including Chicago, the company faced rows of empty seats.

For Merle Armitage every moment of the day was filled with incidents "beyond belief." Diaghilev, he wrote, "detested our democratic ways." He treated subordinates, including those in executive positions, as menials. He had no use for Ben Stern, to whom the Met had entrusted the management of the tour, and on even minor matters he insisted on wiring Kahn for advice. Diaghilev's high-handedness raised tension behind the scenes. In one particularly unpleasant incident, he struck a busy stagehand with his walking stick when the worker refused to carry out an order. A dozen men rushed to their coworker's defense, and only Armitage's timely appearance saved Diaghilev from harm. Later that night, a chunk of pig iron fell from the grid ninety feet above the stage, stripping the rim from Diaghilev's derby. An explanation of the "accident" was never found.[18]

The tour ended on 29 March. Five days later the company began a four-week season at the Metropolitan Opera House. Two works were added to the repertory: *Le Spectre de la Rose*, which had its premiere on opening night, and *Cléopâtre*, which the company gave two days later. But the real excitement centered on the arrival of Nijinsky. For months Diaghilev had pulled strings to secure the dancer's release. But it was only when the American government, still neutral in the European conflict, stepped in that the Austrian authorities were persuaded to let Nijinsky and his family go. Otto Kahn played a crucial role in the undertaking, not only because of his prestige as chairman of the Met's board of directors, but because, as a major underwriter of the Allied war effort, he exerted influence at the highest levels of government. On 7 February he received a telegram from Robert Lansing, the U.S. secretary of state, relaying a message from the American ambassador to Austria-Hungary. "Have succeeded getting promise government permit Nijinsky and wife start immediately New York provided you cable personal guarantee that they will return this monarchy immediately conclusion engagement Metropolitan Opera. Nijinskys can start soon as I transmit your agreement to government." By 28 February Nijinsky was free at Bern.[19]

Far from ending the Met's troubles, the dancer's release only added to them. In Switzerland Nijinsky demanded money and in early March, not without misgiving, the Met cabled its representative, Henry Russell, the $7,000 the dancer claimed he needed for debts. But this was only the beginning. Having arrived in New York, Nijinsky flatly

16 Bernays, 105-108.

17 Serge Diaghilev, letter to Otto Kahn, 3 February 1916, Otto Kahn papers, Princeton University.

18 Merle Armitage, DANCE MEMORANDA, ed. Edwin Corle (New York, 1947), 26-27. For a lengthy account of the tour, see Macdonald, 151-167.

19 Robert Lansing, telegram to Otto Kahn, 7 February 1916; John Brown, cable to Henry Russell, 28 February 1916, "Diaghilev Correspondence 1915-1916," Metropolitan Opera Archives.

rejected the contract offered him by John Brown, the Met's business manager. He told reporters that he was not under contract to Diaghilev (which was true), and that he was astonished to learn on arriving in New York that he was advertised to appear with his former company (which could not have been true given the $7,000 he had already accepted from the Met). Nijinsky also threatened to begin legal proceedings against Diaghilev for back pay. The newspapers went to town; armies of lawyers went to work. On 9 April a truce was reached: Nijinsky would dance. Two days later Diaghilev agreed to give Nijinsky $13,000 in back pay. He also agreed to pay Nijinsky $1,000, considerably more than the annual income of most Americans, for each of the eleven performances he was to dance in New York.[20]

Nijinsky made his debut on 12 April in *Le Spectre de la Rose* and *Petrouchka*. For some critics his performance was disappointing. It "scarcely provided," as the *New York Times* said, "the sensational features that this public had been led to expect." Others, however, recognized the dancer's genius at once. "Mr. Nijinsky is a male dancer such as New York has not seen in this generation, and perhaps, in any," stated the *Tribune*. "As a dancer pure and simple, as an interpretative artist, as an original personality, he stands alone." In the two and one-half weeks remaining in the season, audiences saw him in other guises—the Poet in *Les Sylphides*, the Golden Slave in *Schéhérazade*, Harlequin in *Carnaval*, the title roles in *Narcisse* and *Faune*. All of these revealed additional facets of his artistry. He was praised for his gift of impersonation, his fantasy in reimagining the different roles of his repertory. There was praise, too, for his polished technique, his mastery of detail, and the way every part of his body—head, limbs, torso, face—seemed alive with expression. Several critics commented on what today we would call his musicality, the subtle dialogue of his body with the music. Many also spoke of the inner rhythm and flow of his dancing, and the effect this created of uninterrupted movement.[21]

Nijinsky's presence had a bracing effect on his colleagues, who danced now with a brilliance and vitality that before they had not always shown. The ballets also benefited from his presence. In *Petrouchka* the *New York Times* remarked upon the many new touches that clarified the action, while in *Les Sylphides* the *Sun* noted that some of the groupings had been modified for the better and that in several places the poses and steps of the principals had been altered to their advantage. Changes were also made in *Spectre*, and these, too, were mentioned approvingly. Several critics referred to tales of Nijinsky rehearsing the ballets in which he appeared, and he may well have done so. Certainly, in one of his first statements to the press after reaching New York, he expressed a desire to rehearse the company so as to bring Fokine's ballets into the "shape in which they were originally created."[22] Nijinsky's concern for the integrity of Fokine's works speaks of the high regard in which he continued to hold them. But his concern also implies that in the brief period since Fokine's departure from the company, his ballets had changed. What America was seeing was the first copy of an original, rather than the original itself.

The changes in *Schéhérazade*, however, went far beyond details. With only a modest troupe at his command, Diaghilev had drastically reduced the number of dancers. For photographer Baron de Meyer, who knew the original ballet well, the small scale of the American version had unfortunate artistic consequences:

"Sheherazade," as shown in New York . . . was but an interpretation, in a minor and reduced key, of the amazing and bewildering orgy which we saw in Paris in former days when a multitude of dancers seemed to whirl in a frenzy. Now the multitude is reduced to eight bayadères, eight negroes, six fruit-bearers and a half-dozen or so principals. There is

20 For the Nijinsky-Met parlays in Switzerland, see Henry Russell, cable to John Brown, 5 March 1916; John Brown, cable to Henry Russell, 6 March 1916; Otto Kahn, cable to Henry Russell, 15 March 1916; Henry Russell, cable to Otto Kahn, 16 March 1916, "Diaghilev Correspondence 1915-1916," Metropolitan Opera Archives. The events following Nijinsky's arrival are pieced together from the following: "Nijinski at Odds with Ballet Russe," NEW YORK TIMES, 8 April 1916; "Nijinsky's Debut in Striker's Role," TRIBUNE, 8 April 1916; "Nijinski Will Dance," NEW YORK TIMES, 10 April 1916; "Nijinsky Ready To Dance Now," TRIBUNE, 9 April 1916. The letter contract signed by Diaghilev and Nijinsky on 11 April 1916 is in the Metropolitan Opera Archives.

21 "Nijinski Puts Life in Ballet Russe," NEW YORK TIMES, 13 April 1916; "Nijinsky Charms in First Dances," TRIBUNE, 13 April 1916. Other reviews that mention the dancer's various qualities are "Nijinsky Dances into Glory on Debut Here," WORLD, 13 April 1916; "Nijinsky Joins the Ballet Russe," EVENING POST, 13 April 1916; "Nijinsky Appears in Two Ballets," SUN, 16 April 1916; "Nijinsky and the Ballet Russe," EVENING POST, 15 April 1916; "Nijinski Dances Again," NEW YORK TIMES, 15 April 1916; "Interest Growing in Ballet Russe," SUN, 18 April 1916.

22 Quoted in "Nijinski at Odds with Ballet Russe," NEW YORK TIMES, 8 April 1916.

23 Baron de Meyer, "The Ballet Russe–Then and Now," VANITY FAIR, January 1917, 120.

no doubt that a certain spirit and atmosphere remains . . . but to anyone like myself who actually was present at the première in Paris, "Sheherazade" . . . is a poor performance and, at times, far from enjoyable. [23]

The *Schéhérazade* we know today is a descendant of this imperfect American copy, not Fokine's 1910 original.

There was one aspect of Nijinsky's dancing that did not go down well with New York critics–the elegance that many perceived as effeminate. "There was a discordant note," wrote the *New York Times* of his performance in *Spectre*, "in a super-refinement of gesture and posture that amounted to effeminacy." Some critics, while noting the absence of virility, qualified their remarks, drawing attention to the masculine "strength" of his dancing. *Narcisse*, however, proved too much for the critical brotherhood–and for many in the audience as well. There were giggles in the house and thundering reviews in the newspapers. The critics had a field day with Nijinsky's costume, not one of Bakst's happiest inspirations. Wrote one: "It was to laugh, as the French say. Such a lovely costume! A nice white shimmy and a nice white knee skirt, and such dear little white unmentionables underneath!" [24] Not surprisingly, *Narcisse* never received a second performance.

24 Quoted in Macdonald, 178.

In the main, however, Nijinsky's appearances drew large and enthusiastic houses, and the season ended on a high note. As the curtain fell on the last performance word came that the company would return to America in the fall, on a visit that would include a long coast-to-coast tour. Although sponsored by the Met, the project was described as "a personal artistic enterprise" of Otto Kahn. [25] Three days later the company, minus Nijinsky, sailed for Spain.

25 Quoted in Macdonald, 183.

26 For Kahn's negotiations with Nijinsky, see Otto Kahn, letter to Laurence A. Steinhardt, 16 May 1916; Laurence A. Steinhardt, letter to Otto Kahn, 19 May 1916; Otto Kahn, letter to Laurence A. Steinhardt, 22 May 1916; Otto Kahn, letter to Laurence A. Steinhardt, 25 May 1916; Laurence A. Steinhardt, letter to Otto Kahn, 27 May 1916; Otto Kahn, letter to Laurence A. Steinhardt, 31 May 1916, Otto Kahn papers, Princeton University. Nijinsky's formal contract with the Metropolitan Opera Company, which is in the Metropolitan Opera Archives, was signed on 2 August 1916. For Nijinsky's explicit barring of Grigoriev, see Metropolitan Opera, cable to Serge Diaghilev, 5 September 1916, "Diaghilev Ballet Russe 1916," Metropolitan Opera Archives.

27 Grigoriev, 111. An updated draft of Diaghilev's contract with the Metropolitan Opera Company is in the Metropolitan Opera Archives.

Kahn had had enough of Diaghilev. He wanted to show the company to America, but he wanted none of the backstage hysterics and intrigue that had accompanied the first tour with Diaghilev. Even before the season ended, Kahn decided to throw his lot in with Nijinsky. In late April he relayed the Met's new and alluring offer–a twenty-week contract beginning about 1 October in which Nijinsky was engaged both as leading dancer and artistic director of the "Diaghilew Ballet Russe." Diaghilev himself would remain in Europe (as would Grigoriev), while Nijinsky ruled the roost in America. If Kahn thought the first tour had gone badly, he had no idea what was in store for him on the second. [26]

A lesser man than Diaghilev might have balked at the scheme. But Diaghilev was full of plans, and he welcomed the prospect of being quit of the company "to plan a whole new repertoire in peace." "When telling me of this arrangement," Grigoriev observed, "he evidently felt quite happy." From a financial point of view there was ample reason for Diaghilev's optimism. There was the Met's $20,000 advance, which would tide him over the summer, then $9,000 for each week of the twenty-week engagement, in addition to half the tour's net profits. The Met assumed responsibility for the orchestra and all travel and administrative costs, in addition to Nijinsky's $60,000 salary. Diaghilev's commitment was limited to the salaries of conductor Ernest Ansermet, company managers Stanislaw Drobecki and Randolfo Barocchi (who had just married Lopokova), a chief machinist, and forty-one dancers. [27]

Over the summer of 1916 the tour took shape. Dancers were signed up, among them Bolm, Lopokova, and Revalles. Seasoned performers and audience favorites, they would carry the major burden of the repertory, as Massine, Tchernicheva, and Idzikovsky were to remain with Diaghilev in Europe. The Met, anxious to strengthen the distaff side of the company, was deep in negotiations with Captain Philip Lydig, an Allied munitions agent who headed the American Ambulance in Petrograd and served as a Special Assistant at the

28 For the Met's efforts, see
Metropolitan Opera, cables to
Artemieff, 25 July 1916 and 7
August 1916, and to American
Embassy, Petrograd, 7 August
1916 and 13 September 1916;
Captain Philip Lydig, cable to
Metropolitan Opera, 13 September
1916, "Diaghilev Ballet Russe
1916," Metropolitan
Opera Archives.

Embassy, to secure the services of a Maryinsky ballerina. The Met hoped to bring over
Karsavina, but when this proved impossible, it settled for Margarita Frohman and Olga
Spessivtzeva.[28] Fokine's *Papillons* ("rearranged" by Bolm) and a new version of *Sadko* (with
choreography by Bolm and designs by Natalia Gontcharova) were added to the previous
season's repertory (see figures 6 and 7). In addition, the Met undertook to produce two
brand-new works—*Till Eulenspiegel* and *Mephisto Valse*. Both were to be choreographed by
Nijinsky, and like his salary, they were to be paid for by the Met.

On paper the tour looked good. But there was reason for the forebodings Grigoriev
confessed to Diaghilev as the troupe sailed from Bordeaux on 8 September. Most concerned
the administration. Neither Drobecki nor Barocchi got on well with the dancers, and
Nicolas Kremnev, the newly appointed regisseur, lacked both tact and authority. And
Nijinsky, even in the best of circumstances, had no aptitude for administration. Within
days of the company's arrival, trouble was brewing. There were disputes over casting and
disagreements among the company's factions. The dancers, wrote Sokolova, were at
"sixes and sevens. . . . We didn't seem to belong to anybody." Although the company was
smaller, it had several newcomers, and fitting them into the repertory was no easy task.
Nijinsky's new ballets were scheduled to open during the New York season, and the
company arrived three weeks early to rehearse them. But the task proved beyond his

figure 6
Corps de ballet from *Sadko*,
New York, 1916, cat. no. 99.

figure 7
Adolph Bolm in *Sadko*, New York,
1916, cat. no. 98.

29 *Lydia Sokolova*, DANCING FOR DIAGHILEV, *ed. Richard Buckle (London, 1960), 89.*

capacity, and *Mephisto Valse* was temporarily laid aside. The rehearsals for *Till* were a shambles: "Nijinsky would appear and disappear. As ever he had great difficulty in explaining what he wanted, and sometimes it was clear that he did not know himself."[29] Hours at a time were wasted, and the dancers in exasperation went on strike. Things reached such a pass that when Nijinsky sprained an ankle, delaying the premiere by a week, the dancers regarded his injury as a bid for extra time. But even with the extra week Nijinsky could not finish the ballet. Arguments broke out at the dress rehearsal; when Nijinsky left in a huff, the company was called together and asked if it could pull the ballet through. From the "scrappy bits" that Nijinsky had choreographed, the dancers pieced together the second half, and the show went on.

The season at Oscar Hammerstein's Manhattan Opera House began on 16 October, a week late. Nijinsky did not dance, and *Sadko*, rather than *Till*, provided the novelty of the evening. With its brilliant colors, fantastic plot, and exotic music (from Rimsky-Korsakov's opera), *Sadko* mined the Russian vein of Diaghilev's most popular works. The *New York Times* compared it to *Firebird* and *Petrouchka*, and had nothing but praise for Bolm's

30 *"Ballet Russe Gives 'Sadko' Its Premiere,"* NEW YORK TIMES, *17 October 1916.*

choreography, which evoked the strange creatures of an underwater kingdom.[30] *Papillons*, by contrast, sparked little enthusiasm. A spin-off of *Carnaval*, the ballet was one of Fokine's minor efforts, and the critics—despite some praise for Lopokova as the Young Girl and Bolm as Pierrot—treated it accordingly. On 24 October Frohman and Spessivtzeva made their debuts in *Les Sylphides*.

The high point of the season came with the long-awaited premiere of *Till*. The eleventh-hour patch job had worked: the ballet impressed the critics as being one of the finest things the company had done in America. Summed up the *Tribune*: "'Till' has but one fellow in the repertory of the Russian Ballet, and that is 'Petrouchka.'"[31]

31 *"Eulenspiegel in Pantomime,"* TRIBUNE, *24 October 1916.*

Till was Nijinsky's fourth and last ballet and the only one he created independently of Diaghilev. The idea came to him in Budapest. "He had for quite a while thought of creating a ballet of the mediaeval age," his wife Romola later wrote.[32] But it was only when

32 *Romola Nijinsky*, NIJINSKY, *foreword by Paul Claudel (New York, 1934), 287.*

a cousin of hers played Richard Strauss's tone poem "Till Eulenspiegel" that the bits of angular movement he had already choreographed came together as a ballet. The libretto, with minor changes, followed the plan of the music. The rogue-hero of the piece, like the pranks that made up its various episodes, derived from medieval German legend. Till's waggeries were legion, and the score was packed with incident, as was Nijinsky's ballet: Till upsetting the carts of the market women, masquerading as a priest, playing the cavalier, falling in love, mocking the learned; finally, Till on the gallows. By the time the Nijinskys left Europe, most of the ballet's details had been worked out.

figure 8
Robert Edmond Jones,
Costume design for Women in the
Crowd in *Till Eulenspiegel*, 1916.
Courtesy, Sotheby's Inc.,
New York.

33 *Robert Edmond Jones,* "Nijinsky and Til Eulenspiegel," DANCE INDEX *4, no. 4 (April 1945), 47-48.*

In late spring 1916 Nijinsky was introduced to Robert Edmond Jones, the scenic artist who would design both *Till* and *Mephisto Valse*. Jones was then at the beginning of his career, but already his work revealed the imprint of what came to be known as "the new stagecraft." In Bar Harbor that summer, the two went to work. With Nijinsky watching, criticizing, and exhorting, Jones drew. Together they mapped out the design for the front curtain—a huge sheet of parchment emblazoned with Till's device of the owl and the looking-glass. The marketplace of Braunschweig began to take shape in front of the brooding black mass of the cathedral, a Braunschweig seen through Till's own eyes. One by one, the characters came alive: the rosy-cheeked apple woman, the fat blond baker, the scrawny sweetmeat-seller, the cobbler with his rack of oddly shaped shoes, the professors in long robes and ridiculous shovel hats, the three *châtelaines* in towering headdresses and streaming trains, even members of the crowd (figure 8), and Till himself in his various guises—imp, lover, scholar, victim.[33]

Till was performed twice in New York (the second time at the season's only sold-out house) and several times on tour. Because the ballet was never seen in Europe, it has been regarded as a footnote to Nijinsky's career, a retreat from the experimentalism of his earlier works. But the manner of the ballet's creation and the character of the overall design suggest otherwise. Prompted and guided by Nijinsky, Jones went far beyond the aesthetic of the World of Art movement (see Bridgman essay). In their exaggerated proportions and semi-cubist forms, his designs acknowledged the revolution of modernism. Neither Bakst's creations for *Faune* and *Jeux* nor Nicholas Roerich's for *Sacre* had done this. Indeed, as Roger Fry noted, the choreography and music of *Sacre* had far outstripped Roerich's "rather fusty romanticism," had "arrived at a conception of formal unity which demanded something much more logically conceived than the casual decorative pictorial formula of the scenery."[34] Quite independently of Diaghilev, Nijinsky, in *Till*, plowed new artistic ground.

34 Roger Fry, "M. Larionow and the Russian Ballet," BURLINGTON MAGAZINE 34, no. 192 (March 1919): 112.

But *Till* broke new ground in still another way. In working with Jones, Nijinsky took Diaghilev's collaborative method as his model. Within the Ballets Russes, however, designers had always had the upper hand, even in ballets like *Firebird* and *Petrouchka* where Fokine had worked closely with the artists. In *Till*, however, Nijinsky imposed his own vision on the ballet. Seizing the initiative, he made Jones the servant of his imagination, the means of giving flesh to his own creation. In so doing, Nijinsky added a new and essential ingredient to the definition of the modern ballet choreographer—the role of artistic director.

Lincoln Kirstein and others have also remarked on *Till*'s choreographic conservatism. Like *Petrouchka*, Nijinsky's ballet was a social epic, rich in character and historical particularity. The curtain rose on a medieval marketplace with its peasants, priests, knights, noblewomen, and beggars. There were props: a huge roll of cloth, a scholar's parchment, apples, bread, sweetmeats. And there was action, as rapidly changing as a motion picture. In her biography of her husband, Romola Nijinsky claimed that *Till* was "sheer dancing from beginning to end."[35] But critics thought otherwise. Wrote the *Times*:

35 Romola Nijinsky, 347.

As for the chorus movements, Mr. Nijinsky has furnished abundant proof of his genius as a stage director. There is almost none of what the average audience would call "dancing." It would be out of place as Nijinsky has conceived the ballet. Instead, the members of the company have been drilled in strange posturings and queer little movements that constantly pique the interest and remind you that you are in the midst of a medieval fantasy.[36]

36 "Portray in Ballet Strauss's Gay Tale," NEW YORK TIMES, 24 October 1916.

More than any other work, *Till* revealed Nijinsky's debt to Fokine. But the ballet also underscored the extent of their differences. Where *Petrouchka* emphasized naturalism, *Till* aimed for stylization. Nijinsky's very steps, wrote H. T. Parker in the *Boston Evening Transcript*, "were as the tracing of his mockery," and the same might be said of the other characters, whose grotesquely exaggerated forms—rounded, attenuated, thickened—became, in Jones's words, "the impossible figments of an imagination enchained by some ludicrous nightmare."[37]

37 H. T. Parker, "The Russians in Full Glory," in MOTION ARRESTED: DANCE REVIEWS OF H. T. PARKER, ed. Olive Holmes (Middletown, Conn., 1982), 123; Jones, 53.

On 28 October the company danced its last performance in New York. A four-month tour lay ahead, and Kahn no less than Diaghilev laid great stock on its success. Unfortunately for both, the tour was a fiasco. Despite generally good notices and occasionally good houses (some of the best were in San Francisco), the Metropolitan lost a quarter of a million dollars. Its goal of taking between $6,000 and $7,000 a performance proved illusory. In Fort Worth receipts fell as low as $767, and during the first week of December alone the losses amounted to nearly $15,000. Much of the responsibility for this

38 *Ernest Henkel, letter to Alwynn Briggs, 22 May 1917; Metropolitan Opera, letter to J. S. Morissey, 14 September 1916, "Diaghilev Ballet Russe 1916"; Ernest Henkel, letter to Otto Kahn, 11 December 1916, "Diaghilev Ballet Russe 1916-1917," box 2; Ben Franklin, letter to Ernest Henkel, 30 January 1917, "Diaghilev Ballet Russe 1916"; Ben Stern, memorandum to Ernest Henkel, 16 December 1916, "Diaghilev Ballet Russe 1916-1917," box 2; Ernest Henkel, letter to L. A. Steinhardt, 27 February 1917, "Diaghilev Ballet Russe 1916"; Will L. Greenbaum, letter to Maxmillian Elser, Jr., 28 December 1916; R. G. Herndon, telegram to Ernest Henkel, 22 November 1916, "Diaghilev Ballet Russe 1916-1917," box 2, Metropolitan Opera Archives. For a sampling of critics' reactions to the tour, see Macdonald, 199-213.*

39 *Ernest Henkel, letter to R. G. Herndon, 8 December 1916, "Diaghilev Ballet Russe 1916-1917"; R. G. Herndon, telegram to Ernest Henkel, 22 November 1916; Ernest Henkel, letter to R. G. Herndon, 8 December 1916, "Diaghilev Ballet Russe 1916-1917," box 2, Metropolitan Opera Archives.*

40 *Stanislaw Drobecki and Randolfo Barocchi, telegram to Ernest Henkel, 7 January 1917, "Diaghilev Ballet Russe 1916-1917," box 2; Serge Diaghilev, cables to Rawlins L. Cottenet and Ernest Henkel, 11 February 1917, "Diaghilev Ballet Russe 1916"; M. Oustinoff, letter to Metropolitan Opera House, 24 February 1917, "Diaghilev Ballet Russe 1916-1917," box 2, Metropolitan Opera Archives.*

41 *For the Met's remittances, see Metropolitan Ballet Company, Inc., letters to National City Bank, 22 December 1916, 28 December 1916, 4 January 1917, 11 January 1917, 24 January 1917, 25 January 1917, 10 February 1917, 19 February 1917. On 16 November 1916, Diaghilev commissioned Fortunato Depero to*

disaster lay with the Met: the high ticket schedule it had insisted on, incompetent advance men who alienated local newspaper editors, and a failure, generally, to assess what the market would bear in places like Wichita and Tacoma. But part of the blame rested with Nijinsky, who dithered over programs until press deadlines were missed and whose failure to dance as scheduled entitled ticketholders on a number of occasions to refunds. To the chagrin of local managements, he often refused to appear more than once on a program, no more than ten minutes if the scheduled ballet happened to be *Le Spectre de la Rose.* "Just think," complained Will L. Greenbaum, the manager of San Francisco's Valencia Theater, "of asking $5.00 for a show such as you are giving us certain nights and think what Pavlowa gave us for $2.50 and how that wonderful little woman used to work. Nine times a week and on the stage all the time." And, of course, Nijinsky's *Mephisto Valse,* which as late as November was scheduled to enter the repertory in San Francisco, failed to materialize.[38]

Nijinsky was not the only "prima donna" to cause difficulty. Despite the Met's generous salary ($500 a week), neither Frohman nor Spessivtzeva was prepared for the rigors of a cross-country tour. Typical of the grueling schedule were the company's dates for the week beginning 13 November: Monday, Worcester; Tuesday, Hartford; Wednesday, Bridgeport; Thursday, Atlantic City; Friday and Saturday, Baltimore. Frohman began missing performances, and by 8 December Ernest Henkel, the tour's New York-based business manager, thought there was "very little use in carrying these two girls around the country" and that they should "leave at the end of the week of 16 December in Omaha." Frohman and Spessivtzeva left the company in San Francisco. Their dismissal, however, was only one sign of a general belt-tightening by which the Met hoped to stave off the worst of what was obviously a disaster. In late November Henkel proposed eliminating one of the company's railway cars; a few weeks later, he spoke of dropping two musicians and charging to Drobecki the fares of two Russian women traveling with the company as chaperones.[39]

In addition to trimming expenses, the Met also cut back its remittances to Diaghilev. By early January he claimed that the Met owed him $37,500 of the $108,000 due to date. On 11 February he wired both Henkel and Rawlins L. Cottenet, a Met board member then in Paris, to cable $47,000 immediately to his bank. "Delay in payment inexcusable. Have urgent bank drafts." Later that month he brought consular pressure to bear on the Metropolitan through the Russian embassy in Rome; by this time, he claimed, the outstanding balance had mounted to $75,000.[40]

The records show that between 22 December 1916 and 18 February 1917 the Met ordered the Foreign Trade Department of the Wall Street branch of the National City Bank to credit $51,500 to Diaghilev's account. Obviously, some of this went to pay the troupe ($22,500 was forwarded to Drobecki on tour), and doubtless, a fair amount ended up in the pockets of Diaghilev's creditors. But surely there was another reason behind the January-February panic: the commitments Diaghilev had just made to produce *Fireworks, Parade, Le Chant du Rossignol,* and an untitled project with music by Maurice Ravel that (with the exception of the Ravel ballet) were to be the high points of his spring seasons in Rome and Paris. A factor in dropping *Le Chant du Rossignol* and the Ravel project may well have been the unanticipated loss of revenue from the American tour.[41]

Theoretically, the Met's remittances should have covered expenses on both sides of the Atlantic. In practice, they did not. Indeed, as Diaghilev signed up artists in Rome, his company virtually starved in America. On 4 December R. G. Herndon, the Met touring manager, reported from Houston:

design the decor, thirty-five costumes, and other accessories for LE CHANT DU ROSSIGNOL. Less than three weeks later, on 2 December, he commissioned another Futurist, Giacomo Balla, to design the "plastic setting" for Stravinsky's FIREWORKS. Diaghilev signed letter contracts with Pablo Picasso and Erik Satie for PARADE on 11 and 12 January 1917. On 12 January Ravel accepted Diaghilev's commission for a ballet that would have a libretto by yet another Futurist, poet Francesco Cangiullo. For LE CHANT DU ROSSIGNOL, see Leonetta Bentivoglio, "Danza e futurismo in Italia 1913-1933," LA DANZA ITALIANA 1 (Autumn 1984), 66; for FIREWORKS, see Melissa McQuillan, "Painters and the Ballet, 1917-1926: An Aspect of the Relationship Between Art and Theatre," Ph.D. diss., New York University, 1979, vol. 2, 383-384; for PARADE, see Richard Buckle, IN SEARCH OF DIAGHILEV (New York, 1956), 93-94; for the Ravel-Cangiullo project, see CATALOGUE OF BALLET MATERIAL AND MANUSCRIPTS FROM THE SERGE LIFAR COLLECTION, Sotheby's (London), 9 May 1984, lot 203.

42 R. G. Herndon, letter to Ernest Henkel, 4 November 1916, "Diaghilev Ballet Russe 1916-1917," box 2, Metropolitan Opera Archives. The letter is obviously misdated.

43 R. G. Herndon, letter to Ernest Henkel, 11 December 1916, "Diaghilev Ballet Russe 1916-1917," box 2, Metropolitan Opera Archives. Fradkin was the tour's concertmaster.

44 Doris Faithfull, letter to Otto Kahn, 11 November 1916, box 57, Otto Kahn papers, Princeton University. Faithfull was writing on behalf of Anna and Lubov Samarokoff [Sumarokova], Mechkovska, Galina Chabelska, Stas Paerska, and Lila Kachouba.

45 Ben Franklin, letter to Ernest Henkel, 25 February 1917, "Diaghilev Ballet Russe 1916," Metropolitan Opera Archives.

Well, the Diaghileff faction is not leaving a stone unturned to keep going until Diaghileff has instructed the bank to pay over the money. . . . The corps de Ballet have had barely enough to keep alive, most of them haven't a cent to eat with. I have been giving those few small amounts out of my own pocket. Drobecki and Barocchi have sent Diaghileff some stinging cables, as they explained to me they asked him if it is his desire to see his company starve and stranded if not to wire immediately to the bank and release the cash.[42]

By the time the company reached Tulsa, the situation had worsened. "The company," reported Herndon, "are on their last dollars as Lopokova, Monteux, Revalles, Bolm have given up all the money they have at their command, and unless money is forthcoming at Kansas City, I don't think they can go further."[43] The money came through, and the company limped on.

But even when salaries were paid, they barely covered living expenses in costly America. Early in the tour Doris Faithfull, an English dancer, wrote to Otto Kahn on behalf of herself and six other members of the corps de ballet:

I am writing this on some of the girls' behalf, also my own. It is concerning our salaries—we wondered if you could intercede with Mr. Diaghilev on the matter. It is absolutely impossible for us to live on the salary we receive—let alone some who have parents to support. When we arrive in a town we have to go hunting about for cheap rooms (carrying heavy suitcases) because we can't afford to stay at the better hotels. We are very sorry to have to trouble you with our private affairs but we are not in communication with Diaghileff. It seems so futile to think that every penny we earn and work hard for has to go in expenses—so cannot save anything in case of illness etc. A list of the salaries are beneath.[44]

These were thirty-three and thirty-four dollars a week. Kahn's response, if any, has not survived.

The company gave its last performance on 24 February 1917 at Harmanus Bleecker Hall in Albany. Like so many others, the engagement was a "terrible fliver," as Ben Franklin, the Albany manager, put it: "Not one fifth of those who saw [the company] here last season, attended the performance last night."[45] On this less than glorious note, the tour ended.

Neither Diaghilev nor the Ballets Russes ever returned to the United States. Despite this, elements of Diaghilev's aesthetic took root here. Adolph Bolm was among the handful of dancers who remained in America in 1917, and in the next two decades his activities as a teacher, dancer, choreographer, and producer would popularize styles and artistic approaches associated with the Ballets Russes. So, too, would the distinguished collaborations of Robert Edmond Jones, which included *The Birthday of the Infanta* and *Skyscrapers*, ballets by John Alden Carpenter, and such dance pieces as *Die Glückliche Hand* (with Doris Humphrey and Charles Weidman) and *The Crucifixion of Christ*, choreographed by George Balanchine. And in the years to come the inspiration of the Ballets Russes would guide many who first saw the company in 1916-1917 toward the creation of an indigenous American ballet.

Michel Georges-Michel,
The Opening of "Parade," 1917, cat.
no. 40. Left to right: Paul
Rosenberg, Marie Laurencin, Serge
Diaghilev, Misia Sert, Erik Satie,
Georges-Michel, Picasso,
and Jean Cocteau.

Ballets and Opera-Ballets Produced by Serge Diaghilev

Compiled by

Nancy

Van Norman Baer

and

Lynn Garafola

▼

THIS CHRONOLOGY is a synthesis of information obtained from various sources, although it draws primarily from David Vaughan's catalogue of the 1974 Diaghilev/Cunningham exhibition at Hofstra University, Hempstead, Long Island, New York. A separate chronology of operas follows this list.

Titles are given in their original and best-known forms. Where a translation is useful, it appears beneath the title.

Restagings are noted only in the case of Ballets Russes productions that incorporated new choreography, costumes, and/or decor.

1909

LE PAVILLON D'ARMIDE
Choreography: Michel Fokine
Music: Nicholas Tcherepnine
Libretto: Alexandre Benois, from Théophile Gautier's story *Omphale*
Costumes and decor: Alexandre Benois
Premiere: 18 May 1909, Théâtre du Châtelet, Paris
Principal dancers: Vera Karalli, Mikhail Mordkin, Vaslav Nijinsky, Tamara Karsavina
NOTE: 18 May 1909 was the date of the *répétition générale*—a full performance given before an invited audience. 19 May 1909 was the official premiere. An earlier version of this ballet was produced by the Imperial Ballet at the Maryinsky Theater, St. Petersburg, on 25 November 1907.

THE POLOVTSIAN DANCES
Ballet excerpt from the opera *Prince Igor*
Choreography: Michel Fokine
Music: Alexander Borodin
Costumes and decor: Nicholas Roerich
Premiere: 18 May 1909, Théâtre du Châtelet, Paris (see note: *Le Pavillon d'Armide*)
Principal dancers: Yelena Smirnova, Sophia Fedorova, Adolph Bolm
NOTE: This ballet was partly rechoreographed in 1923 by Bronislava Nijinska. The final ensemble, however, retained Fokine's choreography.

LE FESTIN
Suite of dances
Choreography: Marius Petipa, Michel Fokine, Alexander Gorsky, Nicolai Goltz, Felix Kchessinsky
Music: Nikolai Rimsky-Korsakov, Mikhail Glinka, Peter Ilitch Tchaikovsky, Alexander Glazunov, Modest Mussorgsky
Costumes: Léon Bakst, Alexandre Benois, Ivan Bilibin, Konstantin Korovin
Decor: Konstantin Korovin
Premiere: 18 May 1909, Théâtre du Châtelet, Paris (see note: *Le Pavillon d'Armide*)
Principal dancers: Tamara Karsavina, Vaslav Nijinsky, Mikhail Mordkin, Vera Karalli

LES SYLPHIDES
Choreography: Michel Fokine
Music: Frédéric Chopin, orchestrated by Igor Stravinsky, Alexander Glazunov, Sergei Taneyev
Costumes and decor: Alexandre Benois
Premiere: 2 June 1909, Théâtre du Châtelet, Paris
Principal dancers: Anna Pavlova, Tamara Karsavina, Vaslav Nijinsky, Alexandra Baldina
NOTE: 2 June 1909 was the date of the *répétition générale*. An earlier version of this ballet, with the title *Chopiniana*, was produced in March 1908 at the Maryinsky Theater, St. Petersburg.

CLEOPATRE
Choreography: Michel Fokine
Music: Anton Arensky, with additional numbers by Sergei Taneyev, Nikolai Rimsky-Korsakov, Mikhail Glinka, Alexander Glazunov, Modest Mussorgsky, Nicholas Tcherepnine
Libretto: after Alexander Pushkin
Costumes and decor: Léon Bakst
Premiere: 2 June 1909, Théâtre du Châtelet, Paris
Principal dancers: Ida Rubinstein, Anna Pavlova, Tamara Karsavina, Michel Fokine, Vaslav Nijinsky, Alexis Bulgakov
NOTE: 2 June 1909 was the date of the *répétition générale*. An earlier version of this ballet, with the title *Une Nuit d'Egypte* (also known as *Egyptian Nights*), was produced in March 1908 by the Imperial Ballet at the Maryinsky Theater, St. Petersburg. *Cléopâtre* was restaged in 1918 with a new pas de deux by Léonide Massine; decor by Robert Delaunay, and additional costumes by Sonia Delaunay.

1910

CARNAVAL
Choreography: Michel Fokine
Music: Robert Schumann, orchestrated by Nikolai Rimsky-Korsakov, Anatol Liadov, Alexander Glazunov, Nicholas Tcherepnine, Anton Arensky
Libretto: Michel Fokine and Léon Bakst
Costumes and decor: Léon Bakst
Premiere: 20 May 1910, Theater des Westens, Berlin
Principal dancers: Lydia Lopokova, Vera Fokina, Vaslav Nijinsky, Bronislava Nijinska, Adolph Bolm
NOTE: This ballet was first produced by the journal *Satyricon* at Pavlov Hall, St. Petersburg, 20 February 1910.

SCHEHERAZADE
Choreography: Michel Fokine
Music: Nikolai Rimsky-Korsakov
Libretto: Léon Bakst, Alexandre Benois, and Michel Fokine
Costumes and decor: Léon Bakst
Premiere: 4 June 1910, Théâtre National de l'Opéra, Paris
Principal dancers: Ida Rubinstein, Vaslav Nijinsky
NOTE: *Schéhérazade* is based on the first tale of *A Thousand and One Nights*.

GISELLE
Choreography: after Jean Coralli, Jules Perrot, and Marius Petipa, revised by Michel Fokine
Music: Adolphe Adam and Friedrich Burgmüller
Libretto: Vernoy de Saint-Georges and Théophile Gautier, after a theme by Heinrich Heine
Costumes and decor: Alexandre Benois
Premiere: 18 June 1910, Théâtre National de l'Opéra, Paris
Principal dancers: Tamara Karsavina, Vaslav Nijinsky, Elena Poliakova
NOTE: This ballet was first produced in 1841 at the Paris Opéra.

L'OISEAU DE FEU
(Firebird)
Choreography: Michel Fokine
Music: Igor Stravinsky
Libretto: Michel Fokine
Costumes: Alexander Golovin and Léon Bakst
Decor: Alexander Golovin
Premiere: 25 June 1910, Théâtre National de l'Opéra, Paris
Principal dancers: Tamara Karsavina, Vera Fokina, Michel Fokine, Alexis Bulgakov
NOTE: This ballet was restaged in 1926 with costumes and decor by Natalia Gontcharova.

LES ORIENTALES
Choreographic sketches
Choreography: Michel Fokine
Music: Edvard Grieg and Christian Sinding, orchestrated by Igor Stravinsky, Anton Arensky, Alexander Borodin, Alexander Glazunov
Costumes: Konstantin Korovin and Léon Bakst
Decor: Konstantin Korovin
Premiere: 25 June 1910, Théâtre National de l'Opéra, Paris
Principal dancers: Ekaterina Geltzer, Tamara Karsavina, Michel Fokine, Vaslav Nijinsky, Alexandre Volinine, Alexander Orlov

1911

LE SPECTRE DE LA ROSE
Choreography: Michel Fokine
Music: Carl Maria von Weber, orchestrated by Hector Berlioz
Libretto: Jean-Louis Vaudoyer, from a poem by Théophile Gautier
Costumes and decor: Léon Bakst
Premiere: 19 April 1911, Théâtre de Monte-Carlo
Principal dancers: Tamara Karsavina, Vaslav Nijinsky

NARCISSE
Choreography: Michel Fokine
Music: Nicholas Tcherepnine
Libretto: Léon Bakst
Costumes and decor: Léon Bakst
Premiere: 26 April 1911, Théâtre de Monte-Carlo
Principal dancers: Tamara Karsavina, Bronislava Nijinska, Vaslav Nijinsky, Vera Fokina

SADKO
Au Royaume Sous-marin
Scene 6 from the opera *Sadko*
Choreography: Michel Fokine
Music: Nikolai Rimsky-Korsakov
Costumes: Boris Anisfeld and Léon Bakst
Decor: Boris Anisfeld
Premiere: 6 June 1911, Théâtre du Châtelet, Paris
NOTE: This ballet was restaged in 1916 with choreography by Adolph Bolm and costumes and decor by Natalia Gontcharova.

PETROUCHKA
Choreography: Michel Fokine
Music: Igor Stravinsky
Libretto: Igor Stravinsky and Alexandre Benois
Costumes and decor: Alexandre Benois
Premiere: 13 June 1911, Théâtre du Châtelet, Paris
Principal dancers: Tamara Karsavina, Vaslav Nijinsky, Alexander Orlov, Enrico Cecchetti

LE LAC DES CYGNES
(Swan Lake)
Choreography: Marius Petipa and Lev Ivanov, with additions by Michel Fokine
Music: Peter Ilitch Tchaikovsky
Libretto: Vladimir Begichev and Vasily Geltzer
Costumes: Alexander Golovin
Decor: Konstantin Korovin and Alexander Golovin
Premiere: 30 November 1911, Royal Opera House, Covent Garden, London
Principal dancers: Mathilde Kchessinska, Vaslav Nijinsky
NOTE: This production was a two-act condensation of the four-act version by Marius Petipa and Lev Ivanov presented at the Maryinsky Theater, St. Petersburg, 1895. The decor and costumes, purchased by Diaghilev, were created for the 1901 Bolshoi production in Moscow.

1912

LE DIEU BLEU
Choreography: Michel Fokine
Music: Reynaldo Hahn
Libretto: Jean Cocteau and Frédéric de Madrazo
Costumes and decor: Léon Bakst
Premiere: 13 May 1912, Théâtre du Châtelet, Paris
Principal dancers: Tamara Karsavina, Lydia Nelidova, Vaslav Nijinsky, Max Frohman, Bronislava Nijinska

THAMAR
Choreography: Michel Fokine
Music: Mily Balakirev
Libretto: Léon Bakst, after a poem by Mikhail Lermontov
Costumes and decor: Léon Bakst
Premiere: 20 May 1912, Théâtre du Châtelet, Paris
Principal dancers: Tamara Karsavina, Adolph Bolm

L'APRES-MIDI D'UN FAUNE
(Afternoon of a Faun)
Choreography: Vaslav Nijinsky
Music: Claude Debussy
Libretto: after a poem by Stéphane Mallarmé
Costumes and decor: Léon Bakst
Premiere: 29 May 1912, Théâtre du Châtelet, Paris
Principal dancers: Lydia Nelidova, Vaslav Nijinsky
NOTE: This ballet was restaged in 1922 with a backdrop by Pablo Picasso.

DAPHNIS ET CHLOE
Choreography: Michel Fokine
Music: Maurice Ravel
Libretto: Michel Fokine, after Longus
Costumes and decor: Léon Bakst
Premiere: 8 June 1912, Théâtre du Châtelet, Paris
Principal dancers: Tamara Karsavina, Vaslav Nijinsky, Adolph Bolm

1913

JEUX
Choreography: Vaslav Nijinsky
Music: Claude Debussy
Costumes and decor: Léon Bakst
Premiere: 15 May 1913, Théâtre des Champs-Elysées, Paris
Principal dancers: Tamara Karsavina, Ludmilla Schollar, Vaslav Nijinsky

LE SACRE DU PRINTEMPS
(The Rite of Spring)
Choreography: Vaslav Nijinsky
Music: Igor Stravinsky
Libretto: Igor Stravinsky and
Nicholas Roerich
Costumes and decor: Nicholas
Roerich
Premiere: 29 May 1913, Théâtre
des Champs-Elysées, Paris
Principal dancers: Maria Piltz,
M. V. Guliuk, (?) Vorontzov
NOTE: This ballet was restaged
with choreography by Léonide
Massine in 1920.

LA TRAGEDIE DE SALOME
Choreography: Boris Romanov
Music: Florent Schmitt
Costumes and decor: Serge
Soudeikine
Premiere: 12 June 1913, Théâtre
des Champs-Elysées, Paris
Principal dancer: Tamara
Karsavina

1914

PAPILLONS
Choreography: Michel Fokine
Music: Robert Schumann,
orchestrated by Nicholas
Tcherepnine
Libretto: Michel Fokine
Costumes: Léon Bakst
Decor: Mstislav Dobujinsky
Premiere: 16 April 1914, Théâtre
de Monte-Carlo
Principal dancers: Tamara
Karsavina, Ludmilla Schollar,
Michel Fokine
NOTE: According to the Russian
edition of Fokine's *Memoirs*, this
ballet was first produced for a
literary fund benefit at the
Maryinsky Theater on 10 March
1912. Irina Proujan [Pruzhan] in
*Léon Bakst: Esquisses de Décors et
de Costumes, Arts Graphiques,
Peintures* (Leningrad, 1986) gives
the date of the first production as
30 September 1912.

LA LEGENDE DE JOSEPH
(Legend of Joseph)
Choreography: Michel Fokine
Music: Richard Strauss
Libretto: Count Harry Kessler and
Hugo von Hoffmannsthal
Costumes: Léon Bakst
Decor: José-María Sert
Premiere: 14 May 1914, Théâtre
National de l'Opéra, Paris
Principal dancers: Maria
Kuznetsova, Léonide Massine,
Vera Fokina, Alexis Bulgakov,
Serge Grigoriev

LE COQ D'OR
(The Golden Cockerel)
Opera-ballet in three tableaux
Choreography: Michel Fokine
Music: Nikolai Rimsky-Korsakov
Libretto: Vladimir Belsky, after
Alexander Pushkin, revised by
Alexandre Benois
Costumes and decor: Natalia
Gontcharova
Premiere: 24 May 1914, Théâtre
National de l'Opéra, Paris
Principal dancers: Adolph Bolm,
Alexis Bulgakov, Tamara
Karsavina

MIDAS
Choreography: Michel Fokine
Music: Maximilien Steinberg
Libretto: Léon Bakst, from Ovid
Costumes and decor: Mstislav
Dobujinsky
Premiere: 2 June 1914, Théâtre
National de l'Opéra, Paris
Principal dancers: Tamara
Karsavina, Adolph Bolm, Max
Frohman

1915

LE SOLEIL DE NUIT
(Midnight Sun)
Choreography: Léonide Massine
Music: Nikolai Rimsky-Korsakov
Costumes and decor: Mikhail
Larionov
Premiere: 20 December 1915,
Grand Théâtre, Geneva
Principal dancers: Léonide
Massine, Nicholas Zverev

1916

LAS MENINAS
Choreography: Léonide Massine
Music: Gabriel Fauré
Costumes: José-María Sert
Decor: Carlo Socrate
Premiere: 21 August 1916, Teatro
Eugenia-Victoria, San Sebastián,
Spain
Principal dancers: Lydia Sokolova,
Léonide Massine, Léon
Woizikovsky, Olga Kokhlova

KIKIMORA
Choreography: Léonide Massine
Music: Anatol Liadov
Costumes and decor: Mikhail
Larionov
Premiere: 25 August 1916, Teatro
Eugenia-Victoria, San Sebastián,
Spain
Principal dancers: Maria
Chabelska, Stanislas Idzikovsky

TILL EULENSPIEGEL
Choreography: Vaslav Nijinsky
Music: Richard Strauss
Libretto: Vaslav Nijinsky, after
Charles de Coster
Costumes and decor: Robert
Edmond Jones
Premiere: 23 October 1916,
Manhattan Opera House, New
York
Principal dancer: Vaslav Nijinsky

1917

FEU D'ARTIFICE
(Fireworks)
Symphonic poem
Music: Igor Stravinsky
*Decor, lighting, and scenic
adjuncts:* Giacomo Balla
Premiere: 12 April 1917, Teatro
Costanzi, Rome

LES FEMMES
DE BONNE HUMEUR
(The Good-Humoured
Ladies)
Choreography: Léonide Massine
Music: Domenico Scarlatti,
orchestrated by Vincenzo
Tommasini
Libretto: after Carlo Goldoni
Costumes and decor: Léon Bakst
Premiere: 12 April 1917, Teatro
Costanzi, Rome
Principal dancers: Lydia
Lopokova, Lubov Tchernicheva,
Léonide Massine, Enrico
Cecchetti, Stanislas Idzikovsky,
Léon Woizikovsky, Josephine
Cecchetti

CONTES RUSSES
Choreography: Léonide Massine
Music: Anatol Liadov
Libretto: Léonide Massine
Costumes: Mikhail Larionov and
Natalia Gontcharova
Decor and drop curtain: Mikhail
Larionov
Premiere: 11 May 1917, Théâtre
du Châtelet, Paris
Principal dancers: Lubov
Tchernicheva, Lydia Sokolova,
Léon Woizikovsky, Stanislas
Idzikovsky, Jean Jazvinsky

PARADE
Choreography: Léonide Massine
Music: Erik Satie
Libretto: Jean Cocteau
Costumes and decor: Pablo Picasso
Premiere: 18 May 1917, Théâtre
du Châtelet, Paris
Principal dancers: Lydia
Lopokova, Maria Chabelska,
Léonide Massine, Nicholas
Zverev

1919

LA BOUTIQUE
FANTASQUE
Choreography: Léonide Massine
Music: Gioacchino Rossini,
orchestrated by Ottorino Respighi
*Costumes, drop curtain, and
decor:* André Derain
Premiere: 5 June 1919, Alhambra
Theatre, London
Principal dancers: Lydia
Lopokova, Léonide Massine

LE TRICORNE

Choreography: Léonide Massine
Music: Manuel de Falla
Libretto: Gregorio Martínez
Sierra, after Pedro Antonio de
Alarcón
*Costumes, drop curtain, and
decor:* Pablo Picasso
Premiere: 22 July 1919, Alhambra
Theatre, London
Principal dancers: Tamara
Karsavina, Léonide Massine,
Léon Woizikovsky

1920

LE CHANT DU ROSSIGNOL
(Song of the Nightingale)

Choreography: Léonide Massine
Music: Igor Stravinsky
Libretto: Igor Stravinsky and
Léonide Massine, after Hans
Christian Andersen
*Costumes, drop curtain, and
decor:* Henri Matisse
Premiere: 2 February 1920,
Théâtre National de l'Opéra, Paris
Principal dancers: Tamara
Karsavina, Lydia Sokolova, Serge
Grigoriev, Stanislas Idzikovsky
NOTE: This ballet was restaged
with choreography by George
Balanchine in 1925.

PULCINELLA

Choreography: Léonide Massine
Music: Igor Stravinsky, after
Giambattista Pergolesi
*Costumes, drop curtain, and
decor:* Pablo Picasso
Premiere: 15 May 1920, Théâtre
National de l'Opéra, Paris
Principal dancers: Tamara
Karsavina, Lubov Tchernicheva,
Vera Nemchinova, Léonide
Massine, Stanislas Idzikovsky,
Enrico Cecchetti

LE ASTUZIE FEMMINILI

Opéra-ballet in three tableaux
Choreography: Léonide Massine
Music: Domenico Cimarosa,
orchestrated by Ottorino Respighi
Costumes and decor: José-María
Sert
Premiere: 27 May 1920, Théâtre
National de l'Opéra, Paris
Principal dancers: Tamara
Karsavina, Lubov Tchernicheva,
Vera Nemchinova, Lydia
Sokolova, Stanislas Idzikovsky,
Léon Woizikovsky, Zigmund
Novak
NOTE: See also *Ballet de L'Astuce
Feminine,* 1924.

1921

CHOUT
(Le Bouffon)

Choreography: Mikhail Larionov
and Thadée Slavinsky
Music: Serge Prokofiev
*Costumes, drop curtain, and
decor:* Mikhail Larionov
Premiere: 17 May 1921, Théâtre
de la Gaîté-Lyrique, Paris
Principal dancers: Catharine
Devillier, Tadeo Slavinsky, Jean
Jazvinsky

CUADRO FLAMENCO

Suite of Andalusian
songs and dances
Music: arranged by
Manuel de Falla
Costumes and decor: Pablo Picasso
Premiere: 17 May 1921, Théâtre
de la Gaîté-Lyrique, Paris
Principal dancers: María
Dalbaicín, La Rubia de Jérez, La
Gabrielita del Gorrotín, La
López, El Tejero, El Moreno

THE SLEEPING PRINCESS

Choreography: Marius Petipa,
with additional dances by
Bronislava Nijinska
Music: Peter Ilitch Tchaikovsky,
partly reorchestrated by Igor
Stravinsky
Libretto: Ivan Vsevolozhsky and
Marius Petipa, after Charles
Perrault
Costumes and decor: Léon Bakst
Premiere: 2 November 1921,
Alhambra Theatre, London
Principal dancers: Olga
Spessivtzeva, Lydia Lopokova,
Pierre Vladimirov
NOTE: *The Sleeping Princess* was
Diaghilev's revised version of
Marius Petipa's classical ballet *The
Sleeping Beauty,* which had its
premiere at the Maryinsky
Theater, St. Petersburg, 1890.

1922

LE MARIAGE D'AURORE
(Aurora's Wedding)

Choreography: Marius Petipa,
with additions by Bronislava
Nijinska
Music: Peter Ilitch Tchaikovsky,
reorchestrated by Igor Stravinsky
Costumes and decor: Alexandre
Benois and Natalia Gontcharova
Premiere: 18 May 1922, Théâtre
National de l'Opéra, Paris
Principal dancers: Vera Trefilova,
Pierre Vladimirov
NOTE: Bronislava Nijinska created
Le Mariage d'Aurore from the first
and last acts of *The Sleeping
Princess.* The production used
Benois's set and costumes from *Le
Pavillon d'Armide* (1909), with
additional costumes for the fairy-
tale characters by Natalia
Gontcharova.

LE RENARD

Choreography: Bronislava Nijinska
Music: Igor Stravinsky
Libretto: Igor Stravinsky
Costumes and decor: Mikhail
Larionov
Premiere: 18 May 1922, Théâtre
National de l'Opéra, Paris
Principal dancers: Bronislava
Nijinska, Stanislas Idzikovsky,
Jean Jazvinsky, Michel Fedorov
NOTE: This ballet was restaged
with new choreography by Serge
Lifar in 1929.

1923

LES NOCES
(The Wedding)

Choreography: Bronislava Nijinska
Music: Igor Stravinsky
Libretto: Igor Stravinsky
Costumes and decor: Natalia
Gontcharova
Premiere: 13 June 1923, Théâtre
de la Gaîté-Lyrique, Paris
Principal dancers: Felia
Doubrovska, Nicholas Semenov

LA FETE MERVEILLEUSE

Choreography: Bronislava Nijinska
Music: Peter Ilitch Tchaikovsky,
reorchestrated by Igor Stravinsky
Costumes: Juan Gris
Premiere: 30 June 1923, Hall of
Mirrors, Palace of Versailles
NOTE: This gala benefit pageant
was composed of excerpts from *Le
Mariage d'Aurore,* with added
vocal interludes.

1924

LES TENTATIONS DE LA BERGERE, OU L'AMOUR VAINQUEUR
(The Temptations of the Shepherdess, or Love Triumphant)
Choreography: Bronislava Nijinska
Music: Michel de Montéclair, arranged and orchestrated by Henri Casadesus
Libretto: Boris Kochno
Costumes and decor: Juan Gris
Premiere: 3 January 1924, Théâtre de Monte-Carlo
Principal dancers: Vera Nemchinova, Léon Woizikovsky, Anatole Vilzak, Thadée Slavinsky

LES BICHES
Choreography: Bronislava Nijinska
Music: Francis Poulenc
Costumes, drop curtain, and decor: Marie Laurencin
Premiere: 6 January 1924, Théâtre de Monte-Carlo
Principal dancers: Bronislava Nijinska, Vera Nemchinova, Lubov Tchernicheva, Lydia Sokolova, Anatole Vilzak, Léon Woizikovsky, Nicholas Zverev

BALLET DE L'ASTUCE FEMININE
Choreography: Léonide Massine
Music: Domenico Cimarosa, orchestrated by Ottorino Respighi
Costumes and decor: José-María Sert
Premiere: 8 January 1924, Théâtre de Monte-Carlo
Principal dancers: Vera Nemchinova, Lubov Tchernicheva, Lydia Sokolova, Stanislas Idzikovsky, Léon Woizikovsky, Anatole Vilzak
NOTE: This work was a suite of dances excerpted from *Le Astuzie Femminili* (1920). The title was subsequently changed to *Cimarosiana*.

LES FACHEUX
Choreography: Bronislava Nijinska
Music: Georges Auric
Libretto: Boris Kochno, after Molière
Costumes, drop curtain, and decor: Georges Braque
Premiere: 19 January 1924, Théâtre de Monte-Carlo
Principal dancers: Lubov Tchernicheva, Anatole Vilzak, Anton Dolin, Bronislava Nijinska

LA NUIT SUR LE MONT CHAUVE
(Night on Bald Mountain)
Choreography: Bronislava Nijinska
Music: Modest Mussorgsky
Costumes and decor: Natalia Gontcharova
Premiere: 6 April 1924, Théâtre de Monte-Carlo
Principal dancers: Lydia Sokolova, Michel Fedorov
NOTE: *La Nuit sur le Mont Chauve* is the ballet act from the opera *La Foire de Sorotchintzi* (*Sorochintsy Fair*).

LE TRAIN BLEU
Choreography: Bronislava Nijinska
Music: Darius Milhaud
Libretto: Jean Cocteau
Costumes: Gabrielle (Coco) Chanel
Decor: Henri Laurens
Drop curtain: Pablo Picasso
Premiere: 20 June 1924, Théâtre des Champs-Elysées, Paris
Principal dancers: Bronislava Nijinska, Lydia Sokolova, Anton Dolin, Léon Woizikovsky

1925

ZEPHIRE ET FLORE
Choreography: Léonide Massine
Music: Vladimir Dukelsky (Vernon Duke)
Libretto: Boris Kochno
Costumes and decor: Georges Braque
Premiere: 28 April 1925, Théâtre de Monte-Carlo
Principal dancers: Alice Nikitina, Anton Dolin, Serge Lifar
NOTE: Masks and symbols by Oliver Messel were added after the premiere, and in 1926 the ballet was partly rechoreographed by Massine.

LES MATELOTS
(The Sailors)
Choreography: Léonide Massine
Music: Georges Auric
Libretto: Boris Kochno
Costumes, drop curtain, and decor: Pedro Pruna
Premiere: 17 June 1925, Théâtre de la Gaîté-Lyrique, Paris
Principal dancers: Vera Nemchinova, Lydia Sokolova, Léon Woizikovsky, Serge Lifar, Thadée Slavinsky

BARABAU
Choreography: George Balanchine
Music: Vittorio Rieti
Libretto: Vittorio Rieti
Costumes and decor: Maurice Utrillo
Premiere: 11 December 1925, Coliseum Theatre, London
Principal dancers: Léon Woizikovsky, Serge Lifar, Tatiana Chamié, Alice Nikitina, Alexandra Danilova, Tamara Geva

1926

ROMEO AND JULIET
Choreography: Bronislava Nijinska, with entr'acte by George Balanchine
Music: Constant Lambert
Libretto: Boris Kochno, after William Shakespeare
Front curtain, back curtain for Act I, and scenic adjuncts: Joan Miró
Back curtains for Act II: Max Ernst
Premiere: 4 May 1926, Théâtre de Monte-Carlo
Principal dancers: Tamara Karsavina, Serge Lifar

LA PASTORALE
Choreography: George Balanchine
Music: Georges Auric
Libretto: Boris Kochno
Costumes, drop curtain, and decor: Pedro Pruna
Premiere: 29 May 1926, Théâtre Sarah-Bernhardt, Paris
Principal dancers: Felia Doubrovska, Tamara Geva, Serge Lifar, Thadée Slavinsky

JACK-IN-THE-BOX
Choreography: George Balanchine
Music: Erik Satie, orchestrated by Darius Milhaud
Costumes and decor: André Derain
Premiere: 3 July 1926, Théâtre Sarah-Bernhardt, Paris
Principal dancers: Alexandra Danilova, Stanislas Idzikovsky

THE TRIUMPH OF NEPTUNE
Choreography: George Balanchine
Music: Lord Berners
Libretto: Sacheverell Sitwell
Costumes: Pedro Pruna, adapted by Prince Alexander Schervashidze
Decor: after George and Robert Cruikshank, adapted by Prince Alexander Schervashidze
Premiere: 3 December 1926, Lyceum Theatre, London
Principal dancers: Alexandra Danilova, Lubov Tchernicheva, Lydia Sokolova, Serge Lifar, George Balanchine

1927

LA CHATTE
Choreography: George Balanchine
Music: Henri Sauguet
Scenario: Sobeka (Boris Kochno), after Aesop
Costumes and decor: Naum Gabo and Antoine Pevsner
Premiere: 30 April 1927, Théâtre de Monte-Carlo
Principal dancers: Olga Spessivtzeva, Serge Lifar

MERCURE
Choreography: Léonide Massine
Music: Erik Satie
Costumes and decor: Pablo Picasso
Premiere: 2 June 1927, Théâtre Sarah-Bernhardt, Paris
Principal dancers: Vera Petrova, Léonide Massine
NOTE: This ballet was originally produced in 1924 by Comte Etienne de Beaumont's Les Soirées de Paris.

LE PAS D'ACIER
Choreography: Léonide Massine
Music: Serge Prokofiev
Libretto: Serge Prokofiev and Georgii Yakulov
Costumes and decor: Georgii Yakulov
Premiere: 7 June 1927, Théâtre Sarah-Bernhardt, Paris
Principal dancers: Lubov Tchernicheva, Alexandra Danilova, Vera Petrova, Léonide Massine, Serge Lifar, Léon Woizikovsky

1928

ODE
Choreography: Léonide Massine
Music: Nicolas Nabokov
Libretto: Boris Kochno
Costumes and decor: Pavel Tchelitchev
Premiere: 6 June 1928, Théâtre Sarah-Bernhardt, Paris
Principal dancers: Irina Beline, Felia Doubrovska, Alice Nikitina, Léonide Massine, Serge Lifar
NOTE: The projections and lighting effects were by Pierre Charbonnier.

APOLLON MUSAGETE
Choreography: George Balanchine
Music: Igor Stravinsky
Libretto: Igor Stravinsky
Costumes and decor: André Bauchant
Premiere: 12 June 1928, Théâtre Sarah-Bernhardt, Paris
Principal dancers: Alice Nikitina, Lubov Tchernicheva, Felia Doubrovska, Serge Lifar
NOTE: In 1929 this ballet was given with new costumes by Gabrielle (Coco) Chanel.

THE GODS GO A-BEGGING
(Les Dieux Mendiants)
Choreography: George Balanchine
Music: George Frideric Handel, arranged by Thomas Beecham
Libretto: Sobeka (Boris) Kochno
Costumes: Juan Gris (from *Les Tentations de la Bergère*)
Decor: Léon Bakst (from *Daphnis et Chloë*)
Premiere: 16 July 1928, His Majesty's Theatre, London
Principal dancers: Alexandra Danilova, Lubov Tchernicheva, Felia Doubrovska, Léon Woizikovsky, Constantin Tcherkas

1929

LE BAL
Choreography: George Balanchine
Music: Vittorio Rieti
Libretto: Boris Kochno
Costumes and decor: Giorgio de Chirico
Premiere: 9 May 1929, Théâtre de Monte-Carlo
Principal dancers: Alexandra Danilova, Felia Doubrovska, Anton Dolin, Léon Woizikovsky, George Balanchine, Serge Lifar

LE FILS PRODIGUE
(The Prodigal Son)
Choreography: George Balanchine
Music: Serge Prokofiev
Libretto: Boris Kochno
Costumes and decor: Georges Rouault
Premiere: 21 May 1929, Théâtre Sarah-Bernhardt, Paris
Principal dancers: Felia Doubrovska, Serge Lifar, Léon Woizikovsky, Anton Dolin

Operas

Produced by

Serge Diaghilev

━━━━━

Compiled by

Lynn Garafola

▼

THIS CHRONOLOGY draws principally on contemporary programs and reviews. Titles are given in their best-known forms. In the case of names, the spelling generally follows *The New Grove Dictionary of Music and Musicians*. The names of performers not listed in *Grove* or other standard sources are given as they appeared on programs or in the press.

When a *répétition générale* preceded the official premiere, the earlier date is given followed by an asterisk (*)

1908

BORIS GODUNOV

Music: Modest Mussorgsky, revised and orchestrated by Nikolai Rimsky-Korsakov
Libretto: Modest Mussorgsky, after Alexander Pushkin
Conductor: Felix Blumenfeld
Chorus master: Ulric Avranek
Stage direction: Alexander Sanin
Sets: Alexander Golovin, Alexandre Benois, Konstantin Yuon
Costumes: Ivan Bilibin, Dmitri Stelletsky, Alexander Golovin, Boris Anisfeld, Eugene Lanceray, Stepan Yaremich, Konstantin Yuon, Alexandre Benois
Premiere: 19 May 1908, Théâtre National de l'Opéra, Paris
Principal singers: Feodor Chaliapin, Natasha Yermolenko, Vladimir Kastorsky, Elisabeth [Elisabeta] Petrenko, Dagmara Renine, Jean [Ivan] Altchevsky, Basile [Vasily] Sharonov, Dmitri Smirnov, Claudia Tugarinova, Nikolai Kedrov, [?] Tolkatchev, Mitrofan Chuprynnikov, Mikhail Kravchenko
NOTE: This opera was first produced in 1890 in St. Petersburg.

1909

PRINCE IGOR

Polovtsian Scenes and Dances
(Act II of the opera)
Music: Alexander Borodin, completed and partly orchestrated by Nikolai Rimsky-Korsakov and Alexander Glazunov
Libretto: Alexander Borodin, after a scenario by Vladimir Stasov
Conductor: Emile Cooper
Chorus master: Ulric Avranek
Sets and costumes: Nicholas Roerich
Scene painting: Boris Anisfeld
Rehearsal director: Alexander Sanin
Choreography: Michel Fokine
Premiere: 18 May 1909,* Théâtre du Châtelet, Paris
Principal singers: Elisabeth [Elisabeta] Petrenko, Basile [Vasily] Sharonov, Dmitri Smirnov, Kapitan Zaporojetz, Michel d'Arial
Principal dancers: Adolph Bolm, Sophia Fedorova, Yelena Smirnova
NOTE: This opera was first produced in 1890 in St. Petersburg.

IVAN THE TERRIBLE
(The Maid of Pskov)

Music: Nikolai Rimsky-Korsakov
Libretto: Nikolai Rimsky-Korsakov, after Lev Mey
Conductor: Nicholas Tcherepnine
Chorus master: Ulric Avranek
Stage direction: Alexander Sanin
Sets: Alexander Golovin, Nicholas Roerich
Costumes: Dmitri Stelletsky
Scene painting: [?] Vnoukow (Scene 1), Boris Anisfeld (Scenes 2, 4, 5), Nikolai Charbé (Scene 3)
Premiere: 24 May 1909,* Théâtre du Châtelet, Paris
Principal singers: Feodor Chaliapin, Alexander Davydov, Vladimir Kastorsky, Lydia Lipkowska, Elisabeth [Elisabeta] Petrenko, Basile [Vasily] Sharonov, Basile [Vasily] Damaev, [?] Pavlova
NOTE: The third and final version of this opera was first produced in 1895 in St. Petersburg.

RUSLAN AND LUDMILLA

(Act I)
Music: Mikhail Glinka
Libretto: Konstantin Bakhturin, Valerian Shirkov, and others, after Pushkin
Conductor: Emile Cooper
Chorus master: Ulric Avranek
Stage direction: Alexander Sanin
Sets and costumes: Konstantin Korovin
Premiere: 2 June 1909,* Théâtre du Châtelet, Paris
Principal singers: Vladimir Kastorsky, Lydia Lipkowska, Basile [Vasily] Sharonov, Dmitri Smirnov, Kapitan Zaporojetz, Yevgenia Zbruyeva
NOTE: This opera was first produced in 1842 in St. Petersburg.

JUDITH

(Act III)
Music: Alexander Serov
Libretto: A. Maykov and others, after the Book of Judith
Conductor: Emile Cooper
Chorus master: Ulric Avranek
Stage direction: Alexander Sanin
Sets: Valentin Serov, Léon Bakst
Costumes: Léon Bakst
Premiere: 7 June 1909, Théâtre du Châtelet, Paris
Principal singers: Feodor Chaliapin, Félia Litvinne, Dmitri Smirnov, Kapitan Zaporojetz, Yevgenia Zbruyeva
NOTE: This opera was first produced in 1863 in St. Petersburg.

1 9 1 3

BORIS GODUNOV

Music: Modest Mussorgsky, revised and orchestrated by Nikolai Rimsky-Korsakov
Libretto: Modest Mussorgsky, after Alexander Pushkin
Conductor: Emile Cooper
Chorus master: [?] Pokhitonov
Stage direction: Alexander Sanin
Sets: Konstantin Yuon, Léon Bakst (Act II) *Costumes:* Ivan Bilibin, Léon Bakst, Konstantin Yuon
Premiere: 22 May 1913, Théâtre des Champs-Elysées, Paris
Principal singers: Feodor Chaliapin, Nicolas Andreyev, Paul [Pavel] Andreyev, Basile [Vasily] Damaev, Hélène Nikolaeva, Elisabeth [Elisabeta] Petrenko, Marie Brian, Alexandre Belianin, Kapitan Zaporojetz, [?] Davidova, Nikolai Bolshakov, [?] Alexandrovitch
NOTE: The opera, in its original form, was first produced in 1874 in St. Petersburg, and in Rimsky-Korsakov's revised version in 1896. The first performance in London of the Diaghilev production was on 24 June 1913 at the Theatre Royal, Drury Lane.

KHOVANSHCHINA

Music: Modest Mussorgsky, completed and orchestrated by Nikolai Rimsky-Korsakov, with additional passages orchestrated by Maurice Ravel and Igor Stravinsky
Libretto: Modest Mussorgsky, Vladimir Stasov
Conductor: Emile Cooper
Stage direction: Alexander Sanin
Sets and costumes: Feodor Fedorovsky
Choreography: Adolph Bolm
Premiere: 5 June 1913, Théâtre des Champs-Elysées, Paris
Principal singers: Feodor Chaliapin, Paul [Pavel] Andreyev, Nicolas Andreyev, Alexandre Belianin, Nikolai Bolshakov, Marie Brian, Basile [Vasily] Damaev, Hélène Nikolaeva, Elisabeth [Elisabeta] Petrenko, Kapitan Zaporojetz, [?] Alexandrovitch, [?] Strobinder
NOTE: This opera was first produced in 1886 in St. Petersburg. The first performance in London of the Diaghilev production was on 1 July 1913 at the Theatre Royal, Drury Lane.

IVAN THE TERRIBLE
(The Maid of Pskov)

Music: Nikolai Rimsky-Korsakov, after Lev Mey
Libretto: Nikolai Rimsky-Korsakov, after Lev Mey
Conductor: Emile Cooper
Sets and costumes: Alexander Golovin
Premiere: 8 July 1913, Theatre Royal, Drury Lane, London
Principal singers: Feodor Chaliapin, Nicolas Andreyev, Paul [Pavel] Andreyev, Marie Brian, Basile [Vasily] Damaev, Hélène Nikolaeva, Elisabeth [Elisabeta] Petrenko, Kapitan Zaporojetz
NOTE: The third and final version of this opera was first produced in 1895 in St. Petersburg.

1 9 1 4

LE COQ D'OR
(The Golden Cockerel)

Music: Nikolai Rimsky-Korsakov
Libretto: Vladimir Belsky, after Alexander Pushkin, revised by Alexandre Benois
Conductor: Pierre Monteux
Chorus master: Nicolas Palitzine
Stage direction: Michel Fokine
Sets and costumes: Natalia Gontcharova
Choreography: Michel Fokine
Premiere: 24 May 1914, Théâtre National de l'Opéra, Paris
Principal singers: Jean [Ivan] Altchevsky, Alexandre Belianin, Aurelia Dobrovolska, Elisabeth [Elisabeta] Petrenko, Hélène Nikolaeva, Basile [Vasily] Petrov
Principal dancers: Tamara Karsavina, Adolph Bolm, Alexis Bulgakov
NOTE: This opera was first produced in 1909 in Moscow. The first performance in London of the Diaghilev production was on 15 June 1914 at the Theatre Royal, Drury Lane.

LE ROSSIGNOL

Music: Igor Stravinsky
Libretto: Igor Stravinsky and Stepan Mitusov, after Hans Christian Andersen
Conductor: Pierre Monteux
Chorus master: Nicolas Palitzine
Stage direction: Alexandre Benois, Alexander Sanin
Sets and costumes: Alexandre Benois
Scene painting: Nikolai Charbé
Choreography: Boris Romanov
Premiere: 26 May 1914, Théâtre National de l'Opéra, Paris
Principal singers: Paul [Pavel] Andreyev, Alexandre Belianin, Marie Brian, Aurelia Dobrovolska, Fedor Ernst, Nicolas Goulaiev, Elisabeth Mamsina, Elisabeth [Elisabeta] Petrenko, Basile [Vasily] Sharonov, Alexandre Varfolomeev
Principal dancers: Max Frohman, Nicolas Kremnev
NOTE: The first London performance was on 18 June 1914 at the Theatre Royal, Drury Lane.

PRINCE IGOR

Music: Alexander Borodin, completed and partly orchestrated by Nikolai Rimsky-Korsakov and Alexander Glazunov
Libretto: Alexander Borodin, after a scenario by Vladimir Stasov
Conductor: Leon [Lev] Steinberg
Choreography: Michel Fokine
Premiere: 8 June 1914, Theatre Royal, Drury Lane, London
Principal singers: Feodor Chaliapin, Nicolas Andreyev, Paul [Pavel] Andreyev, Marie Brian, Maria Kuznetsova, Elisabeth Mamsina, Elisabeth [Elisabeta] Petrenko, Basile [Vasily] Sharonov, Alexandre Varfolomeev
NOTE: This opera was first produced in 1890 in St. Petersburg.

MAY NIGHT

Music: Nikolai Rimsky-Korsakov
Libretto: Nikolai Rimsky-Korsakov, after Nikolai Gogol
Conductor: Leon [Lev] Steinberg
Premiere: 26 June 1914, Theatre Royal, Drury Lane, London
Principal singers: Paul [Pavel] Andreyev, Alexandre Belianin, Marie Brian, Fedor Ernst, Elisabeth Mamsina, Elisabeth [Elisabeta] Petrenko, Basile [Vasily] Sharonov, Dmitri Smirnov
NOTE: This opera was first produced in 1880 in St. Petersburg.

1 9 2 2

MAVRA

Music: Igor Stravinsky
Libretto: Boris Kochno, after Alexander Pushkin
Conductor: Gregor Fitelberg
Stage direction: Bronislava Nijinska
Sets and costumes: Léopold Survage
Premiere: 3 June 1922, Théâtre National de l'Opéra, Paris
Principal singers: Zoia Rosovska, Hélène Sadoven, Stephan [Stefan] Belina-Skupevsky, Oda Slobodskaya

1924

LA COLOMBE

Music: Charles Gounod, with new recitatives by Francis Poulenc
Libretto: Jules Barbier and Michel Carré, after Jean de La Fontaine
Conductor: Edouard Flament
Stage direction: Constantin Landau
Sets and costumes: Juan Gris
Scene painting: Vladimir and Violet Polunin
Premiere: 1 January 1924, Théâtre de Monte-Carlo
Principal singers: Maria Barrientos, Jeanne Montfort, Théodore Ritch, Daniel Vigneau
NOTE: This opera was first produced in 1860 in Baden-Baden.

LE MEDECIN MALGRE LUI

Music: Charles Gounod, with new recitatives by Erik Satie
Libretto: Jules Barbier and Michel Carré, after Molière
Conductor: Edouard Flament
Chorus master: Amédée de Sabata
Stage direction: Alexandre Benois
Sets and costumes: Alexandre Benois
Choreography: Bronislava Nijinska
Premiere: 5 January 1924, Théâtre de Monte-Carlo
Principal singers: Jacques Arnna, Inès Ferraris, Jeanne Montfort, Théodore Ritch, Daniel Vigneau, Albert Garcia
Principal dancers: Anton Dolin, Lubov Tchernicheva
NOTE: This opera was first produced in 1858 in Paris.

PHILEMON ET BAUCIS

Music: Charles Gounod
Libretto: Jules Barbier and Michel Carré
Conductor: Edouard Flament
Chorus master: Amédée de Sabata
Stage direction: Alexandre Benois
Sets and costumes: Alexandre Benois
Scene painting: Vladimir and Violet Polunin
Premiere: 10 January 1924, Théâtre de Monte-Carlo
Principal singers: Maria Barrientos, Nazzareno De Angelis, Alesio De Paolis
NOTE: This opera was first produced in 1860 in Paris.

UNE EDUCATION MANQUEE

Music: Emmanuel Chabrier, with new recitatives by Darius Milhaud
Libretto: E. Leterrier, A. Vanloo
Conductor: Edouard Flament
Stage direction: Alexandre Benois
Sets and costumes: Juan Gris
Premiere: 17 January 1924, Théâtre de Monte-Carlo
Principal singers: Inès Ferraris, Théodore Ritch, Daniel Vigneau
NOTE: This opera was first produced in 1879 in Paris.

1927

OEDIPUS REX

Music: Igor Stravinsky
Libretto: Jean Cocteau, after Sophocles, in a Latin translation by Jean Daniélou
Conductor: Igor Stravinsky
Premiere: 30 May 1927, Théâtre Sarah-Bernhardt, Paris
Principal singers: Stephan [Stefan] Belina-Skupevsky, Michel d'Arial, Georges Lanskoy, Hélène Sadoven, Kapitan Zaporojetz
Narrator: Pierre Brasseur

Jean Cocteau,
Karsavina in "Le Spectre de la
Rose," 1911, cat. no. 1.

Checklist
of the
Exhibition
▼

OBJECTS have been organized by medium and are listed alphabetically by artist and then chronologically by date. Archival material is listed chronologically. Dimensions are given in inches, height preceding width.

POSTERS

Jean Cocteau
(French, 1889-1963)

1 *Karsavina in* LE SPECTRE DE LA ROSE
Châtelet/Grande Saison de Paris/ Ballet Russe, 1911
Lithograph poster, 77 × 48 in.
Severin Wunderman Museum

2 *Karsavina in* LE SPECTRE DE LA ROSE
Théâtre de Monte-Carlo/Ballet Russe, 19 April 1911
Lithograph poster, 38¾ × 25 in.
Severin Wunderman Museum

3 *Nijinsky in* LE SPECTRE DE LA ROSE
Théâtre de Monte-Carlo/Ballet Russe, 19 April 1911
Lithograph poster, 38¾ × 25 in.
Severin Wunderman Museum

Pablo Picasso
(Spanish, 1881-1973)

4 *Ballets Russes/Théâtre Lyrique Municipal de la Gaîté*, 13-21 June 1923
Lithograph poster, 48⅜ × 33½ in.
Nijinska Archives

Valentin Serov
(Russian, 1865-1911)

5 *Pavlova in* LES SYLPHIDES
Théâtre du Châtelet/Saison Russe/Opéra et Ballet, May-June, 1909
Lithograph poster, 69⅞ × 90⅞ in.
Collection Mr. and Mrs. Nikita D. Lobanov-Rostovsky

DRAWINGS, PRINTS, AND PAINTINGS

Léon Bakst
(Russian, 1866-1924)

6 Design for decor for *Schéhérazade*, 1910
Pencil, watercolor, gouache, and metallic paint on paper, 29 × 40½ in.
Collection Robert L. B. Tobin

7 Fabric design for *Schéhérazade*, 1910
Pencil and watercolor on paper, 19⁹⁄₁₆ × 24 in.
Cooper-Hewitt Museum, the Smithsonian Institution's National Museum of Design

8 Costume design for the Sultan Zeman in *Schéhérazade*, 1910
Pencil, watercolor, and gold paint on paper, 12 × 9¼ in.
The Fine Arts Museums of San Francisco, Achenbach Foundation for Graphic Arts, Gift of Mrs. Adolph B. Spreckels

9 *Le Secret du Harem*, ca. 1912
Oil on canvas board, 17½ × 23½ in.
Collection Robert L. B. Tobin

10 Design for decor for *Le Dieu Bleu*, 1912
Gouache on paper, 10 × 14 in.
Collection George Riabov

11 Costume design for a Negro Dancer in *Le Dieu Bleu*, 1922, after 1912 original
Pencil, charcoal, watercolor, gouache, and gold paint on paper, 25⅛ × 18⅛ in.
Collection Robert L. B. Tobin

12 Fabric design for *Le Dieu Bleu*, 1912
Transfer lines, gouache, and metallic paint on paper, 11½ × 17⅝ in.
Collection Robert L. B. Tobin

13 Variation for decor, Scenes 1 and 3, *Daphnis et Chloë*, 1912
Pencil on paper, 10½ × 15½ in.
Collection Robert L. B. Tobin

14 Costume design for the Brigands in *Daphnis et Chloë*, 1912
Pencil and watercolor on paper, 10½ × 15⅝ in.
Cooper-Hewitt Museum, the Smithsonian Institution's National Museum of Design

15 Costume design for a Warrior in *Daphnis et Chloë*, 1912
Pencil, watercolor, and silver paint on paper, 10⅝ × 6⅜ in.
The Fine Arts Museums of San Francisco, Achenbach Foundation for Graphic Arts, Gift of Mrs. Adolph B. Spreckels

16 Costume design for Potiphar's Wife in *La Légende de Joseph*, 1914
Pencil, watercolor, and gold paint on paper, 19 × 13 in.
The Fine Arts Museums of San Francisco, Achenbach Foundation for Graphic Arts, Gift of Mrs. Adolph B. Spreckels

17 Design for decor for *The Sleeping Princess*, 1921
Pencil, charcoal, and watercolor on paper, 11⅝ × 17¾ in.
Collection Robert L. B. Tobin

18 Design for decor for *The Sleeping Princess*, Act II, The Forest Scene, 1921
Charcoal, watercolor, and gouache on paper, 12¼ × 19 in.
Collection Robert L. B. Tobin

19 Design for decor for *The Sleeping Princess*, Act III, The Forest of the Lilac Fairy, 1921
Pencil, watercolor, and gouache on paper, 12¾ × 19 in.
Collection Robert L. B. Tobin

20 Costume design for the Lilac Fairy in *The Sleeping Princess*, 1921
Pencil, watercolor, and silver paint on paper, 17¼ × 11 in.
Collection Robert L. B. Tobin

21 Costume design for the Master of Ceremonies in *The Sleeping Princess*, 1921
Pencil, watercolor, gouache, and gold and silver paint on paper, 19 × 12 13/16 in.
Collection Robert L. B. Tobin

22 Costume design for a Minister of State in *The Sleeping Princess*, 1921
Pencil, gouache, and gold paint on paper, 11 7/8 × 9 in.
The Fine Arts Museums of San Francisco, Achenbach Foundation for Graphic Arts, Gift of Mrs. Adolph B. Spreckels

23 Costume design for a Huntsman in *The Sleeping Princess*, 1921
Pencil, gouache, and gold paint on paper, 12 3/4 × 8 1/2 in.
Collection Parmenia Migel Ekstrom

24 Costume design for Puss-in-Boots in *The Sleeping Princess*, 1921
Pencil, watercolor, gouache, black chalk, and metallic paint on paper, 19 × 12 13/16 in.
Collection Robert L. B. Tobin

25 Costume design for a Dancer and Slave, 1921
Pencil, crayon, and watercolor on paper, 24 5/8 × 18 1/2 in.
The Fine Arts Museums of San Francisco, Achenbach Foundation for Graphic Arts, Gift of Mrs. Adolph B. Spreckels

Alexandre Benois
(Russian, 1870-1960)

26 Design for decor for *Le Pavillon d'Armide*, Scene 2, Armide's Garden, 1909
Pencil, pen and ink, and watercolor on paper, 8 5/8 × 11 1/4 in.
The Fine Arts Museums of San Francisco, Achenbach Foundation for Graphic Arts, Gift of Mrs. Adolph B. Spreckels

27 Costume design for a Gentleman of the Court in *Le Pavillon d'Armide*, 1909
Pencil, pen and ink, and watercolor on paper, 14 3/4 × 10 1/2 in.
Collection George Riabov

28 Costume design for a Lady of the Court in *Le Pavillon d'Armide*, 1909
Pencil, pen and ink, and watercolor on paper, 14 3/4 × 10 1/2 in.
Collection George Riabov

29 Costume design for the Old Marquis in *Le Pavillon d'Armide*, 1909
Pencil, pen and ink, and watercolor on paper, 12 1/4 × 9 1/4 in.
The Fine Arts Museums of San Francisco, Achenbach Foundation for Graphic Arts, Gift of Mrs. Adolph B. Spreckels

30 Design for decor for *Giselle*, Act I, 1924, after 1910 original
Pen and ink, watercolor, and gouache on paper, 18 7/8 × 24 1/8 in.
The Fine Arts Museums of San Francisco, Achenbach Foundation for Graphic Arts, Gift of Mrs. Adolph B. Spreckels

31 Design for decor for *Giselle*, Act I, 1924, after 1910 original
Pencil and watercolor on paper, 20 × 25 1/4 in.
Collection Robert L. B. Tobin

32 Design for decor for *Giselle*, Act II, 1924, after 1910 original
Pencil, ink, and watercolor on paper, 18 3/4 × 25 in.
Collection Robert L. B. Tobin

33 Design for program cover with decor for *Petrouchka*, Act I, 1956, after 1911 original
Pencil and watercolor on paper, 12 1/2 × 9 1/2 in.
The Fine Arts Museums of San Francisco, Achenbach Foundation for Graphic Arts, Gift of Mrs. Adolph B. Spreckels

34 *View of the Fairground in* PETROUCHKA, 1956, after 1911 original
Pencil and watercolor on paper, 6 × 7 1/2 in.
Collection George Riabov

35 Costume design for Petrouchka in *Petrouchka*, inscribed 1911
Pencil, pen and ink, and watercolor on paper, 12 × 8 7/8 in.
The Fine Arts Museums of San Francisco, Achenbach Foundation for Graphic Arts, Gift of Mrs. Adolph B. Spreckels

36 Costume design for the Man with the Peep Show in *Petrouchka*, inscribed 1911
Pencil, pen and ink, and watercolor on paper, 11 3/4 × 9 3/8 in.
The Fine Arts Museums of San Francisco, Achenbach Foundation for Graphic Arts, Gift of Mrs. Adolph B. Spreckels

Jean Cocteau
(French, 1889-1963)

37 *Serge Diaghilev*
Pen and ink on paper, 10 3/8 × 8 1/4 in.
Collection Parmenia Migel Ekstrom

38 *Serge Diaghilev*, 1930
Blue crayon on paper, 10 1/4 × 8 in.
Severin Wunderman Museum

39 *Serge Diaghilev and Vaslav Nijinsky*
Pencil on paper, 14 1/2 × 9 1/4 in.
Collection Robert L. B. Tobin

Michel Georges-Michel
(French, 1883-1985)

40 *The Opening of* PARADE, 1917
Oil on cardboard, 17 5/8 × 13 3/4 in.
The Fine Arts Museums of San Francisco, Achenbach Foundation for Graphic Arts, Gift of Mrs. Adolph B. Spreckels

Alexander Golovin
(Russian, 1863-1930)

41 *Feodor Chaliapin in* BORIS GODUNOV, 1908
Gouache on paper, 18 3/4 × 12 in.
Collection George Riabov

42 Decor for *Le Chant du Rossignol*, Petrograd, 1919
Pencil and watercolor on paper, 25 1/4 × 32 7/8 in.
Collection Masha K. Engmann

43 Costume design for the Emperor in *Le Chant du Rossignol*, Petrograd, 1919
Pencil and watercolor on paper, 12 7/8 × 9 3/4 in.
Collection Masha K. Engmann

44 Costume design for a Mourner in *Le Chant du Rossignol*, Petrograd, 1919
Pencil and watercolor on paper, 12 7/8 × 9 3/4 in.
Collection Masha K. Engmann

45 Costume design for Death in *Le Chant du Rossignol*, Petrograd, 1919
Pencil and watercolor on paper, 12 7/8 × 9 3/4 in.
Collection Masha K. Engmann

Natalia Gontcharova
(Russian, 1881-1962)

46 *Serge Diaghilev*
Pencil on paper, 9 1/2 × 7 1/2 in.
Collection Parmenia Migel Ekstrom

47 Project for the front curtain for *Le Coq d'Or*, 1914
Pencil, watercolor, and gouache on illustration board, 21 × 27 1/8 in.
Collection Robert L. B. Tobin

48 Project for decor for *Le Coq d'Or*, Act I, 1914
Pencil, watercolor, and gouache on illustration board, 19 3/8 × 27 1/8 in.
The Fine Arts Museums of San Francisco, Achenbach Foundation for Graphic Arts, Gift of Mrs. Adolph B. Spreckels

49 Design for decor for *Le Coq d'Or*, Act I, 1914
Pencil and watercolor on paper, 12¼ × 16 in.
Collection Robert L. B. Tobin

50-51 Two studies for details in the decor for *Le Coq d'Or*, 1914
Gouache on illustration board, ea. 21 × 7⅜ in.
Collection Robert L. B. Tobin

52 Costume design for a Princess in *Le Coq d'Or*, 1914
Pencil and watercolor on paper, 9¼ × 6 in.
Collection George Riabov

53 Costume design for the Astrologer in *Le Coq d'Or*, 1914
Pencil and watercolor on paper, 9¼ × 6¼ in.
Collection George Riabov

54 Costume design for a Man in *Le Coq d'Or*, 1914
Pencil, watercolor, and gouache on paper, 18½ × 12 in.
Collection George Riabov

55 Costume design for an Apostle in *Liturgie*, 1915
Watercolor on illustration board, 18⅝ × 11⅝ in.
Collection Robert L. B. Tobin

56 Costume design for Apostle Mark in *Liturgie*, 1915
Pochoir, 25⅝ × 21 in.
Collection Robert L. B. Tobin

57 Costume design for Apostle John in *Liturgie*, 1915
Pochoir, 25⅝ × 21 in.
Collection Robert L. B. Tobin

58 Costume design for Apostle Andrew in *Liturgie*, 1915
Pochoir, 28⅝ × 21 in.
Collection Robert L. B. Tobin

59 *Igor Stravinsky*
Pencil on paper, 13¾ × 9¾ in.
Collection Robert L. B. Tobin

Mikhail Larionov
(Russian, 1881-1964)

60 *Serge Diaghilev*
White chalk and black crayon on paper, 15 × 11½ in.
Collection George Riabov

61 *Serge Diaghilev*
Signed etching, 5½ × 4¾ in.
Private collection

62 *Serge Diaghilev and Igor Stravinsky*, ca. 1917
Pencil on paper, 9½ × 7¾ in.
Collection Parmenia Migel Ekstrom

63 *Guillaume Apollinaire and Serge Diaghilev*, 1917
Pen and india ink on paper, 10⅝ × 8¼ in.
Collection Sylvia Westerman

64 *Caricature of Diaghilev's Circle*, ca. 1920
Pen and ink on paper, 9¼ × 8½ in.
Collection Robert L. B. Tobin

65 *Self-portrait*
Gouache on paper, 11½ × 8 in.
Collection George Riabov

66 Project for the curtain for *Le Soleil de Nuit*, 1915
Pencil, watercolor, and gouache on paper, 22⅞ × 31⅜ in.
The Fine Arts Museums of San Francisco, Achenbach Foundation for Graphic Arts, Gift of Mrs. Adolph B. Spreckels

Pablo Picasso
(Spanish, 1881-1973)

67 *The Chinese Conjuror in* PARADE, 1917
Color woodblock print, 10⅜ × 8½ in.
The Fine Arts Museums of San Francisco, Achenbach Foundation for Graphic Arts, Gift of Mrs. Adolph B. Spreckels

68 *Four dancers*, 1925
Pen and ink on paper, 13⅞ × 10 in.
The Museum of Modern Art, New York. Gift of Abby Aldrich Rockefeller

Nicholas Remisoff
(Russian, 1887-1979)

69 *Léon Bakst*
Color pencil on paper, 15½ × 7½ in.
Collection George Riabov

Attributed to
Auguste Rodin
(French, 1840-1917)

70 Nude study of Ida Rubinstein, ca. 1910
Pencil and brown wash on paper, 23⁹⁄₁₆ × 18¹⁄₁₆ in.
Nijinska Archives

Nicholas Roerich
(Russian, 1874-1947)

71 Costume design for a Man in *Le Sacre du Printemps*, 1913
Gouache on paper, 9½ × 6 in.
Collection George Riabov

72 Costume design for a Maiden in *Le Sacre du Printemps*, 1913
Gouache on paper, 9½ × 6 in.
Collection George Riabov

73 Design for decor for *Le Sacre du Printemps*, 1944, after 1913 original
Tempera on cardboard, 12 × 17¾ in.
Nicholas Roerich Museum

74 Design for decor for *Le Sacre du Printemps*, 1944, after 1913 original
Tempera on cardboard, 12 × 17¾ in.
Nicholas Roerich Museum

75 Design for decor for *Le Sacre du Printemps*, 1944, after 1913 original
Tempera on cardboard, 12 × 17¾ in.
Nicholas Roerich Museum

76 Design for decor for *Le Sacre du Printemps*, 1944, after 1913 original
Tempera on cardboard, 12 × 17¾ in.
Nicholas Roerich Museum

77 Design for decor for *Le Sacre du Printemps*, 1944, after 1913 original
Tempera on cardboard, 12 × 17¾ in.
Nicholas Roerich Museum

John Singer Sargent
(American, 1856-1925)

78 *Vaslav Nijinsky in "Le Pavillon d'Armide,"* 1911
Charcoal on paper, 24¹⁄₁₆ × 18⅝ in.
Private collection

José-María Sert
(Spanish, 1874-1945)

79 Design for decor for *La Légende de Joseph*, 1914
Black and white chalk on cardboard, 27 × 30¼ in.
The Fine Arts Museums of San Francisco, Achenbach Foundation for Graphic Arts, Gift of Mrs. Adolph B. Spreckels

Serge Soudeikine
(Russian, 1882-1946)

80 *Igor Stravinsky*, 1921
Pencil on paper, 20 × 14¼ in.
Collection George Riabov

SCULPTURE

Maurice Charpentier-Mio
(French, 19th-20th century)

81 *Tamara Karsavina and Vaslav Nijinsky in* LE SPECTRE DE LA ROSE, 1911, authorized 1920 edition by Sèvres
Red bisque, H. 10½ in.
The Fine Arts Museums of San Francisco, Gift of Mrs. Adolph B. Spreckels

Malvina Hoffman
(American, 1885-1966)

82 *Vaslav Nijinsky in* L'APRES-MIDI D'UN FAUNE, ca. 1912
Bronze with mottled green patina, L. 17¼ in.
Signed; stamped *Modern Art Fdry N.Y.*
Collection Robert L. B. Tobin

Emanuele Ordoño de Rosales
(Italian, 1873-1919)

83 *Vaslav Nijinsky as Harlequin in* CARNAVAL, ca. 1910, cast 1922
Bronze with dark brown patina, H. 17 in. with base
The Fine Arts Museums of San Francisco, Gift of Mrs. Adolph B. Spreckels

84 *Michel Fokine as Harlequin in* CARNAVAL, ca. 1914, cast 1926
Bronze with dark brown patina, H. 16 in. with base
The Fine Arts Museums of San Francisco, Gift of Mrs. Adolph B. Spreckels

Séraphin Soudbinine
(Russian, b. 1867)

85 *Anna Pavlova as Giselle in* GISELLE, ca. 1911
Bronze with black-green patina, H. 13 in.
Signed; stamped *Alexis Rudier/ Fondeur. Paris.*
The Fine Arts Museums of San Francisco, Gift of Mrs. Adolph B. Spreckels

86 *Tamara Karsavina as the Ballerina Doll in* PETROUCHKA, ca. 1911
Bronze with green patina, H. 13¼ in.
Signed; stamped *A. Rudier/ Fondeur. Paris.*
The Fine Arts Museums of San Francisco, Gift of Mrs. Adolph B. Spreckels

87 *Tamara Karsavina,* ca. 1912
Gilt bronze with brown glaze, H. 13¼ in.
Signed; stamped *Alexis Rudier/ Fondeur. Paris.*
The Fine Arts Museums of San Francisco, Gift of Mrs. Adolph B. Spreckels

PHOTOGRAPHS

E. O. Hoppé
(British, 1878-1972)

88 Studies from the Russian Ballet
London: Fine Art Society, 1911
15 photogravures, ea. 9½ × 14 in.
Courtesy Paul M. Hertzmann, Inc.

Vaslav Nijinsky
(Russian, 1889-1950)

89 Serge Diaghilev, Bois de Boulogne, Paris, 1910
Gelatin-silver print, 1½ × 2½ in.
Nijinska Archives

90 Léon Bakst and Serge Diaghilev, Bois de Boulogne, Paris, 1910
Gelatin-silver print, 1½ × 2½ in.
Nijinska Archives

91 Léon Bakst and Serge Diaghilev, Bois de Boulogne, Paris, 1910
Gelatin-silver print, 1½ × 2 ½ in.
Nijinska Archives

Sasha
(nationality and dates unknown)

92 Jean Cocteau and Serge Diaghilev at the opening of *Le Train Bleu,* Monte Carlo, 1924
Signed gelatin-silver print, 12 × 10 in.
Nijinska Archives

White Studio
(American)

93 Adolph Bolm and Flore Revalles in *Schéhérazade,* New York, 1916
Toned gelatin-silver print, 12⅜ × 10¼ in.
Collection Parmenia Migel Ekstrom

94 Adolph Bolm in *Schéhérazade,* New York, 1916
Toned gelatin-silver print, 12½ × 9⅝ in.
Collection Parmenia Migel Ekstrom

95 Enrico Cecchetti and Flore Revalles in *Schéhérazade,* New York, 1916
Toned gelatin-silver print, 13¾ × 10⅞ in.
Collection Parmenia Migel Ekstrom

96 *Le Soleil de Nuit,* New York, 1916
Toned gelatin-silver print, 10¼ × 13 in.
Collection Parmenia Migel Ekstrom

97 *Le Soleil de Nuit,* New York, 1916
Toned gelatin-silver print, 9⅜ × 13 in.
Collection Parmenia Migel Ekstrom

98 Adolph Bolm in *Sadko,* New York, 1916
Toned gelatin-silver print, 12½ × 9⅝ in.
Collection Parmenia Migel Ekstrom

99 Corps de ballet in *Sadko,* New York, 1916
Toned gelatin-silver print, 9½ × 13½ in.
Collection Parmenia Migel Ekstrom

Anonymous

100 Serge Diaghilev, 1912
Gelatin-silver print, 3½ × 2½ in.
Nijinska Archives

101 Serge Diaghilev, Vaslav Nijinsky, and Igor Stravinsky, 1912
Gelatin-silver print, 3½ × 2½ in.
Nijinska Archives

BOOKS AND ARCHIVAL MATERIAL

102 Sergei Diaghilev, ed.
Mir iskusstva (vols. 1-2, 1898-1899; vols. 3-4, 1900; vol. 7, 1902)
St. Petersburg
The Bancroft Library, University of California, Berkeley

103 Sergei Diaghilev, ed.
Russkaia zhivopis v XVIII v. Tom pervyi. D. G. Levitsky
St. Petersburg: Evdokimov, ca. 1902
The Institute of Modern Russian Culture, Los Angeles

104 Catalogue of exhibition of historic Russian portraits organized by Sergei Diaghilev at the Tauride Palace, St. Petersburg
St. Petersburg: Shnel, 1905
The Institute of Modern Russian Culture, Los Angeles

105 *Salon d'Automne. Exposition de l'Art Russe.*
Prefaces by Serge Diaghilev and Alexandre Benois
Paris: Moreau, 1906
The Institute of Modern Russian Culture, Los Angeles

106 *Cinq Concerts Historiques Russes*
Souvenir program, Théâtre National de l'Opéra, Paris, 1907
The Institute of Modern Russian Culture, Los Angeles

107 *Boris Godunov*
Souvenir program, Théâtre National de l'Opéra, Paris, 1908
Nijinska Archives

108 Handwritten, signed contract between Sergei Diaghilev and Feodor Chaliapin
Moscow, 4 October 1908
Collection Parmenia Migel Ekstrom

109 Vaslav Nijinsky
Choreographic notation for *L'Après-midi d'un Faune*, ca. 1911
Pencil on printed letterhead
Nijinska Archives

110 Arsène Alexandre
The Decorative Art of Léon Bakst
London: Fine Art Society, 1913
Jane Bourne Parton Collection, Mills College Library

111 Maurice de Brunoff, ed.
Collection des Plus Beaux Numéros de COMŒDIA ILLUSTRE *et des Programmes Consacrés aux Ballets et Galas Russes depuis le Début à Paris*
Paris: M. de Brunoff, 1922
Jane Bourne Parton Collection, Mills College Library

112 Maurice de Brunoff, ed.
Collection des Plus Beaux Numéros de COMŒDIA ILLUSTRE *et des Programmes Consacrés aux Ballets et Galas Russes depuis le Début à Paris*
Paris: M. de Brunoff, 1922
The Fine Arts Museums of San Francisco, Achenbach Foundation for Graphic Arts

113 André Levinson
The Story of Léon Bakst's Life
New York: Brentano's, 1922
(NO. 112 of 250)
Jane Bourne Parton Collection, Mills College Library

COSTUMES

All costumes are from the collection of The Castle Howard Costume Galleries.

Léon Bakst
(Russian, 1866-1924)

114-115 Two costumes for Temple Servants in *Le Dieu Bleu*, 1912

Purple wool robes decorated with paint, gold braid, appliquéd silk, embroidery, and gold metal studs.

116 Costume for a Bayadère in *Le Dieu Bleu*, 1912

Cream wool skirt lined with blue cotton decorated with paint, flock, embroidery, and casein sequins. Cream wool bolero decorated with metallic braid, metal plates, paint, flock, and painted wooden beads. Cream wool collar. Cream wool headdress.

117 Costume for a Negro Dancer in *Le Dieu Bleu*, 1912

Cream cotton bodice with attached skirt and hanging panels, decorated with casein sequins, braid, and fabric appliqué. Black satin trousers painted with orange spots. Cream wool turban decorated with paint and casein sequins with metal peacock-feather motif at center front.

118 Costume for a Brigand in *Daphnis et Chloë*, 1912

T-shaped tunic with short sleeves made of black facecloth. Painted blue and brown cotton borders at neck and sleeve ends. Painted matching cotton belt.

119 Costume for a Brigand in *Daphnis et Chloë*, 1912
Sleeveless white cotton tunic painted with circles and stripes in black, cream, orange, and brown.
NOTE: This is one of several costumes designed for *Daphnis et Chloë* that were also used in *Narcisse*.

120 Costume for a Brigand in *Daphnis et Chloë*, 1912

Purple cotton T-shaped tunic with deep purple stenciled design and white spots; painted band and checkered design in black and white. Matching checkered belt.

121 Costume for a Brigand in *Daphnis et Chloë*, 1912

T-shaped tunic of yellow cotton decorated with green chevrons with white borders and black stenciled design.

122 Costume for a Brigand in *Daphnis et Chloë*, 1912

Blue cotton T-shaped tunic with painted yellow bands and red chevrons. Matching chevron-patterned belt. Blue cotton breeches with painted white borders.

123 Costume for the Italian Prince in *The Sleeping Princess*, 1921

Red velvet 18th-century-style coat. Revers and waistcoat in green satin decorated with gold buttons and embroidery. Black felt tricorne hat edged and trimmed with gold braid and black feathers.

124 Costume for a Minister of State in *The Sleeping Princess*, 1921

Red 18th-century-style coat with false waistcoat in orange satin, decorated with gold and silver braid and black velvet.

125 Costume for a Footman in *The Sleeping Princess*, 1921

Blue cotton 18th-century-style coat stenciled in gold paint and trimmed with cream silk, silver fabric buttons, gold metallic cord, metallic fringe, and satin ribbon.

126 Costume for a Lady-in-Waiting in *The Sleeping Princess*, 1921

Yellow velvet bodice and skirt in 17th-century style, decorated with gold metallic braid and embroidery, gold metallic fabric, and gold metal studs.

127 Costume for a Duke in *The Sleeping Princess*, 1921

Yellow velvet and silk jacket decorated with gold paint, gold metallic braid, and brown swansdown. Yellow satin breeches trimmed with green satin ribbon loops.

128 Costume for a Duchess in *The Sleeping Princess*, 1921

Green satin coat decorated with gold paint, metallic braid, blue velvet, and gold lace. Brown satin skirt decorated with gold paint and gold metallic fringe. Brown felt hat trimmed with gold braid and ostrich feathers. Green silk sash with metallic gold fringe.

129 Costume for the Page to the Fairy of the Mountain Ash in *The Sleeping Princess*, 1921

Rowan-red velvet jacket trimmed with black satin. White "artificial silk" shirt collar attached. Red velvet breeches trimmed with black satin and white lace. Red velvet hat trimmed with artificial rowan berries.

130 Costume for a Huntsman in *The Sleeping Princess*, 1921

Green velvet 18th-century-style coat with purple velvet cuffs decorated with gold braid. Attached false waistcoat of blue satin with white and gold braid.

131-132 Two costumes for Baronesses in *The Sleeping Princess*, 1921

Green cotton 18th-century-style coats decorated with gold paint. Cream silk cuffs and revers decorated with brown velvet ribbon and gold braid. Attached false waistcoats in green satin decorated with gold braid and gold metal buttons. Brown cotton skirts printed with gold paint and trimmed with gold braid and fringing. Sleeveless yellow cotton blouses with attached brown silk jabots.

133 Costume for a Marquis in *The Sleeping Princess*, 1921

Blue cotton 18th-century-style coat with green velvet cuffs and allover printed pattern in gold, decorated with metallic trimming and braid. False waistcoat in green velvet. Green velvet breeches.

134 Costume for a Marchioness in *The Sleeping Princess*, 1921

Turquoise silk 18th-century-style coat trimmed with silver braid, silver lace, and silver metallic buttons. Attached false waistcoat of green velvet; cream silk cuffs. Blue satin skirt with bands of metallic braid at hem.

135 Costume for a Village Youth in *The Sleeping Princess*, 1921

Orange felt jacket with attached cream and green striped satin skirt and false waistcoat decorated with green braid and silver metallic buttons. Orange velvet jacket belt. Orange felt breeches.

136 Costume for the Princess Royal in *The Sleeping Princess*, 1921

Red-orange 18th-century-style dress in silk-pile velvet. Cream silk bodice with long red-orange sleeves. Red-orange skirt with attached white satin petticoat trimmed with gold braid, matching gold fringing, swansdown, orange-dyed swansdown, and ermine tails. Bodice and skirt decorated with heavily padded silver tissue designs.

Natalia Gontcharova
(Russian, 1881-1962)

137 Costume for a Peasant Girl in *Le Coq d'Or*, 1937, after 1914 original

White cotton blouse with appliqué and embroidery. Green and yellow cotton skirt with colored appliqué, embroidery, and braid. Cotton headscarf stenciled in orange, red, and yellow.
NOTE: Because the original costumes for *Le Coq d'Or* had been lost, Gontcharova redesigned costumes and sets for the 1937 revival based on her earlier designs.

138 Costume for a Nobleman in *Le Coq d'Or*, 1937, after 1914 original

Dark pink, ribbed silk coat decorated with fabric appliqué and gold embroidery. Dark pink wool overcoat decorated with fabric appliqué, gold embroidery, and fur. Red velvet hat trimmed with fur.

139 Costume for a Persian Woman Warrior in *Le Coq d'Or*, 1937, after 1914 original

Gray satin bodice with attached trousers, covered with brown and metallic crocheted "chain mail." Blue wool overskirt decorated with woolen braid, satin ribbon, and wooden beads. Gold and silver *papier mâché* helmet with attached mesh scarf.

140 Costume for the Queen of Shemakhan in *Le Coq d'Or*, 1937, after 1914 original

Pink taffeta robe with attached cape lined in black silk, decorated with fabric appliqué, embroidery, leather, lace, beads, sequins, and metallic tassels. Cream silk blouse and georgette trousers embroidered with flowers in gold thread. Overskirt with decoration in appliqué, silver sequins, pearls, and metallic beads. Crown of buckram and milliner's wire painted gold and decorated with sequins, diamanté, glass beads, buttons, and leather.

141 Costume for a Sea Monster in *Sadko*, 1916 production

Brown satin under-jacket covered with three red and yellow painted flounces. White cotton under-trousers covered with six red and yellow painted flounces on each leg. Red, yellow, and brown satin carapace, heavily stiffened and wired, decorated with fabric appliqué and gold braid. Stiffened red, yellow, and brown satin headpiece decorated with fabric appliqué and gold braid.
NOTE: The original 1911 production of *Sadko* was designed by Boris Anisfeld and Léon Bakst. Diaghilev asked Gontcharova to redesign the ballet in 1916.

142 Costume for an Attendant to Köstchei, the Immortal, in *L'Oiseau de Feu*, 1926 production

Red wool tunic decorated with blue silk and gold painted squares with black braid, and jet beads.
NOTE: The original 1910 production of *L'Oiseau de Feu* was designed by Konstantin Korovin and Léon Bakst. Diaghilev asked Gontcharova to redesign the ballet in 1926.

143 Costume for an Attendant to Köstchei, the Immortal, in *L'Oiseau de Feu*, 1926 production

White cotton dress with long-sleeved bodice and attached hoop skirt, painted with blue and gold stenciled designs and decorated with silver metallic fabric and gold and silver braid. Blue cotton belt with white cotton appliqué and black painted designs. Padded silk hat with painted decoration.

144 Costume for a Man in *L'Oiseau de Feu*, 1926 production

White cotton doublet with long sleeves and attached skirt. Front and back of doublet painted silver. Blue wool cape.

145 Costume for a Man in
L'Oiseau de Feu, 1926 production

White cotton tunic decorated with
gold cord and fabric. Attached
metallic gold skirt. White cotton
trousers with floral embroidery.
White cap decorated with gold
fabric and pearls.

Henri Matisse
(French, 1869-1954)

146-147 Two costumes for
Mandarins in *Le Chant du
Rossignol*, 1920

Geometrically cut yellow satin
robes decorated with gold lamé
disks that are partly covered and
surrounded by black painted
decoration.

148-149 Two costumes for
Mourners in *Le Chant du
Rossignol*, 1920

Geometrically cut white felt robes
with appliquéd dark blue velvet
triangles. White felt hoods; two
sets of attached ears and attached
back hanging panels decorated
with appliquéd dark blue velvet
chevrons.

Nicholas Roerich
(Russian, 1874-1947)

150 Costume for a Man in
Le Sacre du Printemps, 1913

Cream cotton robe with designs
stenciled and painted in purple
and orange. Helmet-shaped cotton
hat trimmed with brown fur and
painted with a geometric design in
pink, purple, and yellow. Brown
leather waist belt and attached
painted silver wooden dagger with
linear decoration. Yellow suede
ballet slippers with painted purple
and dark pink geometric design
and long cotton ties painted pink
and purple.

151 Costume for a Man in
Le Sacre du Printemps, 1913

Cream cotton robe with designs
stenciled and painted in purple
and orange. Helmet-shaped cotton
hat trimmed with brown fur and
painted with a geometric design in
pink, purple, and yellow. Brown
leather waist belt decorated with
small metal studs and with
attached painted silver wooden
dagger with painted black linear
decoration. Pink leather ballet
slippers with painted blue and red
geometric design and long cotton
ties painted orange.

152 Costume for a Man in
Le Sacre du Printemps, 1913

Cream cotton robe with stenciled
and painted designs in orange and
black. Helmet-shaped cotton hat
trimmed with brown fur and
painted with a light purple and
orange geometric design, with two
painted red appliquéd cotton
triangles. Brown leather waist belt
decorated with small metal studs
and with attached painted brown
wooden dagger with painted gold
linear decoration. Pink leather
ballet slippers with painted green/
blue and red geometric design and
long cotton ties painted orange
with green spots.

Jean Cocteau
Serge Diaghilev and Vaslav Nijinsky,
cat. no. 39.